This book is dedicated to all of the unsung heroines of early archaeology: the unacknowledged women graduate students who did not continue in the field and the wives of archaeologists who toiled on excavations but never saw their names on the publications they helped produce. This is the story of one such woman and it must stand as a proxy for all those whose names and contributions to the field we will never know.

ARCHAEOLOGY, SEXISM, AND SCANDAL

ARCHAEOLOGY, SEXISM, AND SCANDAL

THE LONG-SUPPRESSED STORY OF ONE WOMAN'S DISCOVERIES AND THE MAN WHO STOLE CREDIT FOR THEM

ALAN KAISER

ROWMAN & LITTLEFIELD
LANHAM · BOULDER · NEW YORK · LONDON

Robinson, David Moore. *Excavations at Olynthus: Part VII: The Terracottas of Olynthus Found in 1931*. Frontispiece. © 1938 The Johns Hopkins Press. Reprinted with permission of Johns Hopkins University Press.

Published by Rowman & Littlefield
A wholly owned subsidiary of The Rowman & Littlefield Publishing Group, Inc.
4501 Forbes Boulevard, Suite 200, Lanham, Maryland 20706
www.rowman.com

Unit A, Whitacre Mews, 26-34 Stannary Street, London SE11 4AB

British Library Cataloguing in Publication Information Available

Library of Congress Cataloging-in-Publication Data Is Available

ISBN 978-1-4422-3003-3 (cloth : alk. paper)
ISBN 978-1-4422-3004-0 (electronic)

∞™ The paper used in this publication meets the minimum requirements of American National Standard for Information Sciences—Permanence of Paper for Printed Library Materials, ANSI/NISO Z39.48-1992.

Printed in the United States of America

CONTENTS

ACKNOWLEDGMENTS

I would like to thank the University of Evansville's Alumni Research and Scholarly Activity Fellowship Committee for their support of my research. Also a number of librarians have been very helpful and generous with their time: Jennifer Ford, Jeffrey Boyce, and Jessica Leming of the Special Collections and Archives at the University of Mississippi; James Stimpert of the Ferdinand Hamburger Archives in the Sheridan Libraries at Johns Hopkins University; and Kathryn Bartelt, Margaret Atwater-Singer, and Laura Summers of the University of Evansville's Bower Surheinrich Library as well as interns Hilary Wolkan, Stephanie Marcotte, and Dominique DePriest who have helped to organize and digitize Mary Ross Ellingson's papers and photos. I am also indebted to Barbara Petersen for sharing Ellingson's correspondence with me as well as stories about her mother. Rowman and Littlefield editors Andrea O. Kendrick and Leanne Silverman supported this project from the beginning and put me in touch with excellent peer reviewers who had much useful advice. Countless others, too numerous to mention by name, helped me with my research, particularly the many people at conferences and lectures who told me stories of these archaeologists and gave me ideas for new directions into which I could take my work. Finally I must thank my wife, Christine Lovasz-Kaiser, who patiently combed through archives with me, edited drafts of my work, offered invaluable suggestions, and who helped make a road trip to Oxford, Mississippi, the adventure of a lifetime.

INTRODUCTION

The Ellingson File—A Photo Album

When people meet me for the first time at a party or other social function and they find out I am a classical archaeologist the question they always ask is about my most exciting discovery. I hate that question. The true answer is not what people expect or want to hear. I have worked on projects at Greek and Roman sites in Spain, in northwestern Greece, in Israel, and in Italy at Pompeii and Ostia. One summer I helped search for a lost eighteenth-century synagogue on the Caribbean Island of Nevis. I have found a few exciting artifacts and a large number of unexciting ones but they all pale in comparison to a photo album I found on a shelf outside my office at the University of Evansville. No one wants to hear that at a party. To tell them the real significance of the find would require more attention and time than they are willing to give in such a situation. So I usually tell them some other story that occurred at one of those more exotic locations and keep the story of the photo album to myself. I only tell that story when I have a chance to tell it in full.

This most exciting discovery occurred late one November afternoon in 2003 during my office hours. I should have been grading papers but no one seemed to be around the department offices that afternoon, it was cold and rainy outside, and the next paper at the top of the stack was by a student whom I knew was not a good writer. Suddenly the idea of clearing off a shelf in the room adjoining my office to create a little extra storage space seemed more appealing than continuing to grade papers. Amid the forgotten office supplies and antique computer hardware I spotted the photo album under a large envelope stuffed with yellowing papers resting on a couple of boxes. A letter on top indicated this material had been gathered by Helen Madeline Mary Ross, later to become Mary Ross Ellingson after she married. The boxes were heavy and contained a surprise, a number of plaster casts of ancient Greek terracotta figurines wrapped in paper towels as well as some ancient pot shards. Most of the casts were of figurines that dated to the fifth and fourth centuries BCE. The pot shards were actual artifacts, not casts, with black decoration painted on the orange-red fabric of the clay. Picking up the album, a black-and-white photo of Ellingson fell to the floor. A lovely young woman with a stylish 1930s bobbed hairdo stood beside a large stone grave marker (see figure I.1). I recognized the setting immediately from my own visits to Athens. She stood in the Kerameikos, an ancient cemetery of the city. Intrigued, I opened to a random page in the middle of the album. Ellingson appeared in only a couple of these photos but again I recognized the location. It was a photo of the excavations at Olynthos, or Olynthus as the Greek name of the site was transliterated in the 1930s when the photos were taken, but not a photo I had ever seen before (see figure I.2).

The excavations at Olynthus are counted among the great American-led excavations of the twentieth century. David Robinson of Johns Hopkins University directed four campaigns at Olynthus between 1928 and 1938. Archaeology in Greece had been dominated by excavations of public structures such as temples, theaters, and the buildings around the *agora*, the central square of ancient Greek cities. Robinson was one of the first archaeologists to focus his excavation almost exclusively on houses to better understand domestic life. These were the days of large-scale excavations, which are simply no longer financially feasible today. Robinson used a workforce of hundreds of local laborers each season to uncover enormous portions of the site. While such large-scale excavation precluded careful supervision by enough properly trained staff, Robinson still excavated more houses at Olynthus than had or have since been excavated at any other

Figure I.1. Mary Ross Ellingson in the Kerameikos cemetery, Athens, June 1931. (Photo courtesy of the University of Evansville Archives)

Figure I.2. Overview of Block A VI at Olynthus looking northeast as it appeared on June 4, 1931; House A VI 6 is in the foreground, Mary Ross Ellingson is on the left. (Photo courtesy of the University of Evansville Archives)

site in Greece. All modern studies of the ancient Greek house still begin with the Olynthus excavations. When I was a graduate student I was required to read one of the fourteen volumes of the *Excavations at Olynthus* series for class but had read the rest on my own because I found them so interesting and useful for my own research on ancient urbanism. The thoroughness with which Robinson published was also quite remarkable for his day in that he set out to publish all artifacts he felt were important, not just the most attractive pieces.[1] While modern archaeologists see gaps in his excavation methods and the materials Robinson chose to publish, he set a new standard for his day about which materials warranted recording and publication.[2] The pace Robinson set for the publication of these volumes as well as numerous articles in scholarly journals about the excavation is quite impressive, even dizzying. Some archaeologists are notorious for the slow rate at which they publish their data; Robinson was definitely not one of these.

Olynthus was the perfect place to study Greek domestic structures. Located in northeastern Greece on the Chalcidic peninsula (see figure I.3), citizens of the city became embroiled in the conflicts between Athens, Sparta, and Macedonia in the fifth and fourth centuries BCE. Fearing the people of Olynthus were plotting against him, Philip II of Macedonia, the one-eyed father of Alexander the Great, laid siege to the city in 349 BCE. In three speeches still preserved today, the *Olynthiacs*, one of the great orators of ancient Greece, Demosthenes, urged his fellow Athenians to aid the people of Olynthus and to defy Philip. Despite his warnings, Athens and the other Greek city-states were slow to realize that the conquest of Olynthus was only one phase in Philip's larger and eventually successful plan of mastering all of Greece; they chose to send no troops to help the beleaguered city. Philip eventually took Olynthus by treachery in 348 BCE ordering the city to be looted and destroyed and the survivors of the siege to be sold into slavery. Olynthus was never rebuilt. Although subsequent generations used the site as a quarry, reducing most of the buildings to their foundations, a great deal of evidence survived illustrating life in the city before and during the siege.[3] Indeed, Robinson's team even found six arrowheads and about a dozen lead sling bullets with Philip's name on them amid the ruins of the city.[4]

Ellingson had clearly worked on this excavation. The photos in the album were all carefully pasted to stiff black paper pages and labeled underneath in neat white letters. Accompanying the album was a stack of letters and news clippings as well as the boxes of figurine casts and pot shards. She had been a graduate student at Johns Hopkins University studying classical archaeology and had excavated with Robinson at Olynthus in 1931. Ellingson had penned the letters to her family to tell them about her experiences abroad. After Ellingson's death in 1993 her daughter donated the album to the University of Evansville where Ellingson had taught Latin and English courses in her later years. Someone had placed all this material on the shelf long before the university had hired me.

Figure I.3. Map of Greece showing the location of places mentioned in the text.

The importance of this find slowly dawned on me. Ellingson had participated in an excavation significant in archaeological history and had written about it in a candid and often humorous way as it was happening. I knew of no other behind-the-scenes record like this of the Olynthus excavations. I took the photo album and letters back to my office and sat down to read. Over the next several hours I forgot about student papers and the gathering gloom outside. The ghost of Mary Ross Ellingson came alive, telling me in her own words about her experiences excavating at Olynthus and showing me what she saw through her numerous photographs. Her stories were unique to that time and place. I had known some of the names she mentioned of her fellow excavators only from their later archaeological publications and their highly respected reputations. In her letters they became real people to me. Robinson was witty, flirtatious, and stingy. Gladys Davidson Weinberg, an authority on ancient glass, was a kind, generous, and supportive friend. George Mylonas, who would go on to direct excavations at Mycenae, the Bronze Age site of the legendary Agamemnon's palace, was stiff and formal, never lapsing from the most proper decorum. J. Walter Graham, later to become an authority on the Minonan architecture of Crete, was an energetic supervisor with a large appetite who was always happy to help Ellingson with her work. Sarah Freeman, who would eventually be a recognized expert on ancient coins and medals, came to dislike Ellingson, a feeling that was apparently mutual. Long after they shared their season at Olynthus, some of her fellow excavators became professors, museum curators, and respected excavators. One would be wounded aiding the Greek opposition of the Italian invasion at the beginning of World War II, another is rumored to have joined the American intelligence effort against the Nazis, many years later two would be awarded the Archaeological Institute of America's Gold Medal in recognition of their contribution to the field, and one would die in a gruesome murder fifty years after working at Olynthus. Yet here in her letters they all were young, unknown graduate students excited by their first field experience, playing bridge, swimming in the clear blue water of the Gulf of Cassandra, and enjoying a night of dining and dancing. Virtually no candid snapshots or personal written accounts of the excavations at Olynthus survive making Ellingson's letters and photos a rare archive of a significant pre–World War II excavation.

While the details of her stories are unique to Olynthus in 1931, the themes are universal to all excavations and in them I recognized echoes of my own experiences in the field. Everyone who has worked on an excavation has felt the excitement of being the first person in centuries to lift an artifact from the ground, has made lifelong friendships with fellow excavators, has complained about the food rations, and has delighted in discovering the modern culture of the place they are working. In articulate and artful language she captured all aspects of life in the field in a way few others have.

A few scholars have noted that Robinson made some crucial changes to his goals and techniques over the years that he excavated at Olynthus. Ellingson unknowingly captured glimpses of those changes and their consequences in her letters and photographs proving that 1931 was a critical year in the development of the project. Robinson is celebrated for being one of the first archaeologists to focus a research project solely on Greek domestic structures but that was not his original intent. During his first season at Olynthus in 1928 he sought to find temples and civic structures, as was usually done at classical sites at the time. Ellingson's letters show that Robinson only really began to focus on houses as *the* unit of study in earnest in 1931. The shift in focus required a radical revamping of his excavation and recording procedures to allow him to gather the data he needed. The 1931 season is when these new techniques made their debut.

It was also during that season that Robinson first engaged in an experiment to see if women could oversee trench work for an entire season. Unlike the 1928 season, in 1931 Robinson planned from the beginning to have the three women, Ellingson, Weinberg, and Freeman, work in the trenches and supervise Greek workmen instead of having them primarily wash, mend, and inventory finds in the dig house. Robinson helped create a new generation of women archaeologists. Ellingson, Weinberg, and Freeman were part of the so-called second generation of women in archaeology. Unfortunately this new generation was appearing at a time when opportunities for women were beginning to contract. A complex array of evolving economic and social factors would limit their opportunities to participate in archaeology and academia and would make their work less visible than that of their contemporary male counterparts. This has led to the muting or elimination of their contributions from written accounts of the history of classical archaeology; Ellingson's archive helps add the voices of women back into the history of the discipline.

The three women were not the only people whose career trajectories developed or changed as a result of the 1931 excavation season—the same was true for several of the men. Graham and a fellow graduate student, Alexander Schulz, decided during that season that they would use the material from Olynthus for their thesis and dissertation respectively, the most important decision any graduate student has to make. Another man, Arthur Parsons, made the opposite decision after spending the season with Robinson and sought a dissertation topic elsewhere. This decision changed the course of his career and even his life quite radically. The 1931 season at Olynthus did not simply launch careers, however, it also saved one. Robinson, an aging archaeologist who seemed unaware of the change in archaeological techniques that had taken place around him, was panned for the poor quality of his work at Olynthus in 1928. There were veiled suggestions that his excavation permit should be revoked. The shift in focus and techniques he followed in 1931 saved his reputation as well as his career, and helped establish him as one of the great American classical archaeologists. Much changed in 1931 at Olynthus and even in classical archaeology and I could see it all through Ellingson's eyes.

Engrossed in my discovery, I did not realize that Ellingson's ghost was telling me something else, the final reason the 1931 season at Olynthus was significant. I was soon to uncover a clue she had intentionally left behind that would lead me to expose one of the most shocking plagiarism scandals yet publically recorded in the history of the discipline. Robinson himself left a second clue, a message hidden within a painting currently on display at the University of Mississippi, which would confirm the scandal and offer a silent apology that only Ellingson could have understood. As it all unfolded I found myself telling friends stories about discoveries that sounded more like they came from a mystery novel than the halls of academe.

Uncovering her secret was one of two unexpected twists in what was to turn into a multiyear research odyssey. In seeking to understand the secrets of Olynthus I would eventually discover that some members of the generation of archaeologists who worked in Greece preceding mine knew Ellingson's secret. While they deemed such tales worthy of relating at dinner parties and discussions over drinks at conferences, they sought to thwart my attempts to document the scandal in print. Some members of that older generation wanted the secret to die with them.

PART I

MARY ROSS ELLINGSON'S ARCHAEOLOGICAL ADVENTURE

Mary Ross Ellingson at the Greek site of either Tiryns or Mycenae in June 1931.
(Photo courtesy of the University of Evansville Archives)

ONE

JOURNEY TO OLYNTHUS

Somewhere on the Atlantic
Tuesday, March 10 [1931]
Dear Family,

Thanks so much for the wire. It was quite exciting getting it. I got it soon after I got on board, & then I got another just a few minutes before we sailed (from the girls in the stacks at Hopkins). Jean & 2 of her friends came down to see me off, & of course there were Sally's family, & a lot of Gladys' friends.

We stayed up to see the harbor. It was really beautiful—all the way from uptown down the river past the Statue of Liberty, black night and twinkling lights shining forth from the many million sky-scrapers that make New York the only city of its kind. The Statue of Liberty, we decided, must be impressionistic art, at night, as only its torch was lit, & we could barely see its outline against the black of the Jersey shore. And then-out to sea.

Ellingson's journey to Olynthus required two weeks during which time she sent several letters home revealing a great deal about her personality. At each stage in her journey she met other Olynthus crew members and as she got to know them, I got to know them as well. I was to discover from clues in Ellingson's letters, as well as from subsequent research, that everyone on the Olynthus staff was at a critical moment in their careers in the spring of 1931. Ellingson and her third-class cabinmates aboard the *Roma*, Weinberg and Freeman, were forming their generation of women's approach to classical archaeology. The "boys," fellow Johns Hopkins graduate students J. Walter Graham, Alexander Schulz, and Arthur Parsons, were searching for dissertation topics that spring. Excavation director Robinson was at a low point in his career having suffered such severe criticism for his field techniques and he knew something had to change to regain his reputation. Greek archaeologist Mylonas was a newly minted PhD facing uncertain work prospects in a Depression-era world. Ellingson and her fellow staff members would make decisions that spring that would direct the course of their lives for years to come.

MARY ROSS ELLINGSON, GLADYS DAVIDSON WEINBERG, AND SARAH FREEMAN

Ellingson began her trip to Olynthus long before she set sail for Europe aboard the *Roma* in March 1931. She was born in Edmonton, Canada, in 1906, thus she was twenty-four years old that night she departed New York.[1] Her family was solidly upper-middle class as her father ran his own real estate and insurance business.[2] On her mother's side Ellingson was descended from an old royalist family that had left the United States for Canada after the American Revolution. Her grandparents were among the early pioneering families who settled Edmonton in the 1890s with her maternal grandparents establishing a farm on the outskirts of town because farming was, according to her grandfather Edward Dean, "the only thing worth doing."[3] Her family took vacations in the more rugged parts of Canada, during which Ellingson developed a lifelong love for hiking and the outdoors. She entered the University of Alberta determined to study law but soon discovered an aptitude for, and love of, classical languages and cultures.[4] Ellingson was a popular student according to an undated article she had clipped from the university's newspaper, *The Gateway*, which was probably printed in late 1930. While classical languages were her primary focus, she also cultivated an interest in journalism, working as an editor for *The Gateway* and contributing articles to the off-campus newspaper, the *Edmonton Bulletin*, one of which was among her letters. She eventually joined the staff at the *Bulletin* as an assistant editor.[5] Her journalistic training helped her observe the excavation, Greek cultures, and people at Olynthus and write about them in a clear and interesting way. At some point either during or before her time as an undergraduate, she studied both French and German well enough to at least read scholarly articles in both languages.[6] In the spring of 1930 Ellingson graduated with honors.

Ellingson held a deep passion for classical Greek culture and an unshakeable belief in the superiority of the ancient Greeks.

Figure 1.1. Mary Ross Ellingson's college graduation photo. (Photo courtesy of Barbara Petersen)

As she dreamed en route of seeing Athens for the first time she effuses in a March 20 letter:

> Oh, I don't want to sound like a guide-book or a circular sent out by the Chamber of Commerce of Athens but you can't imagine the wonderful feeling it gives me to think that tomorrow I shall see [Athens] as it remains to the world today. In the fourth & fifth centuries B.C. Athens reached a perfection in art that never will be equaled again. And I think it a great privilege to be going to gaze upon the relics of the perfection. Oh the more I say the more it sounds like the publicity department but at least it's the way I feel.

During the first half of the twentieth century many of those who studied classical cultures saw themselves as the guardians of ancient Greek art, architecture, poetry, and democracy.[7] This legacy needed protection. The impressionistic movement in art and modernism in architecture, poetry, and literature all represented a rejection of the ideals of the classical Greeks. In 1931 the world was still grappling with the mechanized killing unleashed during World War I and the ever-present threat from Communist revolution and invasion after the beginning of the Russian Revolution in 1917; democracy and humanism seemed under attack. Ellingson had joined a field that was a bulwark of conservatism. Indeed, her own conservatism in art was uncompromising. While reflecting on her visit to the archaeological museum in Naples, Italy, one stop during their long journey to Greece, she tells her family in a March 19 letter "they have a few beautiful original Greek statues but an awful mob of hideous Roman ones & Renaissance paintings, which I hate."

After she had completed her undergraduate studies Ellingson moved to Baltimore to begin studying classical archaeology at Johns Hopkins University having received a scholarship to support her studies.[8] Johns Hopkins was an unusual university in the educational landscape of 1920s and 1930s America. At that time many colleges and universities had at best a mixed, at worst a negative, feeling about allowing women to study. Stanford University epitomized the negative attitudes when it implemented a quota on undergraduate women in 1904; for every one woman there had to be three men accepted, a policy that remained in effect until 1933.[9] Although the first women had not entered the graduate programs in arts and sciences at Johns Hopkins until 1908,[10] the institution would rapidly become one of the American universities most welcoming to women and would be one of the universities to grant the highest number of doctorates to women in the country prior to World War II.[11] This liberal attitude toward women extended to the classics department where the graduate program in archaeology was one of the few in North America to accept women.[12]

It was not just the openness of Johns Hopkins that must have attracted Ellingson there; Robinson had an established reputation in the world of classical art and archaeology and was supported by other highly respected professors. W. F. Albright, one of the greatest Biblical archaeologists of his day, was teaching there when Ellingson arrived. Tenney Frank was working on his monumental multivolume work *An Economic Survey of Ancient Rome*, one of the first and most thorough works to address the topic. Ellingson took classes with all three of these professors. Within a few weeks of their first meeting Robinson was so impressed with Ellingson that he asked the new graduate student to join him on the staff at Olynthus. "I am really awfully enthusiastic about being an archaeologist," Ellingson wrote to her family in an undated letter. Her eager anticipation of fieldwork is equally visible in an undated photo that was most likely taken prior to her departure for Greece (figure 1.2).

Ellingson was well suited for archaeological fieldwork. She had a strong personality and little patience for anyone who underestimated her. While still traveling to Olynthus she complains in a March 20 letter of the Greek hospitality workers:

Figure 1.2. Mary Ross Ellingson (left) elegantly dressed but ready to dig. The photo is unlabeled and so the identity of the woman on the right is unknown but she may be Helen Boyle, Ellingson's traveling companion during her return to the United States. The date and location are also unknown but it is likely this photo was taken at her home in Edmonton in late 1930 or early 1931. (Photo courtesy of the University of Evansville Archives)

There is an automatic Elevator in the hotel which we would like to run but, oh no, they must do it for us. And as for us opening the front door ourselves, oh mercy me, how degrading!

Her letters demonstrate another personality trait essential for a good archaeologist, one that indicates flexibility and an ability to get along with others: a sense of humor. Her letters are filled with quips such as this from March 10:

Oh I forgot to mention that we have several celebrities on board. Ripley (you know, believe it or not Ripley) but of course he's up in 1st class so we haven't had a look at him, and the late Al Capone (you know Scarface Al Capone of Chicago-fame)'s body-guard (being deported) but they are down in steerage so we haven't had a look at them either.

Classmate in the classical archaeology program at Johns Hopkins, Gladys Rachel Davidson, who would later add Weinberg to her name after she married, was born December 27, 1909 (figure 1.3).[13] Although her father, Israel Davidson, was a scholar of Hebrew literature, Weinberg became interested in the ancient Greek language and classical cultures in high school. She attended McGill University in Montreal but graduated with a BA from New York University in 1930 and, like Ellingson, had just started at Johns Hopkins when Robinson asked her to go to Olynthus.[14] Unlike many of his colleagues, Robinson cared little about Weinberg's Jewish heritage. Anti-Semitism was rife in American higher education at the time;[15] Princeton, Harvard, Yale, Columbia, Cornell, even the University of Virginia were a few of the many institutions that adopted explicit discriminatory admissions policies.[16] Discrimination existed in hiring as well; by 1940 only 2 percent of the faculty in American colleges and universities were Jewish. A recent study has been unable to locate a single Jewish faculty member teaching in the humanities in any American institution of higher learning prior to 1940. Jewish women like Weinberg who entered academia prior to the Second World War have been dubbed the "lone voyagers," indicating how rare they were.[17] The liberal admissions policy of Johns Hopkins and Robinson's welcoming attitude surely brought Weinberg to attend graduate school there.

Weinberg was popular and likeable, as Ellingson indicates in the quote at the beginning of this chapter when she mentions the large number of friends who came to see Weinberg off when the *Roma* set sail from New York. Ellingson also felt very close to Weinberg even though she was three years younger than Ellingson, being only twenty-one when they watched the Statue of Liberty disappear from sight from the deck of the *Roma*.[18] Ellingson was unaware of this, writing in an April 9 letter "I am the youngest on the party [(]I think Gladys is about the same age but she seems older)," which is an unintended commentary on Weinberg's maturity.

Figure 1.3. Gladys Davidson Weinberg taking notes with her feet in a cistern on the South Hill at Olynthus. (Photo courtesy of the University of Evansville Archives)

"Gladys Davidson [Weinberg], of course I am very fond of. We are very good friends. Sally Freemen & I aren't so thick but we get along O.K. I don't care much for her," Ellingson states in a letter dated April 9. Sarah "Sally" Elizabeth Freeman was a year younger than Ellingson having been born in 1907[19] in Blairstown, New Jersey[20] (figure 1.4). A graduate of Mount Holyoke College in 1928, she had started at Johns Hopkins before Ellingson. While a graduate student she was a champion tennis player.[21] The competitive personality required for succeeding at tennis may have been one of the traits that rubbed Ellingson the wrong way. Regardless of what it was that annoyed Ellingson, it is clear the two women had very different personalities. While it is dangerous to read too much into such things, it is perhaps telling that in nearly every photo in which Freeman appears from Olynthus she is wearing pants (figure 1.4). Ellingson, on the other hand, is always wearing a skirt or dress in photos. Their choice of field attire speaks to two different approaches women of their generation took to working in archaeology. Wearing male clothing was a direct approach showing a woman was able to do what a man could while wearing female clothing spoke to a softer approach, reassuring men that a woman was not trying to usurp their roles.[22]

Despite their differences, all three women had an adventurous and plucky nature. In a letter dated March 16 Ellingson shows their more mischievous side:

[We] had quite a lark the other night, after the Captain's Dinner Party. We broke the wire on the lock keeping us from 2nd class & crawled under the canvas. I was in the lead, & when I rose up from ungraceful position on hands & knees (from crawling under the canvas partition) I was face to face with one of the ship's officers. Nothing daunt[ed] . . . I waited till

Figure 1.4. Sarah "Sally" Freeman on site at Olynthus. (Photo courtesy of the David M. Robinson Collection, Archives and Special Collections, University of Mississippi Libraries)

Sally & Gladys got thru, & we marched up to the top deck. The officer evidently decided we were harmless. After making ourselves at home in 2nd class, we watched our chances & got thru the 1st class gate, which was much easier, we didn't have to crawl under any canvas. We finally got to the top deck of 1st class, which is really beautifully fixed up. Then we decided we wanted to play shuffle board but it was too dark on 1st, so we went back to 2nd but there the things you play with were all put away & of course we couldn't ask for them. So then what [did] we do but go back to 1st (carefully avoiding all officers, deckhands & stewards) & carry enough poles & quoits or whatever they are, back to 2nd & started to play. We played until a nosey deck-hand came around, & then went off to report us, then we gracefully retired under the canvas again, so that when an officer came to put us off, we weren't there. Fooled him.

CLASSICAL ARCHAEOLOGY AND WOMEN ARCHAEOLOGISTS IN 1931

Ellingson was clear that she wanted to be an archaeologist working in Greece and her two classmates appear to have shared her career goal; Ellingson labeled a photograph of herself, Weinberg, and Freeman taken at Johns Hopkins "The three archaeologists" (see figure 8.2). Classical archaeology is a vocation, not a job of course, so the program at Johns Hopkins prepared students to become college professors and, if that was not possible, museum curators. None of "the three archaeologists" could have understood the full magnitude of the challenges that would face them as they pursued their vocation and careers. It was difficult enough for any American or Canadian to pursue fieldwork in Greece because access to excavations was carefully controlled. Women were not encouraged to join in fieldwork, an activity commonly seen as a masculine occupation, although recent history had shown that some strong-willed women could make a place for themselves. Finding a post, particularly in academia, was also a challenge, although there had been recent signs that more opportunities were opening for women. The novelty of Ellingson, Weinberg, and Freeman heading out to join an archaeological excavation was still unusual enough in 1931 to warrant an article in the *New York Times* with the title "Four College Girls Join Olynthus Quest."[23]

All American archaeology in Greece was, and remains, controlled by the American School of Classical Studies in Athens. The purpose of the American School is to offer an education in classical languages, literature, history, and archaeology to students who live in the school's facilities in Athens, from which students visit museums and sites around the city and country. Spending a year studying at the American School is also an important step toward a career in classics and classical archaeology. The American School was the first American research center abroad when it opened its doors in 1882.[24] Almost from its inception, any American who has wanted to excavate in Greece collaborates with the American School, which then supports his or her application for an excavation permit from the Greek government; for all intents and purposes an American excavator needs the blessing of the American School to get a permit. This power makes the school the center of American archaeological research in Greece.[25] The advantage to this system is that the directors of the American School can insist on the highest levels of excellence when it comes to excavation technique, denying permits to those who fail to meet their standards. In this way the American School developed the first cadre of professional American classical archaeologists by the time World War I broke out.[26] The disadvantages to this monopoly on the permitting process are that it can become politically charged and that new ideas can be discouraged by conservative American School directors.[27] Indeed, the conservatism of the American School is well represented by the classical echoes in the style of architecture directors adopted for the school's buildings. In a 1927 photo of the newly built addition to the School, the Gennadion Library (figure 1.5), the conservative classical Greek influences are literally set in stone.

The American School runs two of its own excavations, one at the ancient port city of Corinth and the other in the commercial, political, and social center of ancient Athens, an area known as the *agora*. Excavations at the latter site began in 1896 and at the former site in 1931, at the same time Ellingson and her colleagues were at work at Olynthus.[28] Although there have been a few significant interruptions, especially during wars, these excavations

Figure 1.5. The recently constructed Gennadion Library of the American School of Classical Studies in Athens as it appeared in 1927. (Photo by Wilhelmina van Ingen, courtesy of Raymond Dessy)

have continued nearly every year up to the present. Both sites are central training grounds; more American classical archaeologists have been trained at Corinth than at any other single site in the Mediterranean basin.[29]

Almost from its foundation, women were eager to study at the American School. The first woman to attend a regular session at the School was Annie S. Peck, a professor of Latin at Purdue University, who arrived in 1885.[30] Directors at the School did not necessarily oppose having women there, they were simply wary about the number of women overwhelming that of men. While they were willing to have women participate as students at the school, early directors opposed women participating in excavations. It was not until 1908 that the first woman was allowed to excavate at Corinth.[31]

Despite this opposition, a first generation of American women came to Greece and participated in excavations. After spending time at the American School and being denied access to the Corinth excavations, Harriet Boyd Hawes left the oversight of the American School directors in Athens for the wild and distant island of Crete to survey for sites. Beginning in 1900 she undertook excavations at several Bronze Age sites on the island including her most famous project at the Minonan palace of Gournia. Boyd Hawes was the first woman of any nationality to direct the excavation of a site and then publish it while being assisted by another woman, Edith Hall Dohan.[32] In 1911 Hetty Goldman and Alice Leslie Walker began directing work at the site of Halae. They continued to work in Greece before and after World War I as well as in Turkey after the war.[33]

These pioneers of the first generation of American female archaeologists have been called the "radicals."[34] Ellingson, Weinberg, and Freeman were the beginning of the second generation. While some excavation directors in the United States and Britain encouraged women of this generation to participate in fieldwork,[35] those in Greece depended on a technique for dealing with the growing number of women who wanted to dig in order to avoid their radicalization: contain by segregation.[36] Many project directors chose to put women to work in the dig house cataloging finds rather than out in the field excavating with the men, a division of labor used to contain some women of the first generation as well.[37] William Henry Fox, director of the Brooklyn Museum, explained the ideological justification for the segregation of women by stating, "Women are especially suited to museum work by their love of the beautiful, their adaptability and their patience in detail work."[38] Working at the excavation home base limited opportunities for women to publish and many wound up writing catalogs of "small finds," the coins, small figurines, bits of metal and glass that turn up at every excavation; it was left to the men to publish grand syntheses explaining the full history of a site and all its features.[39] While cataloging finds may not be as glamorous or heroic as excavating, it is by all means a necessary component of fieldwork without which there would be no grand syntheses. This model for the sexual division of labor prevailed for the most part at the American-led excavations at Corinth and in the Athenian Agora.[40] Of the three future archaeologists aboard the *Roma*, Ellingson makes it clear in her letters that while she looked forward to cataloging, she also wanted to dig, an intention that may have gone unfulfilled if she had worked at a site in Greece other than Olynthus. She does not comment on the goals of Weinberg or Freeman.

Although obstacles existed, there were still a few signs in the 1920s and 1930s Ellingson may have noticed that suggested the field was opening to female participation. The number of women in the field saw a slow but nonetheless significant increase in those years.[41] Although it was three years before she arrived at Johns Hopkins, Ellingson still may have heard that Goldman had taught at the university as a visiting lecturer, a clear demonstration that a woman could make it in the field of classical archaeology.[42] The first American woman had earned her PhD in classical archaeology as early as 1908,[43] and in 1933 a contemporary of Ellingson opened the field of anthropological archaeology to women by earning the first PhD in prehistoric archaeology.[44] The year after Ellingson's season at Olynthus Mary Hamilton Swindler would be appointed editor of one of the flagship scholarly journals in classical archaeology, the *American Journal of Archaeology*; she would come to have the longest tenure in that position of any editor remaining until 1946.[45] The prospects for women in the field of archaeology were not good in 1931 but if Ellingson, Weinberg, and Freeman looked closely enough they would have seen many signs of hope that the situation was changing in their favor.

Whether Ellingson and her cabinmates knew it or not, opportunities for women to be employed in academia also increased during and after World War I. The women's suffrage movement had helped improve the numbers of women teaching at universities as had the labor shortage during the war, a shortage which allowed women to get out of the house and work. The percentage of women faculty in American institutions of higher learning rose from 19.8 during the 1899–1900 academic year to 27.6 in 1929–1930.[46] As Ellingson entered the University of Alberta to begin her undergraduate studies, in the United States the American Association of University Professors' Committee W was examining the gender inequities in faculty employment and pay and was seeking remedies. Committee W published data that, while demonstrating encouraging trends, illuminate serious problems for women who wanted to become professors. According to a 1922 report an average of only 4 percent of full professors at coeducational institutions was women and 23.6 percent of instructor positions were held by women. Instructors had higher teaching loads and therefore less time for research and publication, which was the primary avenue for professional advancement.[47] Any woman entering graduate school in 1930, as Ellingson, Weinberg, and Freeman did, would have hope for advancement in the field and in a career but must have understood that it would be difficult.

J. WALTER GRAHAM, ALEXANDER SCHULZ, AND ARTHUR AND GLADYS PARSONS

The *Roma* docked in her home port of Rome.[48] To get to Greece, the trio had to cross Italy by train to the Adriatic port of Brindisi, stopping to see some of the sites along the way, and then boarded another ship for Greece. They arrived in Athens on March 20 as Ellingson wrote to her family:

> We got in today at 4. The boys, Alex Schulz (from Hopkins, who came over about 5 weeks ago, very nice boy) & Walter Graham (the Canadian who was at Hopkins last year & won a scholarship at the American School here) met us at the boat, & they had a man to arrange all our luggage etc.

The fellow Canadian, James Walter Graham (figure 1.6), was twenty-four years old when he met Ellingson on the docks in the port of Athens. Graham came to Johns Hopkins from Acadia University in Wolfville, Nova Scotia, where he had received his BA in 1927 and MA in 1928.[49] Graham may have been the first Canadian to become a Fellow in Archaeology at the School.[50] He took advantage of his time there to learn the craft of archaeology by attending lectures of, and by talking informally to, prominent archaeologists working in Greece and by participating in the School's Corinth excavation. Graham had received excellent training before joining the Olynthus staff. In 1931 he spent the first of two field seasons at Olynthus. Ellingson clearly liked Graham. In an April 9 letter from Olynthus she writes:

> Walter Graham is a very nice chap, & awfully helpful about showing one how to write reports, etc, & he has loaned me his

Figure 1.6. J. Walter Graham illustrates his hypothesis that houses at Olynthus had second stories reached by wooden staircases, the first step of which was made from stone. (Photo courtesy of the University of Evansville Archives)

cane, which is sure a help. They are convenient to lean on, & also convenient when there are dogs around.

Graham also lent Ellingson his typewriter. She used it to type some of her letters as well as her field reports.

The other person who welcomed Ellingson, Weinberg, and Freeman to Athens the day they arrived was Alexander Heinrich Gottfried Schulz (figure 1.7). In the same letter quoted above Ellingson wrote of him:

Alex Schulz is very nice, too. He is the life of the party type, always, I mean often, not always, making everybody laugh. He is Dutch & German descent. His father is a prof[essor] at the U[niversity] of Illinois.

Figure 1.7. Alexander Schulz demonstrating the use of a sitting ceramic bathtub found at Olynthus while smoking his pipe for comic effect. This photo was probably taken when the Olynthus excavators visited the archaeological museum in Salonica (modern Thessaloniki) in June 1931. (Photo courtesy of the University of Evansville Archives)

Schulz was just a year older than Ellingson and had completed his undergraduate degree at the University of Illinois in Urbana where Ellingson relates his father taught physics. His family appears to have been fairly wealthy; Schulz is the only person in Ellingson's photos holding a pipe and wearing a smoking jacket. He is also the only graduate student among the Olynthus staff in 1931 who did not type his thesis himself as he could afford to hire a typist. Schulz seems to have had a romantic-adventurous streak. Ellingson reports in a May 20 letter that upon leaving Olynthus he intended to rent a motorcycle with a friend and tour Europe.

After a day seeing the sights in Athens, the party of five took the train to Saloniki, which Ellingson also spells as Salonique, and Salonica. Saloniki, modern Thessaloniki, is one of Greece's major cities and offered the last chance for the group to enjoy the comforts of civilization before heading into the Greek back country. Ellingson was impressed with their accommodations as her March 22 letter makes clear:

> The Mediterranean Palace [see figure 1.8], the resort of the idle rich, the pleasure haunt of millionaires, the playground of the wealthy! A room to myself. Davey got us a 70% reduction on the rooms so we decided to stay here, as it is really a lovely hotel, & only about 80 drachmas, or 96¢ a day.

"Davey" Robinson may have been trying to compensate in advance for the living conditions he knew he would be subjecting his crew to once they were on site. He had said of the women joining the excavation, "they will have to rough it with the rest of us. I am afraid it will not prove so dramatic as they think."[51]

Ellingson describes their train journey from Athens to Saloniki in the March 22 letter:

> We came right on to Salonica last night instead of stopping off at Larissa as we had intended. It was raining when we got there

Figure 1.8. Photo of the Mediterranean Palace Hotel in Saloniki (modern Thessaloniki) in June 1931. (Photo courtesy of the University of Evansville Archives)

so we decided that another 3 hours on the train wouldn't kill us, & we can see the Vale of Tempe on the way back. . . . We had a lot of fun on the train. The 2 boys are both very nice, and a lot of fun, so I think we shall get along o.k. Mr. & Mrs. Parsons have arrived also & Mr. & Mrs. Robinson get in this morning.

Arthur Parsons came to Johns Hopkins from California to study classical archaeology. His father was the Protestant Episcopal bishop of his home state.[52] Recently married, he and his wife Gladys joined the staff at Olynthus together in 1931 (figure 1.9). Ellingson liked Arthur but was slow to warm up to Gladys. Nonetheless Gladys Parsons took a motherly interest in the young Ellingson. In the April 9 letter to her family in which she describes her colleagues, she writes of the couple:

Mrs. Parsons (Gladys) is always seeing that I have a flashlight (I had to borrow one of their's permanently). Arthur Parsons is very nice. The Parsons are an awfully nice couple. They are very much in love with each other (married a year). . . . She is quite a bit older than Arthur. She is awfully interesting. Knows all sorts of interesting people, and has travelled a lot. I didn't like her at all when I first met her but I think she is a peach now.

DAVID AND HELEN ROBINSON

The day after Ellingson and the others arrived in Saloniki they met with David Robinson and his wife, Helen. Robinson was born on September 21, 1880, in Auburn, New York, and so was fifty years old at the time he met his graduate-student staff members in Saloniki (figure 1.10).[53] Robinson's father was a Baptist minister who became the pastor of a church in Brooklyn. The young Robinson showed a powerful talent for languages, mastering Latin and Greek as a teen and later French and German. When only thirteen years old he began his course of study at the University of Chicago and by 1898 had completed his bachelor's degree in Greek.[54] Promptly entering the graduate program at Chicago he supplemented his

Figure 1.9. Arthur and Gladys Parsons from a group photo taken at Myriophito. (Photo courtesy of the University of Evansville Archives)

Figure 1.10. David Robinson standing in one of the houses at Olynthus. (Photo courtesy of the David M. Robinson Collection, Archives and Special Collections, University of Mississippi Libraries)

American studies with stints abroad in Germany at Halle, Bonn, and Berlin.[55] At that time the German universities offered the best education in classics. The German approach was known as *Altertumswissenschaft*, literally "the scientific study of antiquity," and put equal weight on all aspects of ancient culture, encouraging students to study the art history, languages, history, and archaeology of the Greeks and Romans.[56] Robinson's career shows he embraced the German approach; while he is known today for his archaeological research he also published works on classical history, epigraphy, literature, philology as well as verse translations of both Latin and Greek poets, particularly his favorite, Sappho.[57] An avid collector of ancient artifacts, he published three volumes on vases in his own collection in the international multivolume catalog of Greek vases, the *Corpus Vasorum Antiquorum*.[58] As would be expected, Robinson went to Athens to study at the American School and gained his first taste of fieldwork in 1902 and 1903 at Corinth. He used material from these experiences as the basis for his dissertation, which earned him his PhD at the University of Chicago in 1904.[59]

The next year he became the first archaeologist Johns Hopkins University hired on a full-time basis for its Department of Art and Archaeology; he would remain there as the department head for more than forty years.[60] Temporary faculty had already turned the department into a major force in the discipline of classical archaeology within the United States by that date. In fact, classics was the first graduate program established at Johns Hopkins after the foundation of the university in 1876. Robinson augmented that reputation and turned the department into one of the preeminent departments in the country. Although professors like Frank and Albright helped, Robinson taught most of the courses his students took.[61] He was a tremendously popular teacher throughout his career and his undergraduate courses were always filled.[62] Producing successful graduates with their MAs and PhDs is another measure of the success of a professor and a graduate program and by this measure Robinson and the archaeology program at Johns Hopkins were highly successful. Robinson's program has been called "an academic factory" for the high number of degrees it granted.[63]

While at Johns Hopkins, Robinson showed leadership in the field in other ways as well. To name just a few of his more outstanding accomplishments, he edited journals and popular magazines such as *Classical Weekly*, *American Journal of Philology*, and *Art and Archaeology*, the latter being the forerunner to the current *Archaeology* magazine. After founding the *Art Bulletin* he served as its first editor. Robinson served as president of the College Art Association and held several posts, including president, of the main umbrella group for archaeologists in North America, the Archaeological Institute of America. He also continued fieldwork in what is now Turkey excavating at the Greco-Roman cities of Sardis in 1910 and Antioch in Pisidia in 1924 (see figure I.3). His leadership of this last excavation came about purely by chance. In May 1924 Francis Kelsey was unexpectedly unable to lead the University of Michigan's excavations at the site.[64] Kelsey asked Robinson to take over at the last minute, no doubt partly because of the formidable reputation he had within the archaeological field.[65]

Robinson's most recent project was the excavation at Olynthus. He had first visited the site in 1902 and picked up shards of ancient black- and red-figured pottery as well as the heads of some small terracotta figurines on the ground surface, all of which indicated the presence of an important site.[66] The first season at the site, in 1928, did not go well. Robinson had failed to keep up with developments in excavation technique and so was digging in a manner several years outdated. One of his graduate student staff members in 1928, Wilhelmina van Ingen, wrote about her experiences in a series of letters to her mother. These letters now reside in the archives at Virginia Tech.[67] The central task Robinson gave to van Ingen and her friend and fellow graduate student, Eunice Couch née Stebbins, was the inventorying of finds. Robinson brought the pair out of the dig house to help supervise the excavation trenches only a few times during the months they were at Olynthus. Even though she was a graduate student working on her first excavation, van Ingen recognized immediately specific problems with Robinson's techniques, which she catalogs in a letter dated April 11, 1928. In this quote she refers to Couch by the nickname Nike, the name of the Greek goddess of victory:

> Nike and I went up to the dig to watch trenches today—a great relief after having been cooped up in the house constantly doing close work. I hope Davy [Robinson] lets us go out more—certainly we are needed for there are so many workmen and trenches that it is impossible to keep close enough watch over things. . . . I have been watching one trench—there were 131 workmen in it today, in an area of about thirty square yards, and it is impossible to keep an adequate record of what is found—and as soon as I get some little orderly plan worked out, Davy comes along and changes everything, so it's all rather futile.
>
> The chief value of this experience to me will be that I shall have formed some ideas of what NOT to do, and shall have had

some opportunity to observe the various sorts of objects which are turned up—if I can remember them until sometime when they can be explained AND dated by someone who knows some archaeology.

In an earlier letter dated March 21 she states, "Things are not developing as easily as they might, and it is possible that the time will come when I will not care to add my presence at this dig to my list of credentials." Rumors drifted back to the American School in Athens that Robinson's techniques of recording the context in which artifacts were found were seriously lacking, causing serious concern.[68]

Upon completion of the 1928 season, Robinson began to publish articles as well as volumes on his findings at Olynthus with unbelievable speed. The first volume in the *Excavations at Olynthus* series appeared in 1929 and was the only volume for which Robinson's name does not appear on the cover page. It was a publication of the dissertation written by his student George Mylonas on a Neolithic settlement at the site. Robinson wrote and published the second volume on the architecture at the site in 1930, less than two years after his initial field season. The following year he managed to complete and publish no less than two additional volumes, *Olynthus III* on the coins found in the 1928 season and *Olynthus IV* on the small terracotta figurines he had uncovered.

Reviews of these volumes were mixed. Some classists were impressed with his arguments for having found the site of Olynthus mentioned by Demosthenes in the *Olynthiacs*, while both numismatists and art historians appreciated the new evidence of well-dated pieces he had found to inform their fields.[69] The archaeologists who reviewed his work were not impressed at all, however, echoing van Ingen's criticisms. Dohan, writing about the terracotta figurines published in *Olynthus* IV, complained about a lack of contextual information stating there was little point in publishing figurines from an excavation if Robinson could not explain specifically where within the site of Olynthus they were found; naturally it matters a great deal for understanding how a terracotta figurine was used if it is found in a temple, or house, or even in the public or private rooms within a house.[70] Alan Wace, director of the British School at Athens and excavator at sites across Greece,[71] made a similar complaint lamenting the lack of information not only about the horizontal but also the vertical find spot of each lamp.[72] Another reviewer made an even more stinging charge:

> In these days when the standard of excavation is already high, and the technique becoming yearly more perfect, there is no excuse for an ill-conducted excavation. Archaeologists make it a matter of principle not to employ large numbers of workmen without the most expert and careful supervision, or to confuse evidence by overhasty search for results. Nor do the Archaeological Schools usually entrust a site, whether large or small, to anyone who has not had adequate training. The methods adopted at Olynthus were, therefore, a shock to those who saw or heard of them, nor will their reputation be retrieved by the volume under discussion.[73]

Another criticism of the 1928 season was about the failure to find fine sculptures, Greek inscriptions, or public architecture. At that time these were the primary prizes classical archaeologists sought when digging. Van Ingen neatly sums up what all were thinking during that season in a letter dated March 16, 1928: "So far they haven't found much that's exciting—lots of private houses, terracotta, vase fragments, coins, etc. but no public buildings or inscriptions."[74] Van Ingen expressed her opinion privately in a letter but others expressed their disappointment in Robinson's finds publically in print, adding to his humiliation.[75] Robinson came to his second season at Olynthus in 1931 looking for redemption.

Ellingson gives no indication that she was aware of these pressures on Robinson; she clearly had a deep respect and affection for the man. Although she was less than half Robinson's age, Ellingson's letters show they had a friendly, even flirtatious relationship. She repeatedly refers to him as "Davey" in her letters and, presumably, in person. Admittedly, she was not the only young woman to be so informal with him; van Ingen, referred to him repeatedly as "Davey" in her letters as well.[76] Nonetheless, in the April 9 letter to her mother quoted above Ellingson writes:

> The other night I asked him [Robinson] where the men were going to be paid, & he said "would you like to pay them? You're the prettiest girl here, you can be Miss Olynthus, & pay the men." And the other day when my hand was swollen from a flea bite, he said, "You have a pretty neck, I hope it doesn't swell up." And on rainy days, he tells me I don't need to go to the dig at all. (I mean on days when it is threatening to rain, we don't go at all on rainy days.)

It seems unlikely that their relationship ever went beyond flirtation. Mentioning the compliments Robinson made to her in a letter to her mother hardly seems the actions of a woman engaged in an adulterous affair. Ellingson also describes the protective attitude Mrs. Robinson had toward the younger woman and Ellingson never mentions anything Mrs. Robinson said or did that indicated she felt jealousy. Quite the contrary, Mrs. Robinson did not hesitate to take trips to Saloniki while her husband remained at Olynthus working with Ellingson. Also in the same letter quoted above to her mother Ellingson writes: "Mrs. R[obinson], is awfully nice to me too, & she calls me 'Little One' just like you do . . . & [she] loans me her own shoes etc."[77] Nonetheless others on the crew must have noticed the pairs' flirtations.

Ellingson's affection for Robinson was not shared by all who worked with him. Van Ingen had carefully contemplated going with Robinson to Olynthus while she was still studying at the American School and as a result anticipated the coming season with trepidation. In a letter sent from Athens dated February 24,

1928, she writes: "The two months in Olynthus may not be un-alloyed pleasure—Davy is exceedingly difficult to get along with and not always entirely to be commended in his actions."[78] A few months later on April 2 writing from Olynthus she sums up her feelings about Robinson: "In brief he is a poor scholar, un-gentlemanly, and not always honest."[79] Her letters record fights and tears and the constant strain of dealing with a man she and her fellow graduate students found to be controlling, egotistical, and vindictive. In a fairly typical letter dated April 11 van Ingen writes:

> Davy is more or less on his good behavior, though he's always sticking sly little digs into the conversation that Nike and I know are meant for us. Also, there is a constant nervous strain trying to keep one's temper and not get wrought up over things, and seeing the dig carried on in such a careless way, and not being able to do anything about it.

In early May van Ingen and her two fellow graduate student colleagues finally decided to depart the excavation ten days before they were scheduled to leave, their flight precipitated by a tremendous fight with Robinson.[80] Van Ingen finally did transfer to Harvard and successfully pursued her graduate studies without Robinson.[81] It is quite telling that of all the staff members from Johns Hopkins or the American School who joined Robinson for the initial season at Olynthus in 1928, only one, George Mylonas, returned for additional seasons at the site.

Robinson was a conundrum, however. While he may have been controlling of his graduate students, he also went far out of his way to take care of Ellingson and his other students by making certain they received what they needed to be successful. He helped them find grants and scholarships to support their studies and travels.[82] The American School offered fellowships to students who scored well on the school's exams in ancient Greek and history and either literature or archaeology, which candidates took at their home institution at the time they were applying to attend the American School. In at least one case Robinson fought fiercely to get one of his students a fellowship. Among the letters of Edward Capps, the chairman of the Fellowship Committee, now archived at the American School, were some from committee members objecting to giving one of Robinson's students a fellowship because of her gender, deafness, and facility on the exams. Letters from Robinson defend her fiercely; in the end the committee gave her the fellowship. By 1934 the director of the American School, Richard Stillwell, was unhappy about the large number of Johns Hopkins students at the American School, a backhanded compliment to Robinson's efforts.[83]

Robinson was willing to do whatever it took to get his students a fellowship at the American School, perhaps even if it was not ethical. In late 1932 a graduate student at Johns Hopkins tipped off the American School's Fellowship Committee that a certain professor was feeding information to his students about specific questions and topics on the exams. An investigation ensued, during which members of the committee discreetly referred to the accused teacher as "Professor Blank," never actually giving his name. The committee made changes to the manner in which they gave the exam to thwart any future attempts to cheat. Incidental clues in the correspondence over the matter have led one historian of the American School to suggest that Robinson was "Professor Blank."[84]

Whether or not Robinson helped his students cheat on the exam, there was clearly tension between him and the leadership of the American School. During the 1920s and 1930s faculty from Princeton University were moving into the leadership positions of the American School and a rivalry developed with students and faculty from other universities, especially Johns Hopkins.[85] Van Ingen's letters show the pleasure she and the other Johns Hopkins students took with Robinson in sharing embarrassing gossip about the Princeton students.[86] This rivalry had consequences for

Robinson that went far beyond mere rumor spreading. In 1928 the Greek government attempted to take the power to issue permits for American-led excavations in Greece away from the American School through legislation making the government the sole entity to decide who received permits. Leaders at the American School fought to have their right to decide which American projects should be recommended for permits to the Greek antiquities authorities. By the end of 1928 the American School had won the dispute and retains the right to this day. At the beginning of 1928, however, before the American School had secured this right and as the dispute with the Greek government was developing, officials at the School asserted that Robinson had to go through them before he sought a permit from the Greeks for his first season of excavation at Olynthus.[87] They also insisted that since this would be an American School–sanctioned excavation he had to bring three students currently attending the school's regular session to work on the excavation. The three student-representatives Robinson and school officials agreed upon were from Johns Hopkins: van Ingen, Stebbins Couch, and Herbert Couch.[88] It is not clear how Robinson reacted to this assertion of power, especially when the person behind it was Capps from Princeton. It is easy, though, to imagine the tension that must have existed, especially since all the excavations Robinson had directed prior to this were outside of Greece in places where Robinson had a great deal more independence. In 1931 Robinson had to have known that officials from the American School would be watching his second season closely after his poor performance during the first season and would be deciding whether or not to allow him to have a third season in the future.

Robinson's tempestuous personality led him to bitter conflicts throughout his life. He was at his most vengeful, however, when he believed his intellectual property rights had been violated. While working on the material from his Antioch excavation in 1924 he became embroiled in a dispute with Sir James

Ramsey over who had the right to publish, and therefore have the claim to have discovered, an important inscription found at the site. The inscription was a copy of the *Res Gestae Augusti*, a document the first Roman emperor, Augustus, wrote at the beginning of the first century CE detailing his accomplishments and justifying his position as the first emperor. Augustus was, without a doubt, one of the most influential of all the Roman emperors and the discovery of portions of his own assessment of his reign was something quite extraordinary. Pieces of the inscription had been found at other sites but having another copy with portions of hitherto unknown text made the find a huge coup. Ramsey had been supervising the area where the inscription was found but when Robinson had agreed at the last minute to lead the excavation in Kelsey's stead part of the agreement was that he would be allowed to publish everything that had been found there, especially the inscriptions.[89] When Ramsey published news of the discovery and his transcription of the inscription, Robinson labeled Ramsey's publication "illegal."[90] The dispute between them spread across the pages of several scholarly journals.[91] Robinson added personal insult to his legalistic invectives against Ramsey. He claimed that he had found additional pieces of the inscription in Ramsey's back-dirt pile, implying Ramsey had missed portions of this major discovery during excavation. Such a charge is the ultimate insult one archaeologist can level against another. Robinson did not stop there—he even claimed to have purchased pieces of the inscription from nearby villagers who had fished them out of Ramsey's back-dirt pile.[92] By relating the story Robinson obliquely suggested rural farmers with no formal training in archaeology were better able to spot important finds than Ramsey.

In 1910 Robinson married Helen Haskell (figure 1.11), who was his constant companion during the Olynthus excavations.[93] Stepdaughter of the Protestant Episcopal Bishop of Maryland, she was a graduate of Bennett College, a women's college in

Millbrook, New York.[94] Ellingson really liked Mrs. Robinson and spoke fondly of her years after their shared experience in the field.[95] George Mylonas writes of her:

His many students will cherish forever the picture of Mrs. Robinson as the graceful hostess who brightened so many of their days, and those who were privileged to participate in the excavations of Olynthus will never forget her kindness, her efficiency and cheerfulness in the midst of adverse conditions, and her understanding of the failings of human nature.[96]

His comments are rather cryptic, perhaps intentionally. Does he suggest that Mrs. Robinson forgave the students' human failings while at Olynthus or that she helped them forgive those of her husband?

Figure 1.11. Photograph by Mary Ross Ellingson taken in Saloniki on the morning of March 25, 1931, as Robinson and his crew prepared to depart for Olynthus. From left to right, George Mylanos, Helen Robinson, David Robinson, an unidentified man, Arthur Parsons, Sarah Freeman, Alexander Schulz, and Gladys Davidson Weinberg. (Photo courtesy of the University of Evansville Archives)

GEORGE AND LELA MYLONAS

The last couple to join the expedition in Saloniki was George Emmanuel Mylonas (figure 1.12) and his wife, Lela. Mylonas was one of the Greek-speaking natives of the western portion of Asia Minor known as Ionia, having been born in 1898 in Smyrna, or modern Izmir. When he was seventeen years old, Mylonas went to Athens to study classics at the University of Athens and during World War I joined the Greek army to fight against the Ottoman Empire and its ally, Germany. He was taken prisoner and almost did not survive his imprisonment. When he was finally released in 1923 he went to Greece at a time of great turmoil. Greece had just concluded a disastrous war with Turkey which ended with an exchange of ethnic Greeks from Turkey and Turks from Greece. Mylonas met another refugee from Turkey, Lela Papazoglu, and the two were married in 1925. He found employment working at the American School in Athens as a bursar and translator.[97] In 1927 the University of Athens awarded Mylonas a PhD after he completed his dissertation on the Neolithic period in Greece. The following year he came to Johns Hopkins to complete a second PhD in only one year.[98] Robinson made Mylonas's Hopkins dissertation the inaugural volume in the *Olynthus* series and gave him the unique honor of allowing Mylonas's name alone to appear as the author of the *Excavations at Olynthus* I.[99] In the introduction to *Excavations at Olynthus* I Robinson expresses his great pride in seeing Mylonas's dissertation published in the *Excavations at Olynthus* series.

When Ellingson met Mylonas at Saloniki, he was thirty-two years old and already a distinguished archaeologist. In 1931 while he worked at the Olynthus excavation Mylonas was caught between two separate worlds and lifestyles, one in Greece and the other in the United States. After arriving at Johns Hopkins, he remained and seems to have been hoping to emigrate but needed a job, preferably a tenure-track position at a university.

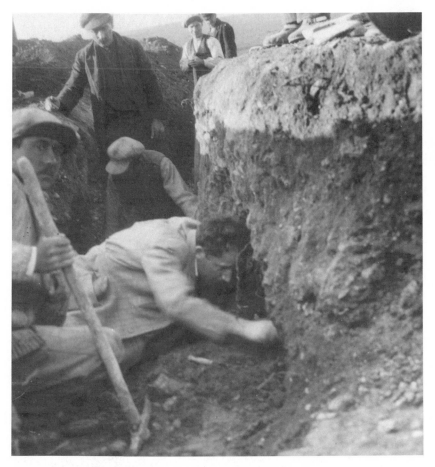

Figure 1.12. George Mylonas excavating at Olynthus. (Photo courtesy of the David M. Robinson Collection, Archives and Special Collections, University of Mississippi Libraries)

At that point he did not know if he would be able to make the move permanently or would have to remain in Greece. Ellingson rarely mentions him in her letters. In the April 9 letter where she describes her fellow staff members she merely says of Mylonas and his wife that they were very formal, always addressing everyone by their surnames preceded by "Mr." and "Miss." Ellingson seems to have found them to be rather aloof.

FROM SALONIKI TO OLYNTHUS

Driving the approximately sixty miles from Saloniki to Myriophito, the nearest town to the site of Olynthus, took the better
part of a day in 1931. Prior to the team's departure in two cars
and a truck on March 25, Ellingson snapped a photograph of
the group (figure 1.11). All are smiling and appear to be in good
spirits, a mood that would not last. In a letter to her family dated
March 26, she writes of the difficulties of the journey, "We had
to drive right thru a river. One sight we saw was a wall of water
coming down a dry river-bed, however we got in OK." The Parsons, Weinberg, and Freeman in the other car and the truck that
accompanied them did not have as easy a journey. Of them she
writes in a March 29 letter:

> As I started to tell, the other car had a terrible time getting out
> here. We didn't start until about 1, as we had been waiting for
> the truck. As Wednesday was a national holiday, there were a
> whole lot of parades etc., so they were held up, and then they had
> a flat tire. As there wasn't any spare, they had to go back and get
> another car. The man drove back on the rim, lickety split, over
> rough cobblestone roads. They got another car, and finally got
> out of Salonica at 3.15. They caught up to the truck, which had
> had a flat tire when we passed it, and when they passed it, it had
> its wheel off and was stuck in the mud. The rain was all over by
> the time they came along, so they had to get out in the mud and
> push while the sun was shining, which was infinitely better than
> getting out in the rain, I suppose. Finally it got dark, and they
> came to the river which they had to cross, and not being able to
> see the road, they went right thru instead of going a little further
> up as we had. And of course when they got in the middle of it,
> they got stuck and Gladys and Sally and Arthur had to get out in
> the water and push. Maybe I was glad I wasn't with them. Finally
> they got to Modania, where Mr. Mylonas had gone to meet them,
> about 9.30, and they went to the inn there, which isn't so hot, I
> guess. They got over [to Myriophito] about noon.

When Ellingson snapped a photo of the group preparing to leave Saloniki (figure 1.11) everyone was very nicely dressed for traveling. Little did Parsons, Freeman, and Weinberg realize that in a few hours their clothes would be filthy from pushing a truck out of the mud and a car out of a river. They were not the only people who had ever had to push stuck vehicles out of a river in the area, however. In 1928 van Ingen snapped a photo of a Model T in a river near Olynthus clearly demonstrating that the rivers in the area could be quite treacherous (figure 1.13).

A LETTER READ, A JOURNEY COMPLETED

After reading her March 29 letter I searched for a magnifying glass to study the fine traveling clothes the team members were wearing in the group photo. My desk lamp now illuminated the letters, news clippings, and other photos from the album that littered my

Figure 1.13. A Model T stuck in a river near Myriophito in the spring of 1928. (Photo by Wilhelmina van Ingen, courtesy of Raymond Dessy)

desk. It was a disorganized mess. Ellingson and her colleagues had finally reached Olynthus and were about to begin excavating. Setting down the magnifying glass and photo, I shuffled through all the papers to find the next letter. Her stories had been entertaining so far but now I had the chance to learn something about one of the great American-led excavations in Greece to take place between the two World Wars. Did she, Weinberg, and Freeman actually get to excavate? Did Ellingson record any information that might change my, and perhaps others', understanding of this moment in the history of archaeology? Might she include details that failed to make it into the fourteen volumes of the *Excavations at Olynthus* series? She did not disappoint.

TWO

THE DAILY ROUTINE

The long journey was over and the team was now eager to get to work. While reading Ellingson's letters it was easy to get caught up in her excitement for her first field experience; in her stories anyone who has ever excavated could see reflections of their own time in the field. Her stories, some matter-of-fact, some rather amusing, are the type of stories all the excavators at Olynthus must have had but only she wrote down. She offers a unique peek at the human experience behind the factual data and conclusions in the pages of the *Excavations at Olynthus* series. Beyond that, however, she lays out the daily schedule, something no other surviving source from the Olynthus excavations does. Her descriptions are particularly useful for the history of archaeology as the style of massive horizontal excavation she describes is no longer practiced. Reading between the lines offers something even more relevant to archaeological history, clues to two major changes in Robinson's thinking that occurred between the 1928 and 1931 seasons. The first change was his decision to allow women to work in the field supervising trenches for the entire season, not just a few days. How much of this decision had to do with the abilities of the three women cabinmates and how much of it was because of his need of supervisors will never be clear. The second change was his decision that houses were a unit worthy of study. During the previous season his main purpose had been to find public buildings, the traditional focus of classical archaeology at the time, and he was deeply frustrated to uncover only private structures. In 1931 he saw opportunity in what he had considered to be of minimal value three years earlier. Both changes were to have a profound impact on Robinson and archaeology in Greece in ways he could never have envisioned nor ever intended. As I read her description of the daily routine's seemingly mundane details I realized Ellingson was offering me a front-row seat to a landmark moment in the history of Greek archaeology, a moment she describes with the breathless enthusiasm of someone discovering fieldwork for the first time and the keen eye of someone trained as a reporter.

STARTING THE DAY

Olynthus, March 27[, 1931].

Dear Family,

Well, here we are settled, real archaeologists. And would you guess what happened? Last night it started to snow, and boy was it cold or was it cold? We three girls and the Parsons had the top floor of a house, and we had those canvas cots. We each had three blankets and lots of sheets. All night long we lay there and wished for it to be 6.30 which was the appointed hour to get up, and of course when the alarm did go off we didn't want to get up. But as there is quite a bit of snow on the ground, we are not working today. We are over in the other house, and have a nice fireplace. [See figure 2.1]

Robinson chose to begin his excavation in late March and to end it in early June before it became too warm.[1] The clothing fashions of the 1930s did not allow excavators to wear the shorts, t-shirts, and tank tops ubiquitous on sites today, therefore excavating while properly attired in the heat of a Greek summer was out of the question. The current widespread availability of air conditioning also helps to cool crew members during breaks as well as during the night but this luxury was obviously not available in rural Greece in 1931. Digging in the spring helped Robinson and his team avoid the heat but they still had to cope with the cold and rain.

Figure 2.1. The main dig house in Myriophito where the entire team ate and worked and where the Robinsons slept. (Photo courtesy of the University of Evansville Archives)

As Ellingson mentions, she, Freeman, Weinberg, and the Parsons shared the upper story of a house while the bottom story was still occupied by a local family. Among Ellingson's papers is an undated news clipping from an unidentified source with the byline Thelma Atkinson.[2] Atkinson writes:

> Miss Ross writes that she found it exceedingly difficult to accustom herself to the morning invasion of the lower portions of the house by chickens, sheep and even pigs, warned by their hunger that breakfast time was near. Up at six, work commenced at seven.

The five would take their breakfast at the dig house with the Mylonas and the Robinsons. Afterward they would walk to the site wading through, or crossing via stepping stones over, the Resetnikia River and climbing a steep hill, a hike requiring some twenty to thirty minutes as Ellingson states in the same letter quoted above. In an April 8 letter she explains further to her father:

> The Retsinikia [sic], the river we have to cross to go to work, is probably impassable by now, as yesterday it was getting pretty high, and it has rained nearly all day, and heavily. When we first arrived here, we crossed the river piggy-back, on the workmen [see figure 2.2] but lately it has been so deep we have had to cross in an ox-cart, and if tomorrow weren't a holiday, I am sure we should have to swim. These Greek rivers are a howl. Half the time they are perfectly dry, and then a rain comes along, and they are raging torrents.

Once they had made it safely to the site the entire team could turn to their various work assignments.

Figure 2.2. A Greek workman carries David Robinson across the Resetnikia River with the village of Myriophito in the background. (Photo courtesy of the University of Evansville Archives)

WOMEN EXCAVATORS WORKING ON SITE

Although Robinson had been criticized for employing such a large workforce in 1928, he insisted on having an equally large number of paid Greek workmen in 1931 to make certain he could uncover large sections of the site. Sample entries in the daily log for the 1931 season give the specific numbers for each day:

> Saturday April 11, 1931—Resumed excavations with 215 men; short-handed on account of [Easter] holiday season.
> Friday, May 1st, Continued excavation with 350 men.[3]

Today it is inconceivable to employ such a large workforce because labor costs are much higher and the expected ratio of workers to supervisors is much smaller. Yet even in 1931 this was an unusually large number of workers. Robinson expected the workers to move a great deal of earth quickly. He utilized Decauville railroad cars, visible in figure 2.3, to move the large volume of soil the workers excavated; these cars were originally designed for use in mining, agriculture, and industry, which suggests the scale at which Robinson conceived of his project. The chaotic excavation conditions created by using so many men at once are well illustrated by a photo of one of the trenches taken from atop a ladder (figure 2.4). Twenty-one men are at work in the trench surrounding Robinson, who is issuing orders to the trench supervisor in the center of the trench. Each of the workers is busy in his own part of the trench.

Robinson needed as many graduate student supervisors as he could get to manage all of these workers. Putting Ellingson, Weinberg, and Freeman in charge of their own trenches to work as equals with the male graduate student supervisors was probably a decision born of necessity rather than from some nascent desire for gender equality in archaeology. The fact that in his interim report on the 1931 season Robinson states after mentioning Mylonas's help that, "Mr. Graham and Mr. Schulz also assisted

Figure 2.3. Mary Ross Ellingson's team of Greek workmen excavating and depositing the dirt in the Decauville railroad cars in the background. (Photo courtesy of the University of Evansville Archives)

in excavating certain sections" without mentioning any of the women would seem to support the conclusion that Robinson had no equity intentions in mind when he put the women to work in the trenches.[4] Ellingson was both eager to meet the challenge and excited about the opportunities that would open to her with some field experience. Robinson started Ellingson out managing eight workmen but by the end of the season she was supervising sixty men at a time. In a letter of recommendation dated March 15, 1939, Robinson wrote of Ellingson, "she showed remarkable executive ability and was able to superintend the Greek workmen in a very efficient way, a thing that is very unusual for a woman and which quite surprised the Greeks themselves." He added, "she is an excellent field archaeologist." Ellingson brushed aside

Figure 2.4. David Robinson (center with left arm extended) issuing orders to a trench supervisor amid the chaos of a crowded trench. (Photo courtesy of the David M. Robinson Collection, Archives and Special Collections, University of Mississippi Libraries)

compliments about her archaeological and supervisory skills stating in an interview in the newspaper *The Albertan* published on September 18, 1931, that the reason the Greek workmen followed the directions of a woman was simply because "they considered us Americans, and they have peculiar ideas about Americans." Nonetheless the fact that a reporter would ask her such a question shows that while it may not have been unprecedented, it was very unusual for a woman to fill a supervisory role on an excavation at the time.[5]

Ellingson describes what it was like to be a trench supervisor in a letter dated April 1:

> Gee it is exciting when you find something. The men all holler, "Madam, anticha!" If they find anything valuable, we give them a slip of paper with the date, our initials, and the amount

of money they get for it, varying from one to four drachmas. The first man that found something for me, I gave a slip of paper, and all the others gathered round to look at it, and they all chuckled in great glee, at the epigraphy, as they call it. I have about 14 men, four with picks, 4 with shovels, three with wheelbarrows, and two with baskets. Then there is the foreman too.

In another letter, dated March 27, she elaborates a bit more on how she worked with her crew:

None of the men can speak English, except one man I have who seems to know a little bit, and I tell him what to tell the others, and then there is the foreman, who really has some archaeological instincts, and knows what it's all about. And of course Dr. R[obinson] and Dr. Mylonas come around periodically and give instructions.

Ellingson notes some of the difficulties she had managing so many men who had so little experience in archaeology and who were working with such speed. A March 27 letter shows her exasperation:

I had one man who was a terrible trial. He thought that the more pieces he gave me the better pleased I would be, and he was tearing up perfectly good terra cotta drain pipes, instead of excavating around them. However I have finally got him partly trained, if he doesn't go and forget it all by tomorrow.

There were other reasons she had to watch the men, as she explains in this May 20 letter:

Well, such excitement as we have had around Section M, which is my dig. A week or so ago, what came up but a hoard of 63 silver coins, four of them being tetradrachms (large coins, very valuable). Well, we could hardly believe our eyes. The tetradrachms are worth about $800 each, and the smaller coins vary in price. Well, I ask you, was that a find, or was it not a find? Well, not to just stop at one hoard, what did one of my houses (I have 5 just now) produce but a hoard of 33 tetra-drachms (worth about $800 each,—figure it out for yourself.) One of the workmen stole two of them. He must have shuffled them into his shoes (they all wear big shoes) and then walked off in the bushes as if he were going to the toilet, and then hid them under a stone. One of the other workmen found them there later, and reported it. So we have had to be very careful, and watch the place where they come from.

EXCAVATING HOUSES

When Robinson began excavating in 1928 he was hoping to find public architecture. As the hoped-for temples and civic buildings failed to turn up, he widened the horizontal extent of his trenches in the vain hope of finding them nearby. To Robinson's frustration each shovel full of earth seemed to uncover yet another house instead and he was slow to understand that houses might be considered a significant find as well; few had yet studied houses and the daily life of the Greeks and no one had yet made this the sole focus of an excavation project.[6] Of the three volumes he published based on the finds from 1928, only one, the second, covered architecture. Less than half of this volume's text discussed the houses, a topic he saved for the third chapter after one on the excavation of a road and a second on a large, difficult-to-identify public building. Robinson was very much a product of his time in seeking public architecture. From the Renaissance through the nineteenth and early twentieth centuries the focus of nearly all studies of ancient Greek architecture was on the public portions of cities and sanctuaries; the structures found there were considered to be the most aesthetically pleasing and worthy of imitation in contemporary architecture. At the

American School's excavation at Corinth, the flagship American excavation in Greece, archaeologists had little understanding of, or interest in, the city's houses or the quotidian aspects of the lives of the city's citizens despite over three decades of digging by the time Robinson began his project.[7] In addition, in 1931 the American School was just beginning to excavate the Athenian Agora, the city's public center, where the obsession with public architecture continued. Nonetheless, a few reviewers of the early volumes of *Excavations at Olynthus* saw the potential for exploring this subject in Greek archaeology and praised Robinson for having excavated and published the domestic structures.[8] Robinson is known to have sought reviews of his work and so it seems reasonable to assume these reviews helped open his eyes to the potential of excavating houses and influenced his planning for his second season at Olynthus.[9]

Robinson's shift in focus required a shift in methodology and recording techniques. Either at Robinson's suggestion or simply with his assent, Graham devised and implemented a new system for recording the context of artifacts.[10] In 1928 Robinson had opened large horizontal trenches that uncovered several houses at once. He had recorded from which trench particular artifacts came but not which house, room, or street, making it difficult to draw conclusions about where and how the artifacts were used in antiquity.[11] To address this problem, Graham assigned every house, every room within each house, and each section of street an identifying label and had the trench supervisors record the specific location where they found each artifact. This change in recording technique answered the criticisms of the previous season's work and vastly improved the quality of the information the team was recovering. Ellingson describes the more rigorous technique in an article she wrote for the *Edmonton Bulletin* on October 19, 1931:

> When anything of value came to light, the staff members would take a knife, a tooth-brush, a piece of straw from a whisk, and dig out the object, taking care not to mar it in any way. Then

the place of finding has to be measured, special attention being given to the level, as a difference of a foot or even less may mean a difference of a hundred or more years. Each find has to be recorded carefully in the daily diary, with all details. Notes have to be made on the nature of the "fill" (earth in the part being excavated). The exact position (whether right side up, sideways, etc.) has to be noted. All these facts are of the greatest importance in making records of the excavation.

Ellingson mentions that the depth of an artifact was a significant piece of information but it is a little more complicated than she lets on. Archaeologists document the stratigraphy of a site which is the record of the different strata of soil and the order in which they appear. Graham had the crew note in which strata they discovered artifacts in order to know the relative dates of all material. Robinson reported finding no stratigraphy during the 1928 season, a claim that was met with skepticism from at least one archaeologist who reviewed his publications.[12] Graham was able to teach the excavators to recognize and distinguish the different layers of soil and debris and to show them what to anticipate in the stratigraphy. They began digging the most recent layer of soil on the surface which had formed as plants decayed and the wind blew dust across the plain. Directly below that they found the collapsed house roofs and mud brick walls dating to the sack of the city in 348 BCE. The individual mud bricks, originally baked in the sun to become hard, had dissolved over the years to form a stratigraphic layer in which the roof tiles were embedded. Surprisingly little dirt had formed over the ruins in the millennia since the town was abandoned and many years of plowing had loosened some of the top soil which had formed, allowing it to erode away. The remains of Olynthus, therefore, were just a few centimeters below the surface. Once the excavators had removed the debris from the collapsed buildings they found the floors of the various rooms with their associated artifacts which had to date to 348 BCE and before.[13] Thanks to the inclusion of these more detailed field data, the records of the 1931 excavation are much more extensive than those from 1928. In addition to the notes kept by each trench supervisor, Graham wrote a log summarizing what happened each day on site. Robinson had completed that task in 1928. Graham's log is three times longer than Robinson's and contains only information about the archaeology with none of the social commentary of Robinson's log listing the archaeologists and socialites who visited the site as well as Robinson's grievances against the kitchen staff.[14]

While Graham's recording technique represents a vast improvement over that employed in the 1928 excavation, Ellingson's letters reveal that gaps in the application of those techniques persisted. She states the careful recording technique was only used for "anything of value." Artifacts lacking value in Robinson's or Graham's mind included items such as iron nails, ground stone tools, ceramic vessels for cooking, and undecorated ceramics. The amount of ceramics recorded in the Olynthus excavations is well below that found at other sites suggesting the team kept little of the ceramics they excavated.[15] Those working in the cemeteries had a more difficult time recognizing different soil layers as the stratigraphy was much more subtle than among the houses and figure 2.5 shows there was no attempt to dig stratigraphically there. The workmen were digging from the side when they came across the amphora in the photograph, not from the top. In this way they mixed the top soil with the earth underneath. They also mixed the soil from the grave with that of the surrounding area. Missing these nuances made it difficult to see later disturbances, common in cemeteries, and thereby to solidly date finds.

These criticisms notwithstanding, Robinson's decision to excavate as many houses as he could in order to study domestic life almost exclusively was something fairly new in 1931. Figure 2.6 is a plan of one of the houses Ellingson excavated, a house with the rather unromantic label of A vii 2.[16] Figure 2.7 is a photograph of the same house from the south so that the room closest to the

Figure 2.5. The moment of discovery: an amphora used as a grave, Grave 114, East Cemetery, Hill R, 0.4 m below the surface. (Photo courtesy of the University of Evansville Archives)

camera when Ellingson snapped the picture is Room G. The North Hill where she was working was the location of a neighborhood newly planned in 432 BCE. Ancient surveyors had laid out the neighborhood in a grid with streets that met at right angles, following the best theory in urban design of the time. Each block was a square allowing there to be exactly ten houses of identical size on each block arranged in two rows of five with the entrances to half facing north and half south. The Greeks attributed the creation of the grid system of urban planning to one man, Hippodamus from the city of Miletus in western Asia Minor. This attribution is almost certainly incorrect; archaeologists have uncovered urban grids at Greek sites that predate Hippodamus.

Regardless of who invented it, the technique became popular for the foundation of new colonies, the expansion of existing cities, and the rebuilding of destroyed neighborhoods. The original city of Olynthus on the south hill had an irregular layout that grew organically over time. The neighborhood on the northern hill, the location of house A vii 2, was laid out on virgin soil toward the end of the fifth century in a grid fashion, making it one of the early examples of this form of urban planning in Europe. According to the main source about him, book II of Aristotle's *Politics*, Hippodamus had very specific ideas about how urban planning could help create a well-functioning city. He had a strong belief in democracy and the political equality of people from different classes. Robinson's discovery of houses of identical size at Olynthus was surprising as it was the first site where Hippodamus' social views appear to have been built into the urban layout. Greeks in other cities utilized the idea of a grid layout but had little interest in Hippodamus' social ideals.[17]

Figure 2.6. Simplified plan of House A vii 2. (after David M. Robinson and J. Walter Graham, *Excavations at Olynthus VIII*, plate 99)

Figure 2.7. Mary Ross Ellingson's photo of House A vii 2 looking north. (Photo courtesy of the University of Evansville Archives)

Although they share certain elements, the internal arrangement of each house differed. They all were inward facing, with probably few windows opening out onto the street. As with the example in figure 2.6, one would enter a paved courtyard from the street (G). Beyond the courtyard was a long, wide hallway/room that Robinson dubbed the *pastas* (D). Several rooms opened off of the courtyard and the *pastas*. Ellingson discovered that all evidence for at least one of the internal walls of Room H, the one at the northwestern corner of the room, had been destroyed without a trace by later plowing, therefore she was unable to determine whether entrance to this room was gained from the courtyard or the *pastas* and the wall is not represented on figure 2.6. It is difficult to assign a specific use to most rooms but features in several offer clues. One room in each house often had a raised platform along the walls on which wooden couches would have been placed. This was the *andron*, or men's dining room (E). Men and respectable women did not dine together in ancient Greece; when the men had a formal dinner party they would recline on couches in this room. The anteroom one had to pass through in order to enter the *andron* in this particular house (F) ensured the men some privacy from prying eyes, separating the *andron* from the rest of the house. A hearth (1) in A indicates this room was a kitchen; again because of later destruction Ellingson was not able to determine where the door giving access to this room was located and so no doorway is represented on the plan. Attached to the kitchens of many houses were often small rooms with paved floors into which bathtubs were set (figure 2.8), although House A vii 2 lacked such a feature. Putting the bathroom near the kitchen probably facilitated hot baths as the water could be heated on a hearth or brazier and quickly transported to the tub. The walls of the houses had been made of mud brick set on top of a stone foundation which, when it dissolved after the collapse of the houses, formed a layer of earth over the house foundations, floors, and the artifacts that rested on them, helping to preserve them. Ellingson uncovered bits of red-painted stucco in room C of house A vii 2, and a white-painted baseboard, evidence that at least one room had decorated walls. A vii 2 also probably had a second story, like most houses at Olynthus, but little can be said of the arrangement of space on that floor as no evidence survived the collapse of the mud brick walls.

At the end of the season architects drew the house plans and a photographer took pictures of them from the top of a tall ladder. Despite the fact that photography was a costly medium at the time Robinson understood its value in recording and publishing data and so spared no expense in getting the shots he wanted. While he took some of the photos himself, he also employed a professional Greek photographer from Saloniki named Euripides Melanides (figure 2.9) who took superb photos using a large-format camera.[18] Ellingson and Melanides struck up a friendship; she photographed him outside his studio in Saloniki and he gave her copies of photos he had taken for Robinson in which she appeared. They also corresponded briefly after she returned to

Figure 2.8. One of the bathtubs Mary Ross Ellingson uncovered possibly in Room G of House A vi 8. (Photo courtesy of the University of Evansville Archives)

North America. Robinson had Melanides experiment with aerial photography, at the time a cutting-edge technology. Unlike the rest of Melanides's work, the aerial photos are of poor quality as they were snapped when the camera was pointing at wildly differing oblique angles rather than at a consistent ninety-degree angle to that ground as good aerial photography requires.[19] As a result, major parts of the photos are out of focus. It appears that Melanides did not have access to a specially designed mount for his camera as none appears on the airplane in figure 2.9. He must have been leaning over the side of the plane, gripping the camera, to take his shots. Robinson never published any of these photos nor mentioned them in print. Nonetheless, the parts of the photos that are in focus remain a valuable record of the site's architecture at the moment of excavation and may yet yield new information.

Figure 2.9. From left to right, David Robinson, Commander Kazakos of the Greek Aeroplane Service, and photographer Euripides Melanides. (Photo courtesy of the David M. Robinson Collection, Archives and Special Collections, University of Mississippi Libraries)

AFTERNOON AND EVENING

The workday was broken up by lunch at noon. Ellingson jokingly labels one of her pictures "Lunch at a depth of .80 m. in the House of the Comic Actor" (see figure 2.10). The quantity and quality of food the crew receives is always a topic of discussion on any excavation. Olynthus was no exception. Ellingson frequently mentions what she is eating, as she does in this April 27 letter:

Andoni the cook, has become our friend for life. We usually get 2 sandwiches, 1 hard boiled egg, 1 orange for lunch when we have it on the hill. (At the house they have more but I don't like a large lunch). On the first day Mrs. R[obinson] was in Salonica, he gave us 3 sandwiches + egg + orange. That night we told him the lunch was "poly oreia", very good. The next day we had 3 sandwiches + 3 meat croquettes + egg + orange. We told him it was poly poly oreia, very very good. The next day we got 3 sandwiches + egg + orange + huge piece of chocolate. Mrs. Robinson has since come home. Last night they were talking about how much Walter Graham ate, & how he had a "bottomless pit", & Mrs. Robinson said "next thing we know you'll be wanting 3 sandwiches for lunch." Gee we howled inwardly & praised Andoni. Not that Mrs. R[obinson] would mind us having 3 sandwiches but Davey is always talking about how much it costs to have lunch up on the hill, at 2 sandwiches per person.

Figure 2.10. Members of the Olynthus staff on a lunch break in Room C of the House of the Comic Actor. Front, left to right: Mary Ross Ellingson, Alexander Schulz, George Mylonas, Gladys Davidson Weinberg. Behind wall, J. Walter Graham. (Photo courtesy of the University of Evansville Archives)

According to the article by Thelma Atkinson, the crew worked until 5:30 or 6:00 pm. Ellingson states in her March 26 letter that upon returning to the dig house at Myriophito they enjoyed "tea, crackers or bread, & the best cherry jam or peanut butter." But their workday was not complete at that point. "From then till dinner we work on our daily reports, and do any cataloging, until dinner, and then finish," she writes in an April 1 letter. The reports she refers to are daily records of where they dug and what they found, complete with the contextual information required by Graham's recording method.

The artifact cataloging had another significance for each graduate student. Robinson chose who would catalog each category of artifact assigning Graham all the lamps and loom-weights they found. The Parsons looked after the coins.[20] All bronze artifacts were the provenance of Schulz.[21] Weinberg was in charge of the pottery.[22] Each of Robinson's graduate students knew that they had to make a serious decision by the end of the season about the artifacts they were cataloging. They all needed topics for their theses or dissertations and each had to determine if the material from Olynthus provided them with what they needed to write the defining document of their scholarly careers. This would be a question they would not be able to answer until the end of the season. They would also have to assess how well they could work with Robinson and determine if he was the kind of person with whom they could work closely in order to complete a thesis or dissertation. Cataloging, therefore, was more than just another duty.

Robinson selected Ellingson to catalog terracotta figurines. Because of their potential artistic merit, terracottas were a prized category of artifact and Robinson had noted from the beginning the potential for the site to produce them. It is another testament to Robinson and Ellingson's relationship that he gave her the pick of the artifacts to catalogue. In a pair of undated letters she writes of her enthusiasm for her assignment:

I have been busy, because we have discovered a most marvelous cache of terra cottas, in what we think is the cemetery. They are simply the most marvelous things I have ever seen, and it gives me a big thrill to be the one to look after them. We got two dancers that are absolutely the most beautiful things I have ever seen. We have about 70 figurines already, and we are sure of lots more. I have given up my house on the North Hill, and have been transferred to the trench where the terra cottas are, so I can see 'em come out of the ground.

I sure got the pick of the inventories. I'd hate to be doing vases or loom weights or something like that. So far I have cataloged 220 terra cottas.

Robinson required Ellingson, and each of his staff, to write an inventory description of each of their artifacts in a specific, standardized way. She described the process in her October 19 article in the *Edmonton Bulletin*, "These [terracotta figurines] had to be measured at all points, and carefully described in regard to color, texture of the clay, pose of the figure, drapery, etc." Ellingson kept her own inventory, however, as she had decided these terracotta figurines would be the subject of her master's thesis. Using Graham's typewriter, she typed her own catalog for her use once she got back to Johns Hopkins.[23] Another part of the cataloging process involved helping Melanides photograph important pieces and keeping a log so they would know which artifact appeared in each photograph. Again Ellingson went beyond this taking her own personal research photographs (figure 2.11) and making a dozen plaster casts, which are now in the possession of the Department of Archaeology and Art History at the University of Evansville, to help her study them in more depth once she returned to the United States. Ellingson clearly threw herself into this project wholeheartedly.

Dinner was at 8 or 8:30 and Ellingson happily relates how much she liked the food in a letter from April 9:

Figure 2.11. Mary Ross Ellingson took this photograph of some of the terracotta figurines she found at Olynthus while she was cataloguing them in Saloniki. (Photo courtesy of the University of Evansville Archives).

You would be amazed if you could see me eating SPINACH. Andoni, the cook, cooks it marvelously, so that it doesn't taste like spinach, we always have oranges or apples for desert at lunch. Lovely oranges too. Andoni makes lovely deserts too. His caramel custard is lovely.

Bed followed dinner fairly quickly, as she explains in this April 1 letter:

We go to bed around 9.30. The three of us girls are in a nice big room, the second story of a house not far from here, and the Parsons have the other room. We have a nice fireplace, and have a fire every night while getting undressed.

In a May 20 letter she elaborates on their accommodations and gives further insight into her relationship with Weinberg and Freeman:

Gladys has a fever but she isn't ill at all. When Gladys got the fever, Sally moved out of our room into the hall, and it makes it ever so much nicer in our room. Before we had three cots side by each in the room, and it always looked so crowded and messy but now there is lots of room for Gladys and me, and we can keep it looking respectable. I have a very comfortable bed, in fact one of the best there are around here, I think.

A FEW UNREAD LETTERS LEFT

Setting down Ellingson's letter mentioning dinner and bed, my own thoughts turned to home and my own dinner. It was getting late. Outside my office all daylight was gone; the evening had begun. I should have been answering a few last minute emails before preparing to go home but I only had a few letters left to read. These letters mentioned what daily life was like in the village of Myriophito and described their routine while the group worked in Saloniki after closing the excavation. Ellingson's photos and letters captured a time and places that simply no longer existed. I had to read on.

THREE

TRAVEL IN GREECE
AND EUROPE IN 1931

April 1[, 1931]
If you could ever see the men [see figure 3.1]. A lot of them
are Turks, some are refugees, and some native Greeks. They
have come from all around the countryside to work, and we
have about 190 I think, altogether. And the outfits they wear.
Especially their shoes. A lot of their shoes are made from old
tires, bound around with pieces of heavy cloth. Some of them
wear woollen [sic] scarves tied around their head, and some the
queerest trousers you ever did see. The village of Myriophito
[see figure 3.2] where we live is simply priceless. It is really
out in the country, everything is genuine, and no fakes. The
peasant costumes are some of them awfully pretty, and some
of them comical. They have picturesque old wells. The houses
are all very cleanly whitewashed. They have all sorts of animals.
In our front yard is a sheep corral, and every morning when we
emerge from the door, there is a swarm of chickens, who run
immediately [when] they see us. There are all sorts of donkeys.

One of the pleasures of working on any excavation, regardless
of where it is taking place, is learning about the modern culture
of the people living in the surrounding area. In this lively quote
Ellingson indicates her keen interest in life in the village of Myriophito. Although work on the site took up the majority of her
time, when she had the chance she sought to learn about the local
cultures and to enjoy all the village and countryside had to offer.
Ellingson immersed herself in life of the village and the villagers

Figure 3.1. One of Mary Ross Ellingson's work crews. (Photo courtesy of the University of Evansville Archives)

Figure 3.2. View of Myriophito from the site of Olynthus. (Photo courtesy of the University of Evansville Archives)

embraced her and her fellow excavators. In a telling photo Ellingson and her colleagues pose with their local housekeepers, cook, and the mayor of Myriophio with Ellingson linking the two groups; a Greek housekeeper stands on one side of Ellingson and an American friend and colleague on the other (see figure 3.3). Her letters make it clear that Ellingson spoke no modern Greek when she arrived at Myriophito but she did try to pick up some words and phrases, peppering her later letters with some of the vocabulary she was learning. Not only did she learn about the contemporary language and daily life in rural Greece but Ellingson was equally happy to rediscover the joys of urban living once the team returned to Saloniki at the end of the season and as she traveled around Greece and Europe afterward.[1]

ETHNICITY IN MYRIOPHITO

Myriophito had a population of only about five hundred people when Ellingson was there although many more lived scattered

Figure 3.3. A photo in front of the dig house in Myriophito, from left to right: Andoni (the cook), an unnamed vase-mender, Argerol (a maid), Smaro (a maid), Gladys Weinberg, Mary Ross Ellingson, Arthur Parsons, Gladys Parsons, J. Walter Graham, Helen Robinson, Sally Freeman, Alexander Schulz, and the mayor of Myriophito, Praedros. (Photo courtesy of the University of Evansville Archives)

around the surrounding countryside.[2] Most of the local inhabitants worked small farms, herded sheep, and raised silk worms while living in small, one-room mud brick homes (see figure 3.4).[3] Despite the small local population there was still strong ethnic diversity. Ellingson elaborates on the refugees to whom she refers in an article that appeared in the *Edmonton Bulletin* on October 19, 1931:

> These men were, for the most part, Greeks, whose forefathers had lived in Asia Minor for generations, until they had become Turks in everything but descent, and were then rudely deported from Turkish soil to their homeland, which was in no condition to receive them. They drag out a meager existence from a small plot of land donated by the Greek government, hail with great joy the "coming of the Americans," for that means that many of them will earn a few drachmas a day. [See figure 3.5.]

As the Ottoman Empire slowly atomized into nation states during the late nineteenth and early twentieth centuries, the resulting territorial wars led to the migration of people from one nascent

Figure 3.4. Unidentified woman and children in front of their home. (Photo courtesy of the University of Evansville Archives)

Figure 3.5. The workmen gathering to be paid. (Photo courtesy of the University of Evansville Archives)

country in the Balkans to another. The most devastating of these wars was the result of a failed attempt by Greece to capture a major portion of western Asia Minor in the 1920s, a culturally mixed region where Greek-speaking people had resided for millennia. In what came to be known in Greece as "The Catastrophe," the Turkish military routed the invading Greek forces. The low point in the debacle came when Turkish forces entered Smyrna on the coast of western Asia Minor (see figure I.3), set fire to much of the city, and massacred many of the Greek-Christian residents. This disaster ensured that George Mylonas, Ellingson's colleague in the excavations, could never return to his hometown. In the subsequent Treaty of Lausanne, Greece ceded claims to the region and Greece and Turkey were required to exchange populations. Greeks, defined as Christians, had to leave Turkey for Greece and Turks, defined as Muslims, had to leave Greece for Turkey.[4] The Greek government settled about half of the more than one million refugees in one of the least populated parts of the country, a region which included Myriophito (figure 3.6).[5] The newcomers had few possessions to bring with them to their new homeland.[6]

Figure 3.6. Mary Ross Ellingson identifies these women spinning wool in front of their home in Myriophito as refugees. (Photo courtesy of the University of Evansville Archives)

Two factors that motivated Robinson to excavate at Olynthus when he did were the fact that the refugees were starting farms in the area and were thus destroying portions of the site through plowing, the thin topsoil offered little protection to the lightly buried ancient remains underneath, and the fact that the refugees provided a workforce that was very inexpensive to hire as they had few other job prospects in the area.[7]

Of course there were people living in the area at the time the refugees arrived. Greek- and Turkish-speaking farmers had lived in Myriophito for centuries. In addition to these groups there was an ethnic minority known as the Vlachs. Vlachs speak a language descended from Latin and they inhabited the Balkans from Greece to Romania in 1931. Ellingson mentions two types of Vlachs that she encountered in and around Myriophito. One group was made of sedentary farmers living a life similar to that of their Greek- and Turkish-speaking neighbors. The other type of Vlachs were nomads who wandered among the Balkan countries making a living tending their herds of sheep and horses, trading wool, cheese, and live animals with the villagers along the way. Over the years Vlach culture has been disappearing. A hardening of borders among the countries that emerged from the collapse of the Ottoman Empire after World War I curtailed their nomadic lifestyle as did the fighting across the Balkans during World War II and the subsequent Greek Civil War. The Vlachs Ellingson saw were in transition even in 1931 as the nomads were settling with their cousins in the villages of Greece and neighboring countries to the north. In less than a decade Vlach caravans like the ones she saw and photographed would never again be seen in Greece (figure 3.7). After World War II, the settled Vlachs migrated from the rural villages to become assimilated into Greek culture in the cities. By one recent estimate the Vlach language and culture will disappear from Greece in less than a generation.[8]

In 1931 the nomadic Vlach mode of life had changed little from earlier centuries. Ellingson took photos of one of these groups of Vlach nomads passing through Myriophito (see figure

Figure 3.7. Group of nomadic Vlachs passing through Myriophito. (Photo courtesy of the University of Evansville Archives)

3.7). This group was still transporting their tents, clothes, and other belongings on the backs of horses and ponies. The children wrapped in furs in figure 3.7 indicate Ellingson took this photo in late March or early April when the weather was still chilly. The distinctive short, hooded jacket the woman wears made her instantly recognizable as a Vlach.

Other groups of Vlachs were more settled in the villages around Myriophito. By chance, Ellingson had the opportunity to participate in a local Vlach wedding procession and then observe the wedding. Two photos in the album show the wedding procession (see figures 3.8 and A.3). Her April 21, 1931, letter is one of the most extraordinary in the collection because of the detail with which she describes the event. She records her observations of a type of wedding ceremony that is fast becoming extinct. The letter also illustrates Ellingson's enthusiastic embrace of cultures in which she was living as well as her great good humor:

> Well such excitement as there was on Sunday! Yours truly rode in a wedding procession and right beside the bridegroom in the place of honor at that! The Greeks still have the same custom as they had in ancient days—the bridegroom sets out from his home—(this one was in Mariana, not far from Myriophyto) in his cart and horse with 2 other carts, and the father riding horseback in front, kind of a herald glorified. He drives to the home of the bride (at Cassandra, about 10 miles from Myriophyto) and she gets in one of the carts with her attendants, 3 women, 2 small girls, and her mother, and the party starts back again. Well here is where I came in . . . Davey [Robinson] and I walked over to the next village, Hagias Mamas to look at some inscriptions on stone. . . .
>
> We were walking along the road, when we heard the tramp of horses' feet and the rhythmic song of the [Vlachs] approaching. Turning around, we saw horses, carts, people, banners approaching at a great rate of speed. Much shouting and firing of guns and pistols. The party stopped when they got to us . . . [they] got out, they passed the cognac around and invited

Davey and me to come along which we did, I being very anxious to ride in a bridal procession. The groom got out . . . so we rode in his cart, me on the front seat between the driver and one of the male attendants. Now I must explain about these carts, there is a board across the front, to sit on, but no place to put your feet or brace yourself. . . . Well off we went, me feeling very tickled the while. . . . Bump no. 1.—Mary slips back a little on the seat. Pistol shot no. 1, horses lurch forward, Mary falls back into cart, upon Davey and other members of the bridal party. After resuming my original place—on we go. Bump no. 2.—Mary slips back a little—Pistol shot no. 2.—horses lurch forward and Mary, by dint of . . . a few friendly pushes from the back retains seat. . . . Oh I forgot to say that he [one of the men riding in the back of the cart] told Dr. Robinson he would like to marry me, and thought I was very beautiful (this being my 3rd proposal during the course of the afternoon). Finally we arrived at Myrio-phyto, where the whole village . . . was out to greet us. Much firing of pistols etc. . . . Andoni, the cook [see figure 3.9], was out to see it too, and when he saw Davey and me sitting up in the front cart, as large as life, and twice as natural,—well his eyes just about popped. After recovering his first surprise he made one dive for the house and shrieked at the bunch—M'sieur Robinson—Mam'selle . . . marriage! They didn't know what it was all about, and wondered if Davey and I were eloping, Mrs. R[obinson] being away in Saloniki for the week-end.[9]

THE EASTER CELEBRATION

The biggest holiday the Olynthus team participated in while residing in the village was Easter, which they celebrated with a mixture of Eastern Orthodox ceremony and Greek tradition. While Ellingson had studied ancient Greek both as an undergrad-uate and graduate student, the Greek spoken in Myriophito had evolved a great deal and she had to start from scratch to learn it. In an April 11 letter Ellingson shows she was trying to remember various words and phrases of the modern Greek she picked up:

Figure 3.8. The Vlach wedding procession. In the center of the cart seat Mary Ross Ellingson sits between the driver (left) and one of the groom's attendants (right). The groom stands beside the cart. David Robinson looks out from the back of the cart. (Photo courtesy of the University of Evansville Archives)

There are great doings around Myriophito now. Easter Time. They sure make a job of it. Last night they had a big ceremony & buried the Savior. (They had a real grave.) Early this morning, before 6, there was a long procession to the church, & the bells rang nearly all night. . . . Yesterday the lambs were all a sight, all washed nice & white, with blue ribbons around their necks. . . .

At 11 the real service started. At 12 sharp, the priest reads from the Bible the passage where it says "Christ is Risen," only in Greek it is Ὁ Χριστός Ἀνέστη—ho Christos anesti—then there is singing until 1.30, and some more service, at 2.30 they start feasting—oh I forgot to say that on Saturday am they kill a lamb in front of every house, & let the blood run over the threshold, & skin the lamb, & hang it up in the front hall. Then at 2.30 they roast it on a spit [see figure 3.9]. There is much feasting during the night, and then all day (Easter Sunday,

Figure 3.9. Andoni (left), the excavation team's cook, roasts the Easter lamb. (Photo courtesy of the University of Evansville Archives)

there is dancing in the village. Everybody you meet says 'ho Christos anesti.' . . . Church again at 11.30 with everybody dressed in their very best. Little babies in spotless white with great chains of Turkish coins around their necks. Mothers in bright garments, long skirts, and large handkerchiefs, some of them beautifully embroidered, some spotless white linen of the finest weave, and their smart little black jackets, fitted tight at the waist with leg o' mutton sleeve. The unmarried girls wear bright ribbons around their heads. They surely are a picturesque sight. Everybody carries a candle to church. The pappas (παππάς) (priest) enters the church with his lighted lamp, and all the men rush to get their candles lit from his, and the women, who have been consigned to ύψηλα (hypsila) the gallery, come shyly around later to get their candles lit. After the ceremony, they make a long parade from the church around the village, and then they dance somewhere. Yesterday afternoon they danced right in front of our house [see figure 3.10]. It was very pretty. Many of them were regular artists. (It was funny to see our workmen trip the light fantastic gracefully, after we had

Figure 3.10. Men dancing in front of the dig house in Myriophito during Easter celebrations in 1928. (Photo by Wilhelmina van Ingen, courtesy of Raymond Dessy)

been watching them sling a pick all day for 2 weeks.) One of them had had too much uzo (a kind of drink, harmless in small quantities but after that rather prone to become intoxicating) and he was a perfect scream. He danced with all the abandon of a wild Bacchante of ancient Greece, dancing in a frenzied celebration of Dionysius, the wine god. (This part of Greece is the country of Dionysius, you know.)

FREE TIME

Ellingson's photos show that in her free time she took an interest in daily life in the village, not just special occasions. In one photo (figure 3.11) Ellingson borrows a book from a mobile lending library in the village carried on the back of a donkey. Other photographs she took in Myriophito and in other parts of Greece during her travels after the excavation was complete show Greeks

Figure 3.11. Mary Ross Ellingson borrows a book from a mobile lending library. (Photo courtesy of the University of Evansville Archives)

engaged in daily tasks using tools that had changed little in millennia. A woman uses a distaff and spindle to spin yarn from sheep's wool (see figure 3.6), fishermen throw a weighted net into shallow water, and a woman uses a sickle to harvest grain (figure 3.12). The distaff, net weights, and sickle blade were similar to the artifacts the team was finding on the hill at Olynthus. Ellingson may have been recording these scenes to help her better understand what she was seeing emerge from the ground.

Of course the Olynthus team did not work every day. As Ellingson wrote in a letter dated April 11, "We only have 2 kinds of days—work days and other days. The other days are either Sunday or holidays and rainy days." On those "other days" Ellingson could sleep a little longer since breakfast was not until 9:00 am. In

Figure 3.12. An unidentified
woman reaps grain with a sickle
near Delphi. (Photo courtesy
of the University of Evansville
Archives)

the morning they would catch up on their field reports or artifact
inventories. Sometimes they would have a bath. Conditions at
Myriophito were primitive. The village had neither electricity nor
phone service, houses lacked air conditioning and the only heat
came from fireplaces and stoves. Villagers had to draw water for
daily use and baths from a well (figure 3.13). Lacking a hot water
heater, water for a bath had to be warmed on the stove, making
a hot bath an extravagant luxury. Without a barber in the village,
Ellingson and her friends had to attend to their own grooming, as
she explains in a May 4 letter:

Yesterday we ran a barber shop. I cut Alex [Schulz]'s hair, &
Gladys [Weinberg's] hair, & Gladys cut mine. None of the cuts

Figure 3.13. Unidentified villagers in Myriophito drawing water from the well beside their house. (Photo courtesy of the University of Evansville Archives)

were too positively terrible, however. That took us all morning, as we are rather slow. [See figure 3.14.]

During the afternoons on free days, Ellingson and various other members of the staff would go somewhere, usually on foot. Communication with the outside world was intermittent. Everyone was grateful for a letter from home and the occasional English-language newspaper, even if they were dated by the time they arrived. In one response Ellingson reports how pleased she is to receive a letter from her mother only seventeen days after she had mailed it from Edmonton; Ellingson thought it arrived with admirable speed. To get mail, telegrams, or newspapers, however, someone had to volunteer to walk to another, larger, nearby village on one of their free days. As Ellingson explained in an April 9 letter:

Figure 3.14. Mary Ross Ellingson cutting David Robinson's hair on the balcony
of the dig house. (Photo
courtesy of the University of
Evansville Archives)

It has been a joke around here ever since we arrived. After
every meal somebody says "well who's going to Modonia today?" And we all say yes we're going. So today Alex [Schulz]
& I really went. It's 5 miles. We had had 2 rainy days, so were
good & rested. When we got there we went to the café & had
uzo (I don't know if that's how you spell it but you pronounce
it ew-z-o.) which is the Greek national drink I think [see figure
3.15]. Tastes like a combination of licorice root and Castoria.
Then we got the mail & came home, eating numerous chocolate bars by the roadside. We made it in 1 hr 40 minutes each
way & think we are pretty smart.

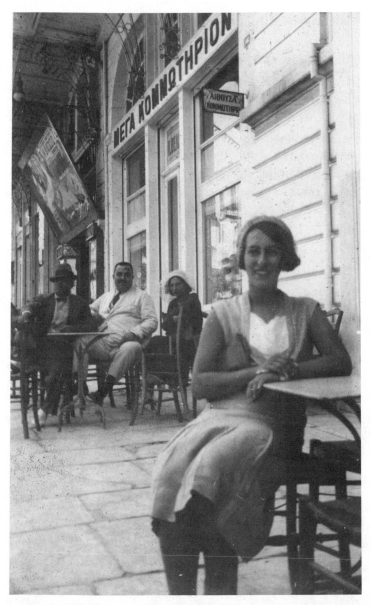

Figure 3.15. Mary Ross Ellingson enjoying a visit to a café on University Street in Athens. (Photo courtesy of the University of Evansville Archives)

Without even a battery-operated radio, the Olynthus staff had to find their own entertainment where they could. In a March 27 letter Ellingson writes:

> I rode part way home on a donkey yesterday afternoon. Gee, it was fun. Mr. Mylonas got home before the rest of us, and came back with a donkey, and let me ride it home. When we got near home, there is a fork in the road, and I wanted to take the one to the right but the donkey evidently thought differently, as his home is on the left, so I had to be rescued.

It certainly helped that the staff got along exceptionally well. Ellingson makes repeated statements such as, "We are having a keen time, it is heaps of fun. And the people are all awfully congenial, we have a fine time at meals, and working."

Figure 3.16. Gladys Weinberg (left) and Sarah Freeman enjoying a donkey ride on their day off. (Photo courtesy of the University of Evansville Archives)

While they worked inside on days when it rained or snowed, jokes and funny stories made the atmosphere bright. In an undated letter she records some ill-informed statements from undergraduate exams and essays that were a great source of amusement to the group. It is not clear from her letter whether these were actual exam answers Robinson and his graduate students had seen or whether they were reading from a magazine titled *College Humor*:

> Vesuvius is a volcano, and if you climb up to the top you can look in and see the creator smoking.
>
> Pompeii was destroyed by an eruption of lava from the Vatican.
>
> All Gaul is quartered into three halves [a mistake for the opening line of Caesar's Gallic Wars: "All Gaul is divided into three parts"].
>
> Pax in Bellum[10] ["peace in the midst of war"] means freedom from indigestion.
>
> The deacon is a mass of inflammable material.
>
> Democracy believes in God, and a republic doesn't.
>
> The process of turning water into steam is called conversation.

The group also enjoyed the game of bridge. In an April 27 letter she reports:

> We were wild & reckless on Saturday night. We stayed up until 12 o'clock, playing cards. Usually we go to bed at 9.30 or 10 at the latest but we decided that it wouldn't kill us to stay up late one night, and it didn't. Sundays we don't have breakfast until 9. (that seems early at home but here it is late when you're used to having it at 5 to 7 every morning).

She adds in a letter dated April 1, "we just had another bridge game, Canada vs. the United States, and of course Canada won." Ellingson and Graham were the two Canadians in the group.

When they could find an excuse for a party, they would take advantage of it as this May 27 letter shows:

> The Sun[day] before we left Myiophito was Mrs. R[obinson]'s birthday so we had a surprise party for her. We got Andoni to make a cake (it was the first one we'd had) & we got wine, & the artist drew cute caricatures of everybody. I enclose mine—it is me in characteristic attitude—cutting hair. [See figure 3.17.]

The caricature she mentions became one of the souvenirs Ellingson pasted into her photo album. The artist, Georg von Peschke, was from an Austro-Hungarian noble family and became enamored with Greece, moving there in the 1920s. Von Peschke married a Greek woman from the Island of Skyros with whom he was deep in love for the rest of his life. By the time Ellingson met him, von Peschke already had a reputation for his Greek Modernist style paintings, prints, and drawings, having already exhibited them in Athens, Paris, and Vienna. It is not clear how Robinson

Figure 3.17. Georg von Peschke's caricature of Mary Ross Ellingson. (Image courtesy of the University of Evansville Archives)

and von Peschke met but the archaeologist convinced the artist to make architectural drawings for him at Olynthus as well as detailed and highly accurate illustrations of some of the mosaics and artifacts. This was von Peschke's first experience illustrating archaeological materials and working with an excavation crew.[11] He clearly liked the work and both he and his wife enjoyed being around the excavators. In a May 17 letter Ellingson writes of an impromptu party the couple threw for the crew one Saturday night: "They brought a radio with them—so after dinner we all went over to their house, & they had the best wine we've had since Athens, & cookies & chocolate, & we danced." Ellingson charmed von Peschke. He had her pose for sketches that he intended to use in a painting depicting the risen Christ and according to the May 27 letter he wanted to use Ellingson's image for Mary Magdalene.

Once the weather warmed as summer approached, swimming became their favorite leisure-time activity both in the nearby Resetnikia River and at the more distant beaches on the Gulf of Cassandra (see figure 3.18). Her May 11 letter relates some of their aquatic exploits:

> We had the best swim today. As soon as the whistle blew we hit for the river, where the boys have made a dam. There is a place where the current flows very fast—you just lie down & boom you sail merrily down the stream about 40 mph. It isn't very deep, however, but you can dive if very careful. Then we ate our lunch & lay on the beach, lovely warm sand until time to come back to work. It was keen fun.
>
> But oh boy swimming in the ocean is the clean stuff tho! Yesterday I went in at Athatal, & the water was simply marvelous. Lovely & warm, & clear as crystal. You could almost see the individual grains of sand. A fish swam along not far from me, & I could see him plain as day.

Although the beaches were some distance from Myriophito, the hike to them was not necessarily unpleasant as she indicates in a May 4 letter:

Figure 3.18. From left to right Gladys Davidson Weinberg, Alexander Schulz, J. Walter Graham, and Mary Ross Ellingson out for a swim. (Photo courtesy of the University of Evansville Archives)

Then in the af[ternoon] Gladys & Sally & Walter & Alex & I went swimming down to the beach—which was much fun. On the way home we came thru the most beautiful place—where a lot of apple trees were in bloom, a clump of tall poplars, the fields just one mass of flowers—yellow and pink and purple and red and white. Really I never saw anything like the wildflowers here. They just absolutely cover the ground. The poppies grow in the grain fields, and are just about as thick as the grain.

RETURN TO SALONIKI

The previous excerpt comes from the latter part of their time at Olynthus. At that point Ellingson and her colleagues had a little over a month until their departure for Saloniki. As the departure date neared, they had less time for leisure. Closing down an excavation at the end of a season requires a great deal of work. They had to complete field reports and artifact inventories, carefully pack the artifacts for transportation back to Saloniki, and stow equipment as well. Amid the chaotic bustle they also had to pack their personal belongings and prepare for the journey themselves. All remembered how difficult the road between Myriophito and Saloniki was and prepared accordingly, as Ellingson describes in this June 7 letter:

> We arrived last Friday night, 5 hours over roads that were terrible—there had been regular cloudbursts the day before—it was a miracle that we got here— it is 85 Kilo[meter]s, about 60 miles I think. We had been expecting mud so we had worn our old clothes, I had on that cotton dress with the short sleeves, it was dirty, too & the boys had on their high boots & breeches & were all muddy when we arrived here at 9 o'clock. . . . But— enter the tragedy—our bags were all on the truck & it hadn't arrived—so here we were looking like tramps. Gladys did have a small bag with her with soap etc. but that was all. And I was so surprised when we arrived in Salonique. It has put on its summer clothes & are the people smart looking? Well I should say. Well anyway we washed our faces, & came back to the Med[iterranean] P[alace] [see figure 1.8] for dinner & sneaked in the back way in our unseemly raiment. The orchestra at the M[editerranean] P[alace] was playing, & it sounded marvel- lous [sic] to us country folks. The tables at the Mediterranean Palace are all moved out on the sidewalk by the water now, & it's lovely. . . . Then oh joy of joys—I had my first hot bath for 2 1/2 months.

The work was not over at this point. According to Greek an- tiquities law and the terms of the permit under which he worked, Robinson did not own the artifacts he had uncovered; they be- longed to the Greek government and people. The permit required Robinson to deposit all the material he had excavated at the na- tional archaeological museum in Saloniki, housed in a building known as the New Mosque (figure 3.19). After the population exchange of 1923 that brought Greek refugees to Greece from

Figure 3.19. View of the National Museum in Saloniki. (Photo courtesy of the University of Evansville Archives)

Turkey and sent Muslims to Turkey from Greece the city of Saloniki turned the mosque into an archaeological museum.[12] Over the next week or so Robinson had his staff of graduate students unpack the artifacts, conduct some preliminary conservation on them, and prepare them for storage in the museum. A rare photo shows Ellingson at work with two of her colleagues in the museum's workspace (figure 3.20). Although Ellingson is clearly visible, all three figures have a ghostly appearance as the camera shutter had to remain open longer in the low light of the room making any motion blur the moving figures.

　After the frenetic pace at the end of the season in Myriophito, Robinson allowed his graduate-student staff to slow their work and enjoy the urbane and sophisticated atmosphere of Saloniki. The city is one of Greece's largest; in 1931 residents had access to the latest cosmopolitan fashions, music, and movies (figure 3.21). Ellingson was dazzled by all she saw and heard and delighted in sharing in an urban night life she and the others had been denied at Myriophito, as she explains in this June 7 letter:

Figure 3.20. Mary Ross Ellingson, forefront in the bottom right-hand corner of the photo, and several of her colleagues at work in the storeroom of the National Museum in Saloniki. (Photo courtesy of the University of Evansville Archives)

It was the opening night of the Med[iterranean] Palace Roof Garden. We had dinner & danced. It was simply marvellous [sic]—had the time of our lives. The roof garden is lovely.

In an undated letter, Ellingson sounds almost breathless as she tries to describe their evening activities in Saloniki:

Then at 4 we started off again, walked down to the tower & had something to eat at one of the café-effects, then we went to the movies—Greek movies (with French also)—Tarzan. Then we came home & changed for dinner. Then dinner put on the street in front of the Med[iterranean] P[alace], then we walked down to the tower, & took a boat for an hour, & went around by a couple of dance places—it [the Saloniki waterfront] looks lovely at night just like Venice so Gladys says. Then we finished up by going up to the roof garden for a few dances—also

Figure 3.21. Ellingson's photo of the view of the Saloniki waterfront from the city's citadel. (Photo courtesy of the University of Evansville Archives)

very enjoyable. . . . It's taking me longer to do my terra cottas then I thought it would but we are having such a good time I don't mind staying here longer.

Saloniki was home to a community of ex-patriot Americans, British, French, and Canadians. The ex-pats welcomed the visitors into their midst. Ellingson describes one extravagant party the excavation team was invited to in an undated letter:

the Americans in Salonique were having a party (cabaret effect) & they had invited us to come. They had the best entertainment features dances, too. A couple of Americans who speak French, & they cracked the best jokes half in English & half in French. They came out dressed in slickers & umbrellas, & sang "Singing in the Rain" & a whole lot of good old American songs. They were a howl, & you'd have to go a long way before you'd get anybody as good. There were about 20 Americans. There was also an English party, about 10, & one Canadian in it with them, whom I met.

Eventually Ellingson and the others did complete their work and the time for departure arrived. The team scattered as each pursued their own travels in Europe. Ellingson mentions a woman named Helen Boyle in a number of letters, a friend who was coming to meet her and possibly the woman pictured in figure 1.2. Together they left Saloniki on June 14 traveling to Athens and then to sites across Greece (figure 3.22). They made their way to Rome, then Paris, ending in London. The pair enjoyed themselves very much, seeing the sites and shopping along the way. Graham accompanied them on the first leg of their trip to Rome before leaving them to pursue his own travels. Coincidentally, Ellingson ran into him again in London, according to a letter dated July 26:

Figure 3.22. Mary Ross Ellingson standing under the cyclopean architecture at the Greek site of Tiryns. (Photo courtesy of Barbara Petersen)

I went to the British Museum yesterday (Helen went to another) & as I was going in who should I meet but Walter. So we went in & were sitting on a bench discussing things in general, & who should rush up but Gladys & Arthur Parsons. So we had a good reunion. We are all going to dinner at the Parsons' tomorrow.

The July 26 letter is the last during her trip and at the end she sums up her entire journey:

Gee we've had a marvellous [sic] trip—everything's just been lovely.

Heaps of love 'n' kisses
Mary.

LAST LETTER, FIRST CLUE

I had read all the letters. According to my office clock I was late for dinner. It was time to venture out into the cold rain and get home. That afternoon I read through nearly all of the material I had found on the shelf and had shared in Ellingson's adventure excavating abroad. I was eager to sit down to dinner to tell my wife, Christine, who is also an archaeologist, all the stories I had read. As I put on my coat and turned out the lights, I thought that night would be the last I would discuss my find with anyone. Little did I realize that I was about to discover eight words written by one of the Olynthus excavators that revealed a secret long buried. I was soon to become the first living person who knew.

PART II

SEXISM AND SCHOLARSHIP

Sarah Freeman, J. Walter Graham, and an exuberant Gladys Weinberg (left to right) on a lunch break at Olynthus. (Photo courtesy of the University of Evansville Archives)

FOUR

THE WOMEN

That night over dinner I told Christine about my find and all of Ellingson's stories. Over the days that followed I told friends, colleagues, students, and anyone who would listen. At one point someone asked me what happened to Ellingson and her fellow excavators; how did the season at Olynthus affect their later lives? The questions piqued my interest, so I did some research to find the answers starting with the three women, and then followed up with the men. What I discovered was that the stories of Ellingson, Weinberg, and Freeman are illustrative of the opportunities and obstacles all women of their generation encountered when seeking a career in archaeology, the sciences, or academia as well as the varied strategies women developed to help them work in fields dominated by men. When they had begun their undergraduate and graduate careers, all three women had a greater chance of becoming college professors than the members of the first generation in the field and it is clear from the letters of their mentor and advisor David Robinson that this is what he was expecting and was the path for which he was grooming all his graduate students, both male and female. The employment landscape in higher education had shifted throughout the 1930s, however, offering fewer opportunities for women, a situation that worsened after World War II. As the door slowly began to close on women who wanted to be professors, they had to develop what one historian of women in archaeology, Mary Ann Levine, has called "alternative career styles," ways of remaining in their chosen field without following the traditional route leading directly to a professorship.[1] Often women wound up on the margins of the field still doing useful and sometimes significant work but never gaining the kind of focused attention that those with university positions did. To make sense of the professional and personal choices each of the three female excavators made after they left Olynthus, it is useful to understand a little of the evolution in attitudes toward women in higher education as well as the change in career opportunities available to them that took place between the 1920s and 1970s. Ideas about marriage and family also evolved during that time as expectations of women developed and redeveloped rapidly before and after the war. Ellingson, Weinberg, and Freeman had to negotiate a swiftly changing America and in doing so each found her own unique path toward the life she wanted.

CHANGES IN CAREER OPPORTUNITIES AND FAMILY EXPECTATIONS FOR WOMEN

When Ellingson was a student, the signs were good that she would be able to get a job in academia once she completed her doctorate. Between the late nineteenth century and the time Ellingson went to Olynthus in 1931, women had made enormous strides in their participation in higher education as undergraduate (figure 4.1) and graduate students (figure 4.2) as well as among college and university faculty (figure 4.3).[2] We have no indication that Ellingson, Weinberg, or Freeman ever consulted or were even aware of the statistics and trends illustrated by the graphs in Figures 4.1–4.3 but it seems plausible that they were aware in an anecdotal way that an increasing number of women had the opportunity to enter the ranks of university faculties. What all three graphs indicate, however, is that the upward trends for women in higher education were beginning to reverse within just a few years of the time they spent at Olynthus. The percentage of

Figure 4.1. Percentage of women among undergraduates at American institutions.[4]

Figure 4.2. Percentage of women awarded PhD's at American institutions.[5]

women within the total undergraduate population in the United States peaked in the early 1920s at 47 percent and had begun a precipitous drop by 1931. The percentage of women receiving PhDs reached a high level in the early 1920s, remained steady for that decade, then began to decline during the 1930s. Women as a percentage of the overall faculty in the United States topped out in the late 1930s before also decreasing. Between the time the three aspiring women professors had started their under-graduate degrees and completed their doctorates, the world of higher education had been transformed in ways that would not help them achieve their goals. The mismatch between Ellingson's expectations and the changing academic world around her is well illustrated by a pair of letters written independently on the same day by two different people. On April 11, 1931, Ellingson wrote to her family about the careful way she had to excavate a badly de-cayed grave; the letter brims with the excitement of someone who is learning skills she hopes to employ in her career. In a letter with the same date Edward Capps, chair of the Managing Committee of the American School of Classical Studies in Athens, suggested the School set a ratio of men to women when awarding fellow-ships to cut down on the number of women studying archaeology at the American School. He complained that there was "a dearth of men archaeologists and a superfluity of women," adding that it would be difficult for "the latter [to] get jobs."[3]

Several intertwining factors led to the decline of female par-ticipation in higher education, particularly as professors, between the 1920s and 1940s. While these factors are laid out here, at their heart was simple sexism; many people held stereotypes about the ability of women to be college professors. Writing in the mid-1970s, a time when notions about the inherent abilities of women were rapidly evolving, the chair of the chemistry department at Trinity College in Washington, Lilli S. Hornig, described the stereotypes she had endured over the previous few decades and which she still encountered:

Figure 4.3. Percentage of women faculty at American colleges and universities.[6]

Women get good grades but have no imagination. They do well in humanities but not in science. They are good at routine work but do not have ideas. They may have jobs but they should not have careers.[7]

Three decades earlier in 1941 sociologist C. Robert Pace published results of a survey focused on the careers of hundreds of recent coed graduates from the University of Minnesota. Pace concludes:

Among the men the job characteristics most clearly related to satisfaction had to do with advancement, opportunity, and the future—suggesting a permanent and sustained vocational drive. Among the women the job characteristics most clearly related to satisfaction had to do with prestige and pleasantness—suggesting a lack of sustained or permanent vocational ambition. Women were most satisfied when their jobs possessed prestige and provided contacts with pleasant people.[8]

Because this is hard data from a scientifically conducted survey, Pace's results justified contrasting stereotypes about men and women: men are aggressive and goal driven while women lack these characteristics and instead prefer to feel important and spend their days with "pleasant people."

These sexist attitudes and beliefs led to institutionalized, self-perpetuating discrimination within higher education. Because women wanted to feel prestigious and liked contact with people, the reasoning went, they made good instructors, while because they lacked drive and focus they made bad researchers. In the 1920s and 1930s female professors were given higher teaching loads and lower salaries than their male counterparts who, it was assumed, needed more time to conduct research and to publish it.[9] With minimal time for nonteaching activities, women professors conducted less research and published fewer articles and books, the yardstick by which their intellect was measured. Among archaeologists women wrote fewer successful research grants than men because women were rarely allowed to lead field projects as fieldwork was primarily a man's job, instead they were often relegated to cataloging artifacts rather than leading excavations.[10] The lower number of publications and grants simply proved the stereotype that women were intellectually incapable of original research and lacked the sustained drive and vision necessary to publish it. As a result, they deserved higher teaching loads and less research time, a conclusion that closed the loop of circular reasoning.[11]

A few extraordinary and lucky women were able to find a way to teach while still researching and publishing in archaeology and the sciences. Their success, however, led to what has been dubbed the "Madame Curie Complex," the idea that if French physicist Marie Curie could teach, publish, discover polonium and radium, and win the Nobel Prize twice, there was no reason other female scholars should not be equally capable.[12] Should a woman prove to be less a researcher than Curie, then she did not deserve time to conduct research. Naturally few male professors could match their accomplishments to Curie's but they were not being measured against her as the women were. In 1924 Goucher College history professor Ella Lon gave a presentation to the American Association of University Women based on a survey she had conducted of the chairs in a variety of departments across the United States seeking to understand their attitudes toward women faculty. While most respected their female professors as teachers, she reported, they lamented their lack of doctorates, publications, and more up-to-date knowledge of their fields. Lon's solution to this problem was that female professors simply had to try harder to become Curie despite their heavy teaching loads; that would be the only way to prove the intellectual abilities of all women. Lon failed to understand that this was not a realistic resolution to an institutionalized problem.[13]

The lack of research and publications became a serious problem for women beginning in the 1920s with the introduction of the tenure system. The American Association of University Professors (AAUP) issued its first statement on tenure in 1925 followed by a revised statement in 1940.[14] As the AAUP's idea came to be applied at most colleges and universities, newly hired professors would have seven years to prove they were good researchers and competent instructors. After seven years if they lacked validation by their peers through peer-reviewed publications, they were clearly not cut out to be college professors. With their higher teaching loads and difficulties in finding grant money, conducting original research, and publishing in multiple venues, the tenure system began to squeeze many women out of colleges and universities.[15] It is no coincidence that the percentage of women professors begins to decline after the AAUP's endorsement of the tenure system.

Figure 4.3 shows the dramatic rise in the number of women on college faculties between 1910 and 1940, with particularly large growth between 1910 and 1920. What would seem to indicate progress in gender equality actually led to backlash. University officials began to worry about the feminization of their institutions; since women were inferior researchers, as proven by the smaller number of publications they produced, male faculty with longer publication lists made an institution more prestigious. During the 1920s and 1930s universities began to seek male candidates for jobs more frequently than female candidates. In an ironic twist, even women's colleges started to aggressively recruit male faculty.[16] The percentage of women on faculties continued to grow, nonetheless, until around 1940 when the result of this hiring policy finally began to be manifest in the statistics. As the graph in figure 4.3 indicates the highs in the percentage of women faculty reached around 1940 would not be equaled again for another four decades.

With the onset of the Depression in 1929 discriminatory hiring against women inside and outside of academia only increased as the number of jobs available decreased. Since women were believed to only be seeking jobs, while men were seeking careers, and because it was the role of men to support their families financially, some politicians became determined in the early years of the Depression to drive women out of the workplace to decrease their competition with men for jobs. The mayor of Syracuse dismissed all women from city government whose husbands had employment. The North Dakota legislature created a ban on women working at state educational institutions. In Maryland a new law required that any woman working at a public school be fired once she married.[17] Across the public and private spheres the number of job opportunities for women decreased dramatically.[18] Colleges and universities across the country adopted another mechanism to limit the number of women faculty they employed: antinepotism policies. If a husband worked at a university it was deemed unfair to hire his wife. While such policies began to appear in the 1920s, their popularity increased during the Depression and many institutions retained them long after the financial crisis had ended.[19] Archaeologists Madeline D. Kneberg and Tom Lewis, specialists in the American Southeast, became involved in a relationship not long after Lewis hired Kneberg to work in the University of Tennessee archaeology lab in 1938. The two chose not to formalize their relationship in order to avoid the invocation of the university's antinepotism rule. Upon Lewis's retirement in 1961 the two married after what Kneberg described as "the longest courtship on record."[20]

The decline in the percentage of women undergraduates reached its lowest point in 1949–1950 according to figure 4.1. The percentage of women receiving doctorates hit bottom during the 1950s (see figure 4.2) while the percentage of women on faculties bottomed out around 1959–1960 (see figure 4.3). Although the downward trends had begun prior to World War II, they accelerated after the war primarily because of the GI Bill, a government program that offered financial support to veterans who wanted to go to college. The male undergraduate and graduate populations quickly skyrocketed as 97 percent of the people taking advantage of the GI Bill in the 1940s were men. Institutions favored returning veterans, quickly filling all available class seats and leaving few for women. Women had to prove their abilities were far superior to men in order to gain admittance to the few remaining spots.[21] The end result was a dramatic drop in women undergraduates which led a few years later to fewer female graduate students and ultimately a dearth of women professors.

While all of these factors influenced the career options available to Ellingson, Weinberg, and Freeman, probably the single biggest factor with which they and other women scholars of their generation had to contend was the question of whether or not to marry and have children. As archaeologist Jane Kelley points out, "women arrive at their penultimate childrearing years about the same time they are well into their PhD program or beginning the critical period of career development," the period requiring them to focus on publishing their dissertations and finding their first jobs.[22] Immediately before and after World War II the commonly held belief was that women could either have a career or a family but not both. In 1941 the sociologist Pace illustrated the stark black and white nature of this decision when he stated flatly, "undoubtedly there are some women who have as intense vocational ambitions as men. But probably most women want to get married."[23] Women, therefore, could only be in the workforce temporarily, pursuing a job until they married rather than pursuing a long-term career. Such a scenario presented a particular problem within academia where, ideally, one would work at one position for many years if not for life. For this reason some department chairs were hesitant to hire a single woman and at some universities the expectation was that once a woman married she would either resign or be forced to resign.[24] When Nobel Prize–winning geneticist Barbara McClintock was beginning her career in the botany department of the University of Missouri in 1936 her enraged chair called her into his office and pointed to a wedding announcement in a local newspaper mentioning a Barbara McClintock. He was prepared to fire her on the spot until she was able to convince him of the truth, that the announcement was not about her but about another woman who by coincidence happened to have the same name.[25]

During the first thirty years that Ellingson, Weinberg, and Freeman were alive the percentage of female college graduates with a bachelor's degree or higher who married increased at a much faster pace than for the general population of women in the United States. Between 1912 and 1937 the increase in the percentage of women graduates who married was over 20 percent while for all American women the figure was a mere 3 percent (figure 4.4).[26] The data in figure 4.4 are based on surveys of graduates from Mount Holyoke, a women's college, but evidence from other colleges and universities show similar patterns. During this same period the women who married were also marrying at an increasingly earlier average age.[27] These changes in marital demographics correlate with the drop in the number of women in bachelor or advanced degree programs. Whether more women chose to marry rather than go to college or increasing discrimination against women in higher education led more women to give up the goal of going to college or graduate school and marry instead is currently an unsolvable chicken-and-egg problem. Nonetheless, just one year after their adventure at Olynthus across the United States 78 percent of college women, and 92 percent of all women, were marrying with those numbers continuing an upward trend. The societal pressure on the three women to marry must have been great. This is not to say women who married saw themselves as left with no other options and so reluctantly walked down the aisle. In his 1941 survey of nearly one thousand male and female graduates from the University of Minnesota, Pace reported that the people who had the highest satisfaction with their current jobs were housewives and that married women were more satisfied with what they were doing than single women.[28]

At a time when women had to choose between a family and career, however, some chose their careers over marriage. Virtually no data exist to enlighten us as to why some women made this highly personal decision, some may have felt they were making a sacrifice while others may have reveled in the freedom of being single, nonetheless not marrying offered some advantages to women researchers and professors. At a time when women had to face the high bar set by the Madame Curie Complex, being able to focus on her research without being distracted by caring for a house, husband, and children certainly allowed a woman who chose this path to excel.[29] A recent book celebrating early women archaeologists presents the biographies of twelve pioneers in the field. The editors of the book note that of these only three married and only two had children, to make their mark the other nine women, or 75 percent, chose to forego marriage.[30]

Naturally a woman's intellectual pursuits did not have to end with marriage. As life spans grew longer and as the average age of

Figure 4.4. Percentage of graduates from Mount Holyoke College who married compared to all women born in the United States.[31]

marriage fell, a growing number of women found themselves with years, even decades, of time to pursue their own interests as their children went to school and eventually left home. Women returning to the workforce later in life became an increasingly common phenomenon after World War II.[32] Precedents exist within the field of archaeology. In 1939 Mildred Mott Wedel, an archaeologist whose research focused on the Native American cultures of the American Plains and Southwest, married a fellow archaeologist and retired from the field. She returned twenty years later, picking up her career where she had left it, expanding her research focus, and publishing popular accounts of archaeological research.[33] Even before World War II archaeologist Boyd Hawes had followed a similar path. She had this advice for women aspiring to work in the field:

> A woman should expect her intellectual life to be interrupted, i.e. she should be prepared to give the first 10 years after marriage . . . to her family interests. . . . Perhaps she can keep alive

her intellectual interests and return to them with new zest and judgment after ten years. Throughout life a woman's work should be more or less interruptible or family and society will suffer. Her happiness in accepting this interruption will depend largely on her having anticipated it as part of the Good Life.[34]

Ellingson, Weinberg, and Freeman faced all of these challenges when pursuing their careers. Each reacted differently to them and found a different way to be satisfied with her career and home life. Their stories nicely illustrate the three most common directions women in archaeology and the sciences went after receiving their doctorates. Careers like these have been documented too rarely.[35]

MARY ROSS ELLINGSON'S CAREER

One of the people to whom I mentioned Ellingson's story was the archivist in the University of Evansville library. She offered to check for Ellingson's personnel file and discovered that it was still on record. The file contains a treasure trove of official documents that allowed me to trace Ellingson's career after she returned from Olynthus. Forces such as sexist attitudes, institutionalized discrimination, and pressures to choose between a career and marriage all influenced the options open to her in the 1930s and beyond. Nonetheless Ellingson charted a course through these difficult waters in a way that allowed her to fulfill both her familial and career desires, although perhaps not in a way she would have envisioned when she was hard at work on the excavation.

After returning to Baltimore from England, Ellingson spent the rest of 1931 and the beginning of 1932 writing her master's thesis, *The Terra-cottas of Olynthus*, which earned her a master's degree in classical archaeology in 1932. While Robinson must have given her access to the excavation records, most of the thesis was based on her own notes, photographs, and the plaster casts of some key pieces she had made independent of Robinson's records (see figure 2.11). The catalog in her thesis is a well-documented history of the evolution of Greek terracotta figurines from the sixth to the mid-fourth century BCE. For each of the 392 figurines she provides a catalog number as well as the contextual information: when the piece was found in a building she gives the building number, room letter, and the piece's depth below the surface; when it comes from a grave she gives the cemetery designation and grave number when an individual grave could be delineated. Each entry has measurements of the figurine and a description of the individual piece along with a list of similar pieces uncovered at other sites or of similar artistic representations in other media. These *"comparanda,"* as they are called, were of particular importance because they had been securely dated by archaeologists working at these other sites, allowing Ellingson to date the similar pieces from Olynthus. Figure 4.5 shows one of the plaster casts Ellingson made while at Olynthus, which is now in the collections of the University of Evansville. In her catalog entry about this piece she identified the figure as a dancer found in the East Cemetery. It stands 24.6 cm high and she noted traces of red paint on the dancer's hair and red and black paint on her clothing. Ellingson dated this figurine to the early fourth century BCE based on dated *comparanda* from other sites. She points out that the artist who made this figure was trying so hard to show the spinning of the dancer that he made a figurine which is quite unbalanced. The break in the middle of the plaster visible in figure 4.5 occurred after Ellingson had made the cast, further showing how unbalanced the original design was.[36]

Ellingson's chronologically organized catalog was a useful contribution to the fields of archaeology and art history.[37] It gave further examples of terracotta figurines known from other sites, offered variations on those known examples, and publicized some previously unknown types. Her analysis of the larger issues surrounding the use of these types of artifacts was also important.

Figure 4.5.
Plaster cast of a
fourth century
BCE terracotta
figurine rep-
resenting a
woman danc-
ing. (Photo by
the author)

Among other conclusions, she observed that terracotta figurines were found in both houses and graves. Until her time most archaeologists believed that the purpose of these figurines was to accompany the dead in their graves or as offerings to deities in their temples. Ellingson was able to show beyond a shadow of a doubt that while many terracotta figurines did end up in graves, many living people at Olynthus also displayed some for decoration and some for worship in their homes. She also noted that nearly all types of terracotta figurines were found in both homes and graves, indicating they were not made exclusively for funerary use. Robinson's publication of the terracotta figurines found during the

1928 season in *Excavations at Olynthus IV* was only a catalog with no analysis. Ellingson's thesis catalogs the figurines from the 1931 season as thoroughly but is more valuable than *Excavations at Olynthus IV* because of the accompanying analysis.

After completing her thesis Ellingson decided to leave graduate school. Her reasons for leaving are not clear but she had been contemplating a temporary departure for a year. In an undated letter from Olynthus that must have been written at some point in April 1931 she explains to her mother: "I wouldn't consider going back to Hopkins for the 2nd year (I mean for Ph.D.) right away but would work maybe a year or two before going on with my Doctor's work." Despite the tight conditions imposed on the job market by the Depression and the sexist attitudes of some in higher education, Ellingson managed to find a position in her native Alberta teaching Latin and classical studies at Mount Royal Junior College in Calgary, a junior college affiliated with Ellingson's alma mater, the University of Alberta.[38] Whether true or not, Robinson credited an old friend of his and a former professor of Ellingson's from the University of Alberta, W. H. Alexander, with making Ellingson aware of the position and helping her get it.[39] Ellingson thrived at Mount Royal; a letter from the school's dean written in 1939 and placed in her University of Evansville personnel file shows she was a good teacher as he wrote, "all who were associated with her either as colleagues or as students are unanimous in considering Miss Ross one of the best and most popular teachers on staff." Her time in Calgary lasted longer than the year or two she had envisioned. It was not until 1938 that she made good on her determination to return to Johns Hopkins to complete her PhD work. What kept her in Calgary for so much longer than she intended is not clear.

Ellingson spent the academic year 1938–1939 in Baltimore writing her dissertation, *The Terra-cotta Figurines of Macedonia and Thrace*.[40] For this document she created a second catalog and compared terracotta figurines excavated at other sites in northern

Greece and Bulgaria to those she and other members of Robinson's team found at Olynthus. The first portion of her dissertation is less interesting as it relates information about figurines found at sites other than Olynthus, information which came from previously published sources. More useful is a pair of tables she added as appendixes that list specific graves and rooms within houses along with all the terracotta figurines found in those locations during the 1931, 1934, and 1938 seasons at Olynthus. These tables make all three volumes of the *Excavations at Olynthus* series mentioning terracotta figurines much easier to use as rather than making the figurines the unit of study, as the catalogs do, the tables make the individual houses and graves the units of study. As with her thesis, the most interesting part of her dissertation is the analysis.[41] While she discusses the movement of certain artistic motifs in terracotta figurines across the Balkans, her most valuable conclusions are again based on the Olynthus material and particularly the data in the two tables. Using those tables, she generates some descriptive statistics that allow her to move beyond a simple art-historical analysis of the figurines and into an archaeological analysis of their use within Olynthian society. For instance, she reconfirms what she had stated in her thesis: that the people of Olynthus placed terracotta figurines in temples, graves, and their homes, a view still not widely held at the time of her writing. She found figurines made from the same mold excavated in graves and houses, proof that they were not made for one use but rather that individuals had some choice as to what they did with them. Figurines in the homes are of two types: religious motifs such as seated goddesses that were probably worshiped and apotropaic or decorative images, such as dancers (see figure 4.5) and caricatures. Most frequently excavators uncovered figurines in the entrance courtyard, *andron*, or *pastas* of the houses, indicating these were the areas in which the people of Olynthus preferred to worship and display these artifacts. Patterns of human behavior also emerge from the placement of figurines in graves. Of the more than six hundred graves Robinson's crews found, about half had some kind of grave good and only a total of fifty-eight had terracotta figurines, indicating they were not common grave offerings. More children than adults had figurines in their graves leading Ellingson to conclude that, contrary to what some had argued, figurines with motifs such as roosters, pigs, tortoises, monkeys, and sphinxes did not have a symbolic significance but rather were toys. Her discussion of the context of the figurines' find spots offers us a glimpse of human behavior that is simply impossible to discern from a catalog of figurines. According to the material in her personnel file, her dissertation earned her a PhD from Johns Hopkins in the spring of 1939.

As she was finishing work on her dissertation, Ellingson met a recent graduate from Johns Hopkins, Rudolph Conrad Ellingson. He was the youngest son of a chemistry professor and department chair at St. Olaf College in Northfield, Minnesota, and had received his PhD in chemistry from Johns Hopkins in 1938. Since that time he had worked as an instructor at Johns Hopkins as he sought a job in industry.[42] According to the Ellingsons' eldest daughter, Barbara Petersen, the landladies of the boarding houses where each of the pair lived were friends and decided to host a dinner in an attempt to get the two to meet and begin dating.[43] While there may be some charm in this story, it certainly is an indication of the societal pressure on single people to marry. The fateful dinner occurred in February; by May 1939 the two were engaged. That same month Ellingson completed her degree in archaeology while her fiancé found work with the pediatric nutrition manufacturer, Mead Johnson in Evansville, Indiana. The wedding took place in August in the bride's family home in Edmonton after which the couple moved to Evansville and established a home there.

Once engaged, Robinson believed Ellingson's career in archaeology and academia was over; like many at the time he was certain that a career and marriage were mutually exclusive life choices. He wrote of his ambivalent feelings at Ellingson's decision to marry in a letter to Alexander at the University of Alberta on May 27, 1939, not long after he had learned of her engagement. He states, "I spent a lot of time on her and it seems too bad that it is to be lost but after all I advised her to get married as she is such a nice girl and probably marriage is better than being a teacher."[44]

Ellingson was convinced that she could be a wife and a professional in the field, waiting on the birth of her first child to decide if she could be a wife, professional, *and* mother. She was following a trend during the first half of the twentieth century as an increasing number of American women continued to work after marriage and only stopped with the birth of their first child.[45] Like today, after earning a PhD the next step toward becoming a professor is to publish one's dissertation as this establishes a candidate as a promising scholar. Ellingson intended to pursue that path as a series of letters between her and Robinson in October and November 1941 make clear.[46] Robinson was supportive and expressed his confidence that her dissertation was worthy of publication if she could condense it a bit and supply illustrations.[47] Other opportunities were presenting themselves, however, which were making it difficult for her to focus on this publication project. In the 1940s there was only one college in Evansville and the surrounding area, Evansville College, later to become the University of Evansville. Contracts in her University of Evansville personnel file indicate that she had found a temporary adjunct professor position teaching art history at the college in 1940 and 1941. She may have been hoping that this would turn into a permanent position but that did not occur. Once Evansville College stopped offering her temporary positions, Ellingson took on a volunteer position in 1944 that allowed her to use her skills and that demanded a great deal of her time. According to her University of Evansville personnel record, she became the Chair of the Department of Archaeology at the Evansville Public Museum where she organized exhibits and events on local archaeology, particularly about a major pre–Columbian Native American site in Evansville

known as Angel Mounds. She also set out to organize and catalog the museum's archaeological collection. At some point in the
1940s Ellingson must have given up on the idea of publishing her
dissertation as discussions of the topic disappear from her letters.

Balancing the demands of career and home proved difficult. In
a letter to Robinson Ellingson confides, "[m]y housekeeping has
gone by the board in the meantime but that's all right."[48] After two
or three miscarriages, she finally gave birth to a healthy daughter,
Barbara, in 1945 (see figure 4.6). Barbara remembers spending
time at the Evansville Public Museum with her mother but by 1949
Ellingson felt the need to give up her work there to concentrate on
her family. The Ellingsons adopted a second daughter in 1951.[49]
As their children grew and became more self-sufficient, however,
Ellingson became restless like so many educated women of her generation. She returned to teach Latin part time at Evansville College
in 1960 according to a contract in her personnel file. In 1963 she
joined the college faculty on a permanent basis teaching courses in
Latin for the Foreign Languages Department and English vocabulary derivatives from Latin and Greek roots for the English Department (figure 4.7).[50] Four years later a rapid increase in student
population led to the renaming of the institution to the University
of Evansville.[51] Since I also work for the same university, I have met
several of Ellingson's former students and in casual conversations
they always repeat that her vast knowledge, wit, and dignity made
her a respected and well-liked teacher. Surprisingly, those former
students when asked all stated that Ellingson never mentioned her
participation in the Olynthus excavation to them and all expressed
surprise to learn of her past. The University of Evansville was more
of a teaching than a research institution, so there was little pressure
on Ellingson to publish any of her archaeological work, which
may be one reason she never mentioned this part of her life to her
students. By the time she retired in 1974 Ellingson had been promoted to full professor and granted tenure even though she had no
publications; at the University of Evansville she was being evaluated

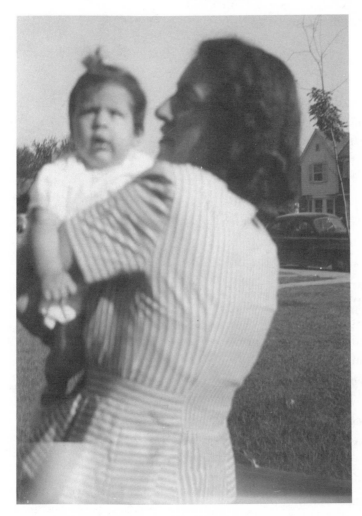

Figure 4.6. Mary Ross Ellingson with her daughter Barbara in 1945. (Photo courtesy of Barbara Petersen)

on her ability to teach, not research. She lived in Evansville another twenty years before her death in 1993.

The "alternative career style" Ellingson pursued left her on the margins of the field and academia for much of her career. While she put in a great deal of work at the Evansville Public Museum and helped to preserve and present the archaeological collection there, her position was unpaid and so lacked any prestige or permanence. She was an adjunct professor for several years depending on the fluctuating staffing needs of the local college but her status as a recently married woman no doubt denied her the opportunity for a regular position as the expectation was that she would soon become pregnant after which point it was assumed she could no longer work. Only when her children were old enough was she able to pursue a tenure-track professorship; it cannot be a coincidence that in 1963, the year Ellingson started working on a permanent basis at Evansville College, her oldest daughter turned eighteen. Since moving from Evansville was not an option as her husband had a good job that he clearly enjoyed there, teaching at Evansville College was Ellingson's only avenue for pursuing her desire of being a professor. Since that institution was a teaching college and not a research institution like Johns Hopkins, working

Figure 4.7. Mary Ross Ellingson teaching at the University of Evansville. (Photo courtesy of the University of Evansville Student Publications, *LinC* *1970*)

there left her outside of the archaeological world as she was not expected to conduct research nor to publish. No one has attempted to quantify how many women who received their PhDs before or after World War II returned to university faculties in the 1960s when the number of undergraduates skyrocketed as the baby boomer generation came of age but Ellingson's story may be fairly common.

THE CAREERS OF GLADYS DAVIDSON
WEINBERG AND SARAH FREEMAN

Like Ellingson, both Weinberg and Freeman wound up on the margins of the university system. Neither became the full-time, tenured professor Robinson had hoped they would become, nonetheless they both used research assistant and curatorial positions quite successfully to further their career goals. Their stories are worth recounting for the creative and sharply contrasting ways they developed their own "alternative career styles" in the face of the same expectations and discrimination Ellingson faced. The choices they made about marriage in particular had a large effect on opening or closing career opportunities to each woman.

After her season at Olynthus, Weinberg did not remain under Robinson's tutelage and decided not to pursue the vases she had cataloged for her dissertation project. She spent 1931–1932 in Baltimore and returned to Greece, studying at the American School in Athens and participating in the excavations at the ancient port city of Corinth between 1933 and 1937.[52] Weinberg completed her dissertation in 1935 focusing on the "small finds" from Corinth as her unit of study, an assignment typical of women at the time.[53] Weinberg had trouble finding a publisher for her dissertation and feared losing a $100 deposit all graduates were required to pay to Johns Hopkins University, refundable as long as they published their dissertations within two years of graduation. In response to a despondent letter from Weinberg in which she announced her intention to publish her dissertation on the shoe-string budget provided by her $100 deposit, Robinson wrote, "I think it would be very foolish to publish a hundred dollars' worth of your excellent dissertation."[54] Presumably he was concerned about the limited number of copies that would be produced and the poor quality that the limited budget would impose. In the same letter Robinson describes steps he took to get Weinberg an extension on the two-year deadline from the Johns Hopkins administration. Even after the expiration of the deadline and the loss of the deposit Robinson continued to encourage his former student to publish. After much delay because of World War II, Weinberg eventually published a revised version of her dissertation in 1952.[55]

Saul Weinberg was a fellow Johns Hopkins graduate who spent the 1937 season at Corinth with Gladys Davidson. Slightly younger than his future wife, the Chicago native had participated in the 1934 season at Olynthus, gaining his first taste of fieldwork under Robinson. Saul Weinberg had graduated in 1936 and soon became an integral part of the staff at the Corinth excavation, producing several important interim articles on the excavation and eventually two volumes in the *Corinth* series. He quickly became a respected archaeologist and a prolific scholarly writer.[56] The Weinbergs married in 1942 amid the chaos of World War II. As all archaeology in Greece had shut down during the war, Gladys Weinberg joined the Foreign Service Auxiliary of the U.S. State Department as a librarian and translator in Athens and Istanbul.[57] Rumors persist that she also worked for the American wartime spy agency, the Office of Strategic Services.[58] Her husband joined the U.S. Army Signal Corps and was stationed in England, France, and Belgium.[59]

After the war Gladys Weinberg's career was inextricably linked to Saul's. With all of the barriers women faced in finding academic positions at the time, it certainly made more sense for Saul Weinberg to seek positions without competition from his wife. Prior to the war the strong strains of anti-Semitism in American academia made such a dream elusive. In 1940 Jewish faculty made up only 2 percent of all the faculty members at American colleges and universities. Fortunately for the Weinbergs, the postwar years saw a reversal in anti-Semitic hiring practices as institutions of higher learning rapidly increased the number of Jewish men they were hiring; the number of Jewish women added to faculties was much more modest and the positions they filled tended to be at the lower levels.[60] While looking for an academic position, the Weinbergs returned to Greece where he became the assistant to the director of the American School.[61] In 1948 the University of Missouri at Columbia hired Weinberg and he remained on the faculty there for the rest of his career helping to re-found the Department of Art History and Archaeology in 1960; the department became a significant center for the training of a new generation of classical archaeologists.[62]

Gladys Weinberg did not compete with her husband for an academic job; instead the couple worked as a team in the field and she pursued her own research interests. In 1957 they founded the Museum of Art History and Archaeology at the University of Missouri with Saul Weinberg as the director and Gladys as the assistant director and curator.[63] In the 1950s Saul Weinberg led several excavations in Greece with the help of his wife.[64] Working in museums and assisting husbands on excavations was a career strategy some women followed to remain active in the field before and after World War II. Most men who have directed excavations in Greece were married and their wives provided valuable logistical and technical support.[65] Although they worked together well, Gladys Weinberg established her own professional identity independent of her husband. She edited the popular magazine *Archaeology* from 1952 to 1967 ensuring that articles were scholarly, well written, and interesting to the general public.[66] Another technique women in archaeology and the sciences used to carve out a niche for themselves that would not compete with men was to focus on some topic that had previously received little scholarly attention.[67] While working on small finds from Corinth, Weinberg had become interested in the glass excavators had found, a type of material that few had studied in depth prior to World War II. She soon made herself a leading expert on ancient and medieval glass and became so curious about the origins of glass production that she, with Saul Weinberg's assistance, organized a joint excavation of the University of Missouri and the Corning Museum of Glass at two sites in Israel with evidence for glass manufacturing, Jalame and a site near

Shavei Zion, during the 1960s.[68] Ancient glass expert Paul Perrot lauded Weinberg for focusing on the "minutiae of scholarship" and "emphasizing the study of those aspects [of archaeology] which for some may hold little glamour," pointing out how neglected the study of glass had been.[69] Between the late 1960s and the mid-1980s the Weinbergs worked together on a significant Hellenistic site in the Upper Galilee of Israel, Tel Anafa. The Archaeological Institute of America awarded Saul and Gladys Weinberg its Gold Medal for Distinguished Archaeological Achievement in 1985.[70] The Israel Museum in Jerusalem awarded the couple the Percia Schimmel award the following year. Saul Weinberg passed away in 1992, Gladys followed a decade later.[71] She was the last surviving member of the team that excavated at Olynthus in 1931.

For Weinberg marrying a fellow archaeologist allowed her opportunities not open to Ellingson. She was able to help Saul Weinberg on the excavations he directed and received his support in those she wanted to conduct. Since Saul Weinberg joined a faculty in a department determined to grow, Gladys Weinberg could help him increase department resources by aiding in the founding of the university museum and by curating its collections. Remaining within this academic and archaeological world also gave Weinberg access to an excellent library, a base from which to apply for grants and raise money for excavations, and the moral support of others interested in similar subjects, all of which made her career advancement possible. Ironically, while Ellingson never published or directed excavations like Weinberg, she did manage to become a full professor with tenure, the one accomplishment that eluded Weinberg.

Freeman took a very different path from Ellingson or Weinberg since she chose not to marry. Nonetheless, it is clear that Freeman continued in the field after participating in the Olynthus excavations but also chose to search for a subject other than material from Olynthus for her dissertation. During the fall of 1931 she remained in Athens as a student at the American School, being drawn to the Corinth excavation as Weinberg had been. Eventually she wrote her dissertation about a Roman-era temple excavated at that site, Temple E, putting the training she had gotten at Olynthus in surveying and architectural drawing to good use. Freeman continued working with the Corinth team for years to come.[72] She graduated from Johns Hopkins with her PhD in 1934 during the height of the Depression when jobs were scarce and discrimination against women inside and outside of higher education was increasing. With what appeared to be no prospects for a job, she remained in Baltimore for a year until Robinson hired her as his research assistant at Johns Hopkins. Freeman held this position from 1935 to 1944,[73] aiding Robinson in the publication of the Olynthus volumes, a position for which she was eminently suited.[74] Johns Hopkins University was a vibrant place for Freeman to work and during the 1920s and 1930s as an unusually large number of highly educated women, some recent graduates and others the spouses of male faculty members, worked in the medical and science labs as well as in individual departments helping prepare publications like Freeman forming a supportive community.[75] In 1944 Freeman finally found a permanent position and was able to leave her research assistantship to become the curator of Fine Arts at the Johns Hopkins museum.[76] During her tenure there she cataloged two extensive collections of ancient coins and medals donated to the museum, becoming an acknowledged expert on the subject and publishing extensively until her retirement in 1972.[77] Her later career echoes those of Ellingson and Weinberg, working at a museum and focusing on a type of small find as her area of study. She remained a loyal assistant to Robinson, helping him to publish more Olynthus volumes even when that was no longer her job. Freeman suffered a horrific death in 1986 when men entered her home, locked her in a closet, robbed her, and fled. Her mailman called the police nine days later when he noticed all of the uncollected mail; officers discovered the body still in the closet. Two men were convicted for the crime.[78]

As is clear from the relationship between Robinson and both Ellingson and Weinberg, advisors can help their graduates in a number of ways. Patronage jobs such as the one Robinson created for Freeman is yet another way.[79] Since Freeman did not have a husband to support her financially or professionally, having a powerful patron like Robinson was vital to her success. This practice continues to this day and is a valuable way for advisors to help the budding careers of their recently graduated students while receiving help on their own projects. Whenever job candidates have gaps in their CVs, indicating periods during which they were not working in the field, employers become suspicious as to their abilities to do the job for which they are interviewing. Research assistantships like this help fill those gaps and give recent graduates the flexibility to quit as soon as they find a better position. During the 1920s and 1930s the number of research assistantships associated with research universities increased, especially in the sciences, and women often filled these positions.[80] While they could help a recent graduate survive until she found another job, the disadvantage to these positions was that the pay was low or nonexistent, funding could unexpectedly disappear, and there was little chance for advancement within a university from a research assistant position.[81]

THREE WOMEN, SEVEN MEN

After conducting all this research, I had satisfied my curiosity about what happened to Ellingson and her roommates and how their experience at Olynthus had affected their lives. In the process I had learned a great deal more than I ever expected to about women in the history of archaeology and academia. Still I was not satisfied. It would not feel like I had reached the end of the story until I learned the fate of Ellingson's male colleagues.

FIVE

THE MEN

Rediscovering the stories of the three women had been eye-opening as only a handful of stories of the second generation of women in classical archaeology have been recorded, requiring me to dig deep in libraries and archives to piece it all together. To complete Ellingson's story for myself, I wanted to find out what happened to the men with whom she worked and see how the 1931 season at Olynthus affected their lives and careers. It seemed to me that it would be much easier to find the stories of the men as several of them became well-known archaeologists, so well known that books on their biographies must have been written. I was wrong; I had to return to the library to piece together the epilogue to the story of Ellingson's male colleagues. It is particularly surprising that Robinson has not yet been the subject of a book-length biography as his brilliant, volatile, and energetic personality has made him into a controversial archaeological legend about whom those who knew him, as well as those who knew those who knew him, still love to tell stories.

J. WALTER GRAHAM AND DAVID ROBINSON

After the 1931 season at Olynthus, Graham and Robinson's fates were linked for years to come. Unlike some of the other graduate student staff from that season, Graham remained under Robinson's tutelage and completed his dissertation on the domestic architecture of classical Greece, receiving a PhD from Johns Hopkins University in 1933.[1] With jobs scarce in Depression-ravaged America, Robinson looked after Graham as he had Sarah Freeman offering him a paid research assistantship so that Graham could help him with the Olynthus publications.[2] During the 1931 season Graham had taken on the responsibility of inventorying lamps and loom-weights[3]; he now worked the inventory into a full catalog including *comparanda* of contemporary lamps from other sites. Robinson published this in 1933 as a separate chapter in *Olynthus V*, giving Graham full credit as the chapter author. When Robinson became aware of a faculty position at Washington University in St. Louis, Missouri, he pushed those he knew at the university to hire Graham but, for reasons that are not clear, Graham did not follow through on the process and chose to remain a research assistant at Johns Hopkins.[4]

During the following two years Graham's personal and professional life changed rapidly. When he returned to Olynthus in 1934 Robinson promoted him to assistant director and put him in charge of the lamps again as well as the "smaller finds."[5] Mylonas, Robinson's previous second in command on site, was not able to come to Olynthus that season, which helps explain Graham's promotion.[6] Robinson seems to have been off site a lot that season, leaving Graham in charge of day-to-day operations. Following up on his own interest in the houses, he had the crew focus on carefully recording specific data about their architecture to provide information for a future *Excavations at Olynthus* volume.[7] After the excavation season wrapped up in July Graham traveled to London, where he married a fellow Johns Hopkins graduate student and graduate of Vassar College, Annie Christine Hare, who was focusing her studies on Latin.[8] Eventually the two would have two daughters and a son.[9] In 1935 he found a teaching position at the University of Missouri where he remained until 1947.[10]

In 1938 Robinson and Graham published *Excavations at Olynthus VIII* jointly; Graham was the first person to share the authorship and the title page of one of the *Olynthus* volumes with Robinson. In the introduction to the volume they state that *Olynthus VIII* incorporates material from Graham's 1933 dissertation which is greatly augmented with data from the 1934 excavation season.[11] Joseph Shaw, a later student of Graham's, has claimed that the names of the authors should have been reversed to acknowledge Graham's majority contribution to the volume.[12] *Olynthus VIII* is probably the most famous of the Olynthus volumes. In a review that appeared just one year after the volume's publication, Lucy T. Shoe[13] made a bold prediction about the volume's lasting value that was to prove true:

> the study of the Hellenic house as set forth here will remain for some time the reference work on domestic architecture of the late fifth and early fourth centuries B.C. It would be hard to overestimate the importance of this contribution to our knowledge of Greek architecture and civilization, filling as it does one of the most tantalizing gaps in our previous information. . . . The authors are to be congratulated on a carefully recorded, well assimilated, correctly evaluated, and well documented presentation of material which makes a real addition to our evidence for one of the outstanding periods of Greek civilization.[14]

Graham had developed a better system of recording where excavators found artifacts than the one Robinson had used in 1928, a system used in the 1931, 1934, and 1938 seasons. The new recording technique was so well-thought-out that even today it is possible to use the publications and excavation records in the archives at the University of Mississippi to determine in which rooms of each house specific artifacts were found, allowing modern archaeologists to reconstruct the use of individual spaces within the houses. Graham's records have allowed at least one recent archaeologist to examine the differences in artifacts found in different buildings and interpret what that tells us about the status, economic decisions, even the aspirations of the residents of each house.[15] For Graham *Olynthus VIII* and the archival records used to produce it were, and continue to be, a triumph.

In 1947 Graham was able to return to his native Canada, taking a position at the University of Toronto where he remained for the rest of his career. Leaving the University of Missouri opened a faculty position that was to be filled by fellow Johns Hopkins alumnus, Saul Weinberg. While teaching in Toronto Graham served as the Keeper of Classical Collection in the Royal Ontario Museum of Archaeology significantly improving the displays there. Up until that point his work at Olynthus had defined Graham's career but after his return to Canada Graham turned his attention to the Bronze Age Minoan architecture, making himself an expert on the subject after repeated trips to Crete and publishing the celebrated work *The Palaces of Crete* in 1962. He retired from the University of Toronto in 1972 and passed away in 1991 after having suffered for some time from Parkinson's disease.[16]

As Graham's career developed Robinson went from being his mentor to his colleague, then to a friend, and finally to an enemy. Throughout most of the rest of Robinson's life the two men's professional and private lives remained intertwined. After the 1931 season Robinson returned to Baltimore and focused on publishing more additions to the *Excavations at Olynthus* series as well as numerous articles on Olynthus and other subjects. He had two more field seasons at Olynthus in 1934 and 1938 and hoped for more but war forced him to postpone those plans. During World War II and the Greek civil war that followed, Robinson was the president of the Maryland Branch of the Greek War Relief Association and a member of the Council for the Restoration of Greece raising money to help the Greek people and nation recover from all they suffered during the 1940s.[17] Robinson returned to Greece in 1947 to investigate the possibility of reopening excavations at Olynthus, but quickly realized that it would not be feasible.[18] While in Saloniki he worked with the staff of the archaeological museum to locate and dig up boxes of artifacts that they had hidden to keep safe during the conflict. Some of the Olynthus pieces had been broken in the process of hiding and rediscovering them, so Robinson paid to have them mended.[19] In the end the 1938 season at Olynthus proved to be the last excavation he would ever direct and Robinson spent the rest of his life preparing publications on the Olynthus material. He completed the fourteenth and final volume in 1952.[20] He planned to write a fifteenth volume to summarize and synthesize his life's work at the site[21] but he had made little progress on it by the time of his death.

The 1931 season was pivotal. Reviewers received the volumes published after that season with more enthusiasm than they had the earlier volumes as Robinson's recording techniques had improved and his exclusive focus on houses and daily life were something fairly new for classical archaeology. Illustrating how unique this focus was, one reviewer states:

> [Olynthus] offers little in the way of public buildings, major sculpture, or civic documents. As if with conscious singleness of purpose, Olynthus is concentrated on the private life of the individual, and on the several subjects which grew from it, i.e., on his dwelling, its multifarious contents, its place in a [city] plan. In this sphere Olynthus is unrivaled, and the fourteen volumes are indispensable.[22]

Another reviewer addressed the harsh commentary on Robinson's pre-1931 Olynthus publications, offering him absolution for his post-1931 work:

> Some earlier volumes have been criticized for not giving 'archaeological contexts' in full. In [Excavations at Olynthus] X the place of discovery at least is given with most items, usually a particular room of a house, or a grave; and Professor Robinson expresses concern at lack of precise information in some cases.[23]

As the final volumes of the series appeared in print the accolades mounted. One reviewer wrote of *Olynthus XII*, "Prof. Robinson and his collaborators are to be thanked and congratulated once more on a solid contribution to our knowledge of Greek life. No pains have been spared in presenting this uniquely interesting material."[24] Another reviewer summed up the feelings of many at seeing the last volume in the *Excavations at Olynthus* series appear in print:

> It is a little overwhelming to realize that the excavation of this extensive significant site has been brought to a conclusion and that all the finds have been published. There may still be room for more excavation at Olynthus or in its vicinity, but this can hardly detract from credit due an excavator who has carried out a great project with vision, determination, and tremendous energy.[25]

The lasting impact of Robinson's work on classical archaeology has to do with not only the scale at which he excavated but also at which he published. Many reviewers used the word "perseverance" when describing Robinson's energetic and unrelenting drive to excavate and publish the site completely. A few numbers may give some indication of Robinson's accomplishments. In the final season he estimated that his crew was removing sixty tons of earth each day.[26] During his four field seasons he uncovered over six hundred graves and more than one hundred houses; no other Greek site can boast the excavation of so many houses even today. The entire cost of the four field seasons at Olynthus was $50,000 of which Robinson contributed $20,000.[27] It took Robinson twenty-three years to publish the fourteen volumes of the *Excavations at Olynthus* series and these run for a total of 4,499 pages of text with 1,902 illustrations describing 11,221 artifacts.[28] While all of this is impressive valid criticisms of Robinson's excavation remain. Even with the increased number of supervisors, Robinson did not have enough people directing and controlling his workers to record all the data he uncovered and the excavation techniques they employed were a bit old-fashioned by 1931. Robinson's dig winds up on the wrong side of any comparison with the supervisor/worker ratio and techniques employed in the contemporary excavation in the Agora of Athens.[29]

Even though he received a great deal of recognition for it, Robinson was never fully satisfied with his shift in focus away from public architecture to private. In a letter to Graham from 1947, long after praise of his work had begun to appear, Robinson makes the rather stunning statement, "I often wish that I'd never put the time and sacrifice into Olynthus . . . [n]aturally, I too was disappointed not to find better houses and I've spent endless time and money trying to locate temples."[30] Despite all he had accomplished, Robinson could not escape the traditional idea that classical archaeology was primarily about life in public, not life in private.

The Olynthus excavations were not Robinson's only legacy; he also trained a new generation of classical archaeologists. George Hanfmann, one of Robinson's former students, claimed, "Professor Robinson's greatest pride was to be a teacher and he gloried in saying of younger scholars: 'He was my student.'"[31] During his many years at Johns Hopkins, Robinson made the Department of Art and Archaeology into a top destination for graduate students interested in classical archaeology. He supervised the writing of a staggering forty-one master's theses and seventy-four dissertations on classical and archaeological topics. Robinson conferred degrees on many of the most influential members of the next generation of classical archaeologists[32] and used his connections to help them acquire jobs. Robinson helped by publishing the work of several of his students, including Mylonas and Graham, in the *Excavations at Olynthus* series. He also started and edited the Johns Hopkins University Studies in Archaeology series and used it as a vehicle to publish the dissertations of some of his other students. Each year Robinson would attend the annual meeting of the Archaeological Institute of America where he would, as one scholar remembers, "hold court" surrounded by his former students, now colleagues.[33]

Not all of Robinson's former students shared feelings of goodwill toward him, nor did he retain similar feelings toward some of them. Loyalty was a characteristic he valued most highly in his students and his rage was implacable when he felt betrayed. Robinson had a very public spat with Graham and another former student, Paul A. Clement, after each wrote a negative review of an *Excavations at Olynthus* volume.[34] Clement joined the Olynthus team in 1934, several years after he had completed his dissertation under Robinson at Johns Hopkins, spending the season cataloging the coins.[35] Together Robinson and Clement published the coins in *Excavations at Olynthus IX*, for which they shared the authorship making Clement the only other person besides Graham whose name appears on the cover page of an *Excavations at Olynthus* volume beside Robinson's. Robinson responded in print to Graham and Clement's critiques by calling them "petty inaccurate rude reviewers"[36]; the lack of commas in his text only highlights the breathless rage Robinson felt, as if he did not want to take the time to pause between insults. In the same response to their reviews Robinson dismisses their comments on his work by adding that both Graham and Clement's statements were "unauthorized and breaking the rule of the School that no information can be printed by any member of the staff without the consent of the Director." He is in fact mistaken as both men based their critiques on published data which they cite.

The sense of betrayal Robinson felt is understandable as Graham was harsh in his assessment of Robinson's excavation. Graham compared *Excavations at Olynthus XII* in his review with the volume he coauthored with Robinson, *Excavations at Olynthus VIII*:

> Most of this new Olynthus volume is devoted to the houses excavated in 1938, a rather generous "supplement" (p. v) to Olynthus, VIII, The Hellenic House. Indeed the question may

well occur whether the size and cost of this "μέγα βιβλίον,"[37] especially under present conditions, is warranted by the amount of new evidence.[38]

It was not just that Graham had written a bad review that bothered Robinson but that he had written a bad review of his former mentor's work. In a letter Robinson wrote to Graham after seeing his review he states, "it is generally considered bad etiquette for a student to review or criticize the work of his own chief. It almost seems like a case of spite, at least of ungratefulness."[39] Robinson was giving voice to an unspoken expectation of many in the field about respect for their intellectual fathers.

Robinson took Clement's review of *Excavations at Olynthus VIII* as a personal attack. The reason the review so galled him was that Clement states *Excavations at Olynthus VIII* was based on Graham's dissertation supplemented by data he gathered during the 1934 season when, according to Clement,

> Graham was again at Olynthus, the de facto field director for the third campaign of the Johns Hopkins University's excavations on the site. Conscious at that time of the responsibility he was to assume for the publication on domestic architecture at Olynthus he made every effort to augment and to correct the data pertinent to the solution of problems connected with that publication—and his success was notable, within limits imposed by circumstances beyond his control.[40]

Even though Robinson and Graham are both listed as authors on the title page of *Olynthus VIII* with Robinson's name first, Clement never uses Robinson's name in the text of his review, giving all the credit for what he assesses to be an excellent work to Graham alone. Clement also absolves Graham of any shortcomings with the caveat about "circumstances beyond his control" which one who knew the personalities of those involved might interpret as interference from Robinson. As if that was not slight enough in his review Clement repeatedly points out interpretations of evidence that differed from the earlier volumes and for which he felt the volume VIII interpretations were always superior. Therefore, according to Clement, Graham did a better job interpreting the evidence than the author of the other volumes on the architecture at Olynthus, Robinson.

While it is not difficult to understand Robinson's resentment, it is a little more surprising to see how time failed to soften his hurt feelings at all; the wounds remained fresh for years. Robinson published the acerbic rebuttal to the two reviews quoted above in 1950, three years after Graham's review appeared and a full eleven years after Clement's. Three years later, in 1953, Robinson still fumed at Graham:

> You will be the death of me. I can't understand your disloyal and bellicose (a word used by one of your friends) and unfriendly attitude after all I have done for you financially and otherwise paying all your expenses at Olynthus (even medical bills) and giving you a good salary as a research assistant for several years. . . . I do not mind friendly criticism and suggestions but as I told you at Olynthus when you acted as if you were in charge and asked me to let you publish Olynthus (into which I have put more than $100,000)[41] and sulked, I was responsible and no one else according to the contract. I have always appreciated your great help and thank you but Olynthus is mine, not yours.
>
> But what I want to say again is that the Olynthus volumes and material are **copyrighted** in my name and nothing can be used without my permission. . . . Better consult your lawyer before you use unauthorized (I have used this word before) copyrighted material as you did in Cleveland in plans, slides, etc.[42]

Robinson's temper not only led him into a conflict that destroyed his friendship with Graham, it also cost him his job at Johns Hopkins in 1946. The circumstances that precipitated Robinson's departure from the university are murky but there is no question that his anger was a major contributing factor. As Jennifer K. West, one historian of archaeology who has studied Robinson's papers at the University of Mississippi, concluded his dismissal was "[a]t least in part due to the fact that he was a 'difficult' person."[43] James Stimpert, an archivist at Johns Hopkins, shared a secondhand story with me that offers a few more details, however he stresses that the full veracity of the story is difficult to confirm from the letters that remain in the university's archives as they are worded very carefully so as to avoid the charge of libel. According to the story Stimpert heard and based on his investigation in the archives, Robinson believed that some of the artifacts he brought back to the university from a trip to Egypt belonged to him personally while the university administration believed they belonged to the university. The disagreement turned ugly when Robinson removed artifacts from campus in perhaps an aggressive attempt to test the strength of the administration's claims. Rather than involve lawyers in the matter, as administrators had to admit that their records on the Egyptian artifacts were incomplete, they forced him to retire citing the fact that he was past the mandatory retirement age. To mollify him the administration named him a Professor Emeritus of Art and Archaeology,[44] a merely ceremonial position, and gave him a year's pay. It is not clear if Robinson had tenure at Johns Hopkins; he began work there in 1904 long before the tenure system became popular in American academia. The Johns Hopkins administration would have found it easy to dismiss an untenured faculty member. Perhaps not surprisingly, Robinson found someone else to blame for these events. In a letter he suggests that Graham's public statements about the Olynthus material challenging some of Robinson's interpretations led to his forced retirement.[45]

Robinson had trouble finding another position. This is a rather unexpected development as he was a highly respected archaeologist by this time, he had many students who were in positions to help him, and colleges and universities across the country were eager to hire professors because of the glut of students arriving on campuses thanks to the GI Bill. One can only wonder if his reputation for being a "difficult person" preceded him. Desperate for another academic appointment Robinson found an opening at the University of Mississippi, an institution that was in a totally different class from Johns Hopkins. The university was equally desperate, having a position they could not fill; they had already offered the job to eight other archaeologists and classicists all of whom declined because of the inadequate compensation the university was offering. Robinson took the job at half his Johns Hopkins salary. He spent the rest of his career at Ole Miss finishing the publication of his Olynthus excavation volumes and teaching classes on art and archaeology. His classes were popular and always well enrolled.[46] In October 1957 Robinson became ill and stepped away from his teaching duties; the following January he died.[47] At the time of his death, Robinson owned an extensive collection of antiquities which his will divided between Harvard University, the American Numismatic Society, the University of Mississippi, and various individuals; the University of Mississippi received all of his papers.[48] The fact that he left none of this material to Johns Hopkins after having worked there for more than forty years may represent one last spiteful jab at the institution for making him leave.

GEORGE E. MYLONAS, ARTHUR PARSONS, AND ALEXANDER SCHULZ

Robinson remained on much better terms with Mylonas, Parsons, and Schulz. He and Mylonas in particular had a lifelong friendship while Parsons and Schulz moved on to other projects, moving to Robinson's outer sphere of influence. Mylonas held several temporary teaching positions in the United States after the 1931 season at Olynthus. In 1933 Washington University in St. Louis, Missouri, hired him as faculty in the Department of Art and Archaeology where he became department chair in 1939 and remained until his retirement in 1969.[49] In a letter he sent to Robinson, Mylonas credits his former advisor with using his influence and connections to get Mylonas the position;[50] this was the same position Robinson had first sought for Graham but in which Graham was ultimately not interested.[51] Holding a permanent position helped Mylonas become a naturalized U.S. citizen in 1937, although he continued to spend much of his time in Greece.[52] Mylonas did not participate in the 1934 season at Olynthus as he was excavating at the Greek site of Eleusis but he returned in 1938 during which time he held the excavation permit jointly with Robinson.[53] During the latter half of his career Mylonas worked at the Bronze Age citadel of Mycenae, famed as the home of the mythical king Agamemnon, becoming one of the noted excavators of the site. In recognition of his work at Mycenae he was allowed to be buried there after his death from a heart attack in 1988.[54] The Archaeological Institute of America awarded Mylonas its Gold Medal for Distinguished Archaeological Achievement in 1970,[55] making him, along with Gladys Davidson Weinberg, one of two staff members at Olynthus in 1931 to win this prestigious distinction. Mylonas continued an interest in Olynthus, contributing to *Excavations at Olynthus XII*, and remained a good friend to Robinson, editing a two-volume work in honor of Robinson's seventieth birthday in which he gathered chapters by Robinson's former students and admirers. The table of contents for these volumes reads like a who's who of early 1950s archaeology including V. Gordon Childe, George Hanfmann, Spyridon Marinatos, W. F. Albright, William Dinsmoor, to name just a few.[56] Perhaps it is not surprising that chapters by neither Graham nor Clement appear in the volume. In the dedication and introduction to the first volume Mylonas writes in glowing terms about his former mentor, showing that the great affection he always had for Robinson never dimmed.

Parsons, on the other hand, broke away from Robinson to pursue his career. Like Freeman, Arthur and Gladys Parsons were fellows at the American School of Classical Studies in Athens in 1931–1932. The couple returned to Olynthus in 1934 to aid in that year's excavation but Arthur Parsons had lost interest in Olynthus for his dissertation research.[57] Between his two seasons at Olynthus, Parsons had become involved in the American School excavations at Corinth and in the Athenian Agora.[58] Parsons rose to be the Assistant Director of the School from 1939 to 1941.[59] With the Italian invasion of Greece in 1940 the Parsons and others at the American School became determined to aid the Greeks in the war effort. At Gladys Parsons's suggestion, members of the American School raised money to build a truck which they used to ferry supplies to the front as well as to transport wounded and exhausted soldiers.[60] Arthur Parsons drove the truck on some of these dangerous missions.[61] Once the Germans took control of the Greek invasion, the Parsons fled.[62] Despite the chaos of war, Parsons managed to complete his dissertation in 1942 based on data he gathered during excavations on the slopes of the Athenian Acropolis[63] which he published the following year.[64] Although he was away from Greece for much of his tenure and worked simultaneously with the U.S. State Department, Parsons was appointed the nominal head of the American School from 1941 to 1946. After the war Parsons served as a liaison officer and representative for the United States to the United Nations Security Council International Investigating Committee in Athens.[65] He died of a heart attack in the fall of 1948.[66]

It is not clear if Alexander Schulz ever took the motorcycle tour of Europe that he told Ellingson he was planning after the excavation season at Olynthus ended. In 1931 he joined Freeman and the Parsons at the American School in Athens. He later spent nine months working with, and learning from, the highly respected artifact conservator and restorer, Apostolos

Kontegeorgos, while working on some of the Olynthus material in the museum in Saloniki.[67] Schulz completed his MA in 1935 with a thesis on the burial customs of prehistoric Greece, a work that makes very little mention of Olynthus.[68] He never published his thesis. Schulz clearly enjoyed conserving artifacts and reassembled one of the ceramic bathtubs which the team had excavated at Olynthus and which the Greek government had allowed Robinson to bring back to Johns Hopkins. The bathtub had been smashed into sixty-five pieces, making it a large and challenging jigsaw puzzle.[69] With the advent of World War II, Schulz joined the navy and upon his discharge in 1945, returned to the University of Illinois to pursue his doctorate in classical archaeology. He was distracted from his goal, however, when the faculty head of the university's Classical, Oriental, and Egyptian Museum died in a boating accident and Schulz was appointed temporary Custodian until a faculty replacement could be found. The "temporary" appointment was renewed every year between 1945 and 1950 and Schulz tirelessly threw himself into caring for the neglected collections and augmenting the displays. Devoting himself to work in the museum forty hours a week left little time to write his dissertation and he abandoned the project in 1950.[70] Schulz married and moved to Florida to become a farmer. He passed away in 1973.[71]

GEORG VON PESCHKE AND EURIPIDES MELANIDES

Both of the men who remained in Greece, the artist von Peschke and the photographer Melanides, disappear for the most part in the years following World War II. Von Peschke clearly enjoyed his first experience drawing the Olynthus material and working with archaeologists and wanted to continue. When he and Robinson returned to Athens after wrapping up the Olynthus excavations in 1931, Robinson introduced the artist to his colleagues at the American School whom von Peschke instantly impressed and charmed. Some of the people at the School bought von Peschke's paintings and a few still hang in the School's halls. In 1933 he joined the excavations at Corinth as the chief architect, a position he maintained until the beginning of World War II. Von Peschke later worked at the site of Isthmia near Corinth as well until his sudden death in 1959. His star dimmed after the war, however, as interest in his artistic work faded and after his death he was quickly forgotten. Recently Von Peschke's work has been rediscovered, however, and the Phillips Museum of Art at Franklin and Marshal College held an exhibit of his paintings as recently as 2012.[72]

After Ellingson returned to the United States in 1931 she exchanged letters with the photographer Melanides who sent her some pictures he had taken at Olynthus in which she appeared.[73] Melanides continued to work with Robinson during the 1934 and 1938 seasons photographing architecture and artifacts from the excavation.[74] With the approach of World War II his hometown of Saloniki suffered a great deal as first the Axis powers bombed strategic positions in preparation for their capture of the city in 1941, only to be followed by Allied bombing prior to the city's liberation in 1944.[75] The rooftop garden of the Mediterranean Palace Hotel where Ellingson and her colleagues spent evenings dancing in 1931 was blown off in one of these raids. Ellingson enquired of Robinson if he had news of Melanides as she feared for his safety with this destruction in Saloniki but, unfortunately, Robinson's response does not survive and so it is not clear how Melanides and his photography business fared during the conflict.[76] He did survive the war, however, and in the last mention Robinson makes of him he was helping Robinson photograph some of the Olynthus artifacts Robinson had salvaged from the museum's wartime hiding places in 1947.[77]

EIGHT WORDS

That should have been it. I had read all of Ellingson's letters. I had satisfied my curiosity about what happened to Ellingson and her colleagues in the years after their work at Olynthus. It had all been a great deal of fun, but it was time to let it go and get back to my own research. Eight words I had seen on one form in Ellingson's personnel file, however, would not allow me to do that. I had tried to forget about the form and those words but they were not so easily dismissed. In 1973 the University of Evansville required professors to fill out a form outlining their credentials. Under the section on publications Ellingson listed two entries, *Olynthus VII, The Terra-Cottas of Olynthus Found in 1931* and the first chapter of *Olynthus XIV, Terracottas, Lamps and Coins Found in 1934 and 1938*. After giving the title of *Olynthus VII*, she added the eight words: "the work is acknowledged as mine in introduction." I was incredulous; Ellingson was claiming to be the author of one of the *Olynthus* volumes and of a chapter in another. I knew her name did not appear on the cover page of these volumes. Ellingson's story was not over yet, there was now a mystery to solve.

PART III

SCANDAL! MARY ROSS ELLINGSON'S WORK PLAGIARIZED

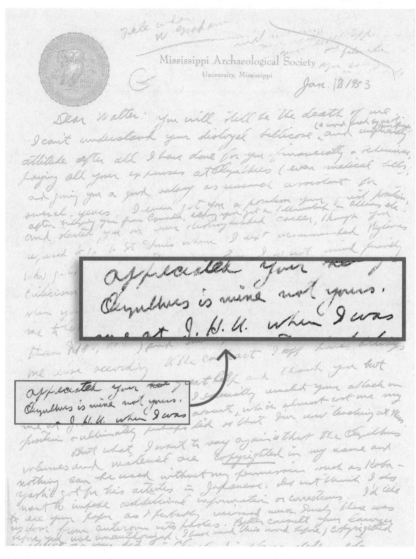

Letter from David Robinson to J. Walter Graham in which he declares "Olynthus is mine not yours." (Image courtesy of the David M. Robinson Collection, Archives and Special Collections, University of Mississippi Libraries)

SIX

A SECRET UNCOVERED

"[T]he work is acknowledged as mine in introduction"; I was dubious when I first saw her words. Mary Ellingson had written this on a personnel form she turned into the University of Evansville in 1973. On the form she claimed to have written *Excavations at Olynthus VII: The Terra-Cottas of Olynthus Found in 1931* as well as the first chapter of *Excavations at Olynthus XIV: Terracottas, Lamps, and Coins Found in 1934 and 1938*. Having read all the Olynthus volumes as a graduate student, I remembered seeing only the names of Robinson, Graham, Clement, and Mylonas on the cover pages of the fourteen volumes in the series, not Ellingson's. Was she lying? Was she exaggerating? Her letters had referred to her work on the terracotta figurines; was she trying to gain some of the reflected glory of Robinson's accomplishment in publishing the terracotta figurines she and the rest of the team had excavated? To find answers to these questions would require a closer look at the *Excavations at Olynthus* volumes, the relationship between Robinson and his graduate students, as well as the relationship between principal investigators and their graduate students both in archaeology and in the sciences between the 1920s and 1950s. I tried to forget about all of this because I did not have time for this new hobby; I had Roman-related articles and a book to write in order to further my career. In the end, however, the mystery of her words got the better of me.

TWO TEXTS, ONE AUTHOR

I could only ignore what I had read for a few days before I found myself returning to the photos and letters I had read that rainy afternoon. There was one other document I had not read that might shed some light on Ellingson's curious claim. A manila folder, discolored with age and tied with a string, had the words "Mary's Thesis" written on the tab. I untied it and began to read. It sounded vaguely familiar.

Since my university does not own any of the *Excavations at Olynthus* series, I had the librarians order volumes VII and XIV through interlibrary loan. The librarians also obtained a copy of Ellingson's dissertation from the Johns Hopkins University archives. It took weeks before I finally had all the documents in hand and was able to spread them out on my kitchen table. The title of Ellingson's thesis is *The Terra Cotta Industry at Olynthus*. The subtitle of Robinson's *Excavations at Olynthus VII* is *The Terra-Cottas of Olynthus Found in 1931*. I read the first few pages of the thesis followed by the first few pages of *Olynthus VII*. They were nearly identical. I read on, alarmed, switching from one document to the other with increasing haste. The same words kept appearing over and over:

Ellingson wrote on page seven:

The district of Olynthus is still rich in clay, and must indeed have been so in antiquity. An especially common clay used in the terra cottas is reddish in color, and heavy in weight; it was used also in local pottery and loom-weights. Twelve figurines from the same mould[13] are of this clay and surely must [be] of native fabric; there are many examples of such products.[14]

Robinson wrote on page three:

The district of Olynthus is still rich in clay, and must indeed have been so in antiquity. An especially common clay used in the terra-cottas is reddish in color, and heavy in weight; it was used also in local pottery and loom-weights. Ten figurines from the same mould (nos. 265–271 and 372, 373, 373a of *The Terra-Cottas of Olynthus Found in 1928*) are of this clay and surely must be of native fabric.

Only two differences appear between these sections. Ellingson listed the figurines from the same molds in a footnote while Robinson listed them in the text. Robinson omits two figurines that Ellingson included for reasons that are not clear. I read on.

On page thirty-two of Ellingson's thesis is:

> [S]tatues of gods were too big to place in the ordinary home, so they were represented merely by masks, herms, and figurines.

On page ten of *Olynthus VII* is:

> Statues of gods were too big to place in the ordinary home, so they were represented merely by masks, herms, and figurines.

Ellingson describes figurines showing satyrs, the half-man, half-goat companions of Bacchus, on page twenty-eight of her work, stating, against the then-current interpretation, that the type first appeared at Olynthus. Robinson makes the same claim on page eight of his work using the exact same words with only slightly different punctuation and spelling. Below Ellingson's version comes first:

> the worship of Bacchus and his attendant cortege is of Thrako-Phrygian origin; its influence spread into Macedonia at an early period. It is not improbable then that Olynthus was the first to seize upon this new idea and create a new type as a result.

> The worship of Bacchus and his attendant cortège is of Thracian-Phrygian origin. Its influence spread into Macedonia at an early period. It is not improbable then that Olynthus was the first to seize upon this new idea and create a new type as a result.

I picked a page at random from *Excavations at Olynthus VII*, found the corresponding section in Ellingson's thesis, and counted the amount of text that was the same: 95 percent. Trying the experiment on other pages yielded similar results. The only changes were editorial, not substantive. Robinson repeated Ellingson's descriptions of the terracottas, her analysis of their styles and production techniques, her chronology, her synthesis placing them in the art historical and archaeological context of ancient Greece, and her conclusions. Ellingson submitted her thesis to Johns Hopkins in 1931. Robinson published *Excavations at Olynthus VII* in 1932 after Ellingson had returned to Canada to take up her position at Mount Royal Junior College. Only Robinson's name appears on the cover page of the volume. I turned to her dissertation and *Excavations at Olynthus XIV*. Although he had edited out some of her work and had added bibliographic references not yet available when Ellingson completed her dissertation in 1939, in the first chapter of Robinson's 1952 volume as well as about half of the second chapter he published most of Ellingson's dissertation.

Ellingson had stated of *Excavations at Olynthus VII* on the 1973 personnel form she filed with the University of Evansville, "the work is acknowledged as mine in introduction." The only mention Robinson made of Ellingson, referring to her by her maiden name, Ross, was on page viii of the introduction:

> Here I should like especially to express my gratitude to Miss H. M. Mary Ross, now instructor in Classics at Mt. Royal College, Calgary, Canada. She was a loyal, tactful, and industrious member of the staff at Olynthus and successfully helped supervise the excavation of the East Cemetery. She kept a careful typewritten inventory of the terra-cottas, separate from my note-books and the daily journal, and I have made abundant use of this and her own valuable suggestions.[1]

The "carefully typewritten inventory of terra-cottas" to which Robinson refers is the same inventory to which Ellingson refers repeatedly in her letters. Robinson clearly saw the inventory as belonging to Ellingson since she made it of her own initiative and not as part of her duties as a staff member of the excavation. Despite Ellingson's claim on her personnel form, this quote does not acknowledge her as the author of *Excavations at Olynthus VII*. Robinson does mention Ellingson in the introduction to *Excavations at Olynthus XIV*, where he published her dissertation but not as an author or contributor:

> I thank especially my former students and members of my staff, Mary Ross (now Mrs. R. C. Ellingson of Evansville, Ind.), Eleanor Lay (now Mrs. Arthur Ross of Syracuse, New York), and I owe much to my deceased daughter (Mrs. Wilson).[2]

His words indicate he did not consider Ellingson's "typewritten inventory" to belong to himself or the excavation but rather to Ellingson alone. To then publish her inventory, as well as her thesis based on that inventory, without listing Ellingson as an author, coauthor, or contributor is inexplicable. Robinson had even less claim to the information Ellingson presented in her dissertation as much of it was based on terracotta figurines found at sites other than Olynthus.

I sat back in my chair not knowing what to think. Something had to be wrong. Robinson, one of the great classical archaeologists, could not have plagiarized the work of one of his graduate students. I tried to find ways to explain what I saw before me. Did an excavation permit holder have *sole* control over all excavated material in 1930s Greece? Did archaeologists routinely exploit their research and graduate assistants back then, taking credit for their work? What about the sciences where research projects also involve a team; did principal investigators use their assistants' work without giving them credit? Had the definition of plagiarism changed in the last fifty to seventy years? Did Johns Hopkins University have a policy on graduate students' and principal investigators' intellectual property rights? There had to be a simple, and ethical, explanation for Robinson's behavior, an explanation about which I understood nothing.

A SIMPLE EXPLANATION

Even though my interest was piqued, I had other research projects to work on including a book based on my own fieldwork studying the streets of Roman cities. The summer before I found Ellingson's materials I had been conducting research in the streets of the Roman cities of Pompeii and Ostia and wanted to get that work written for publication. In the academic world professors have a phrase we repeat to one another, "publish or perish." For untenured faculty, as I was at the time, it is a mantra. There was no time to follow up on something that had happened so long ago and that had nothing to do with my own research and which was outside my field of study. Besides, I had already spent too much time trying to satisfy my curiosity as it was. Once again I tried to forget about it but could not. What had started as a delightful afternoon reading Ellingson's letters was slowly turning into an obsession.

A few weeks later I was in the university library looking for a specific article relating to Roman streets but was easily distracted. Instead of locating the appropriate Roman archaeology journal, I found myself investigating the question of whether Johns Hopkins University had some type of policy about intellectual property rights and graduate student work when Ellingson was a student there. I discovered that in the late 1920s the faculty and administration at Johns Hopkins adopted the rather radical policy of requiring graduates to publish their dissertations within two years of graduation. At that time too few successful PhD candidates published their dissertations, leaving the author's work unavailable to a wider audience some of whom may have found it interesting and useful to their own studies. Johns Hopkins University introduced the policy of requiring graduates to pay the $100 deposit at this time as well,[3] and the policy remained in place at least through the 1940s. Behind the policy is a clear presumption that at Johns Hopkins University the authors of dissertations retained full intellectual property rights to the material in their dissertations. Presumably the same was true for master's theses, although publication appears not to have been required. Even after the expiration of the two-year deadline and the loss of the deposit, the author still retained the intellectual property rights to the dissertation as is clear from the fact that some, like Gladys Weinberg, Saul Weinberg, and Ellingson, continued to work toward publishing their dissertations long after their deposit was forfeited.

This was not the simple explanation I was seeking. If anything, this library research raised more questions in my mind. Did Robinson know about the Johns Hopkins policy? Was archaeology unique in some way because the excavation permit is issued to just one or two people? How did people define the word plagiarism in the first half of the twentieth century and had the definition evolved? Did Robinson ever express an opinion on intellectual property rights? There was only one place where I had any chance of finding answers to these questions. Spring Break was approaching. I really needed to spend the break working on a draft of an article about Roman streets; "publish or perish." Instead I found myself asking my wife if she might enjoy a brief vacation in the South suggesting a day or two in Oxford, Mississippi, home of the University of Mississippi as well as the archive with all of Robinson's papers, might be nice. Luckily she was game to take a road trip south.

The archivists at the University of Mississippi were very friendly and helpful. They brought us box after box of the fifty-three they have containing Robinson's letters and documents. Some of the answers I was seeking began to emerge. There can be no question that Robinson was aware of the Johns Hopkins University policies with regard to the publication of dissertations and, therefore, intellectual property rights. A number of letters passed between Robinson and his recently graduated students asking for help getting extensions on the two-year time limit and expressing fear about losing their deposit. In 1941 Robinson and Ellingson exchanged a series of four letters in which Ellingson sought help with an extension and expressed her continued intention to publish her dissertation, although in the end she was never able to accomplish this goal.[4] Letters between Robinson and several of his graduate students were on a similar theme.[5] The policy and the issue of intellectual property rights were clearly topics of constant discussion in which Robinson engaged with his graduate students.

The issue of intellectual property rights is complicated in the case of a corporate undertaking like an archæological excavation, however. Usually a governing authority issues a permit to one principal investigator that grants not only the right to excavate but also sole possession of the intellectual property produced by that excavation. Robinson's name alone appeared on the permits issued for the excavations at Olynthus in 1928, 1931, and 1934 and with Mylonas's name in 1938.[6] In addition, the rules of the American School of Classical Studies in Athens allowed the permit holder to control all information produced by the excavation.[7]

The rules at Johns Hopkins about rapid publication of dissertations and Robinson's right to control the intellectual property rights of the Olynthus material were not necessarily at odds with one another, however. Robinson seems to have been eager to grant his students permission to publish the material from Olynthus. He helped his students publish their dissertations, particularly as editor of the thirty-eight volume series Johns Hopkins Studies in Archaeology among which the work of several of his students, both those who worked on Olynthus material and those who did not, appeared. He also incorporated material from dissertations by Mylonas, Graham, Clement, and Frank Albright into various volumes and allowed them to share the credit of authorship with himself either as coauthors or as the named authors of particular chapters. In this way his students were able to retain the intellectual property rights to their dissertations while Robinson retained the rights to the Olynthus material. In *Excavations at Olynthus I*, the publication of Mylonas's dissertation and the only volume in which Robinson's name does not appear on the title page, Mylonas thanks Robinson for giving him access to the finds as well as unpublished notes, excavation diaries, and photos. Robinson had read the manuscript, thus making certain that Mylonas was using his material in a way in which Robinson approved.[8] This collaborative process allowed the intellectual property rights of both the student and the mentor to be respected, a process Robinson clearly endorsed in the case of the publication of Mylonas's dissertation. While having many publications can build the reputation of a scholar, having many successful graduate students does as well and this was certainly a yardstick by which

Robinson measured his own success;[9] Robinson was eager to help his students publish.

Perhaps definitions of plagiarism had changed and what seems unacceptable now was acceptable in the 1930s, 1940s, and 1950s. While it is difficult to make a statement about all American academics in the period between the late 1920s and early 1950s, we found evidence among Robinson's papers showing he defined plagiarism as most in academia would define it today. In a letter addressed to the chancellor of the University of Mississippi in 1956 Robinson commented on a draft code of ethical behavior for students which the chancellor had circulated. Ironically, one of the issues Robinson felt was not sufficiently addressed was that of plagiarism. To illustrate how important this issue was, he reported questions students had asked him informally and in so doing he defined the meaning of plagiarism to himself: "Is it honest to erase on a drawing or term paper or examination another name and substitute his or her own—à *la* Shakespeare for Marlowe?"[10] In the same letter Robinson claimed that it was a moral imperative that universities fight ethical transgressions such as plagiarism. He states:

> I quite agree with the President of Columbia University, [Grayson] Kirk, who at Johns Hopkins University the other day said what the Greeks long ago said, "moral integrity is still our [a university's] most important product, and if we or our students are ever allowed to forget it, our society will have been dealt a moral blow."[11]

Plagiarism was not just a technical issue for undergraduates, according to Robinson but instead was a moral issue for professors, the university, and everyone in society. It is quite remarkable that just four years before he wrote these words he had published large portions of Ellingson's dissertation under his own name. Equally astonishing is the simple fact that he could be savage when he felt his intellectual property rights had been violated, as illustrated by his running battle with James Ramsey over the publication of the *Res Gestae* inscription[12] and his accusations against Graham and Clement about publishing information from Olynthus without his permission.[13]

In light of Robinson's understanding of plagiarism, his statement thanking Ellingson at the beginning of *Excavations at Olynthus VII*, his publication of her thesis, takes on special interest. He wrote that Ellingson had, "kept a careful typewritten inventory of the terra-cottas, separate from my note-books and the daily journal, and I have made abundant use of this and her own valuable suggestions."[14] In other words Ellingson wrote her inventory, Robinson wrote *Excavations at Olynthus VII*, and the two are separate documents, a statement that turns out to be false. It is an exceptionally strange thing to write since he makes no similar claim that anyone else was keeping records independent of the excavation records in any of the other thirteen volumes in the series; in this statement Robinson is drawing attention to the very document he plagiarized. The purpose of this statement, I suspect, is to throw any of the participants in the 1931 excavation season off the trail should they grow suspicious of his treachery. Ellingson mentions her independent inventory of the figurines several times in her letters; it was clearly something she put a great deal time into constructing. Her fellow graduate students must have seen her working on this project and heard her talk about it as they were living and working in such close proximity. Robinson must have anticipated that if he then published a volume on the terracotta figurines with only his name on it just months after Ellingson had submitted her master's thesis on the same topic it would have caused suspicion among the other graduate students who had been working at Olynthus. By putting in this disclaimer at the front of the volume he could dampen suspicion by making it appear as if he had written his own catalog and analysis of the terracotta figurines at the same time Ellingson was writing hers. The addition of what he knew was a false statement to the introduction of *Excavations at Olynthus VII* in order to divert suspicion appears to be the actions of a man with a guilty conscience.

Still, I felt like I was misunderstanding something. Today there is an unspoken etiquette shared between the hard sciences and social sciences about what kind of addition to a collective work presided over by one or two principal investigators warranted acknowledgment through a listing as an author, coauthor, or contributor. Perhaps the etiquette in archaeology and the sciences had changed in the last three-quarters of a century. Determining what the rules of publishing etiquette in the social or hard sciences are today, or were in the past, is difficult as no one writes down such rules. Nonetheless people are happy to point out perceived transgressions which help to define where the lines are drawn. Even today academics like to share stories in the halls of their universities or over drinks at private parties about the rare modern principal investigator in archaeology or the sciences, always a man in these stories, who violates those etiquette rules. According to these stories he treats his graduate students like slaves, driving them to write up portions of his research so that he may publish it under his own name, offering the real authors a thank-you in a footnote only if they are lucky. This practice is supposed to be nearly extinct today but it is supposed to have been common in the past. Female graduate students and research assistants of the previous generations in particular are supposed to have been vulnerable to this type of misbehavior. Perhaps that explained Robinson's treatment of Ellingson—he was simply embodying the contemporary culture of archaeology and the sciences.

Two strands of anecdotal evidence allow us to draw a broad picture of what the publishing etiquette was, especially in relation to women's contributions to research projects, in the years before and after World War II. The first strand is actual practice; we can see who received credit in scientific, archaeological, and specifically Greek archaeological publications. One excellent source for comparison material for the *Excavations at Olynthus* series is the publication of the excavations at Corinth, the first volume of which appeared in 1929, the same year Robinson published the first *Excavations at Olynthus* volume. Additional *Corinth* volumes came out throughout the entire period he published the remaining thirteen *Olynthus* volumes. The second strand of anecdotal evidence comes from tales of those who went too far, forcing a rebuke for crossing a line about who deserved acknowledgment. The picture that emerges from these lines of evidence is similar in Greek archaeology, American anthropological archaeology, and the sciences indicating a shared etiquette of publishing women's contributions to large research projects. That culture was tiered with female authors of theses and dissertations at the top, always receiving credit for their work, research assistants in the middle, sometimes receiving credit, sometimes not, and married spouses at the bottom, receiving credit only when their husbands chose to give it, which was not very frequently.

Women who completed theses and dissertations had the most control over their own material. In her 1982 history of women in science, still one of the broadest surveys of the subject, Margaret Rossiter records no cases of a principal investigator in the sciences publishing his students' thesis or dissertation as his own work despite the fact that one section of her book is devoted to the subject of women scientists whose work was not properly acknowledged. It seems to have been the clear understanding that because a thesis or dissertation was independently written, the author controlled it. Weinberg and Freeman represent two examples of this etiquette. Weinberg's reworked dissertation was published as a stand-alone volume in the *Corinth* series with her listed as the sole author[15] and Freeman's appeared as a chapter in *Corinth* I.2, for which her name appears on the cover page and in the table of contents as the sole author of the chapter.[16] I have found only one documented example in archaeology of someone who clearly crossed a line when it came to another's master's thesis. In the late 1920s archaeologist Florence Hawley Ellis wrote a significant thesis on Native American ceramics in the Southwest giving a chronology and demonstrating influences from the cultures of what is now Mexico.[17] When she took a job at the University of Arizona and turned her attention to publishing the thesis, a male colleague, T. T. Waterman, tried to convince her to add his name to the publication even though he had contributed nothing to it. She refused and he sought unsuccessfully to block publication.[18] The fact that this dispute was resolved in Hawley's favor shows Waterman had gone beyond the bounds of proper publishing etiquette.

Women working as research assistants on material that was not part of thesis or dissertation research were in a more precarious position than the women who were working toward their degrees. Research assistants in the sciences and archaeology both before and after World War II were usually highly educated, holding advanced degrees. Most were women who had completed their degrees but were unable to find a job teaching at a university. A mentor or friend would provide the woman a research appointment for his own benefit but also allow her to have an institutional affiliation, an advantage when seeking academic employment. Such positions might or might not be compensated. Research associates were similar to assistants but they had a university appointment and were thus collaborating with their colleagues.[19] The anecdotal evidence indicates the normal etiquette was to offer research assistants and associates some credit, although authorship or coauthorship was not necessarily required. Ignoring a research assistant or associate completely in publication could lead to an embarrassing admonition. Rossiter records the reaction of Agnes Fay Morgan, chair of the Department of Household Science at the University of California, Berkeley, when Herbert Evans of the university's Institute of Experimental Biology suggested that one of Morgan's female faculty work with him on a research project. Morgan vetoed the collaboration for the simple reason that she feared, based on Evans' past behavior, that the research associate's contribution to the project would be "overlooked" when it came time for publication.[20] Another anecdote that demonstrates there were expectations research assistants would receive some credit is that of George Hoyt Whipple, a researcher studying iron-deficiency diseases, and his research associate for thirty-six years, Frieda Robscheit-Robbins. For years Whipple published their joint research under his name alone. When he won the Nobel Prize for his work along with two colleagues, he was chagrined that the committee did not name Robscheit-Robbins as well. From that point forward Whipple made it a point to mention Robscheit-Robbins's collaboration in the research at public appearances and in interviews and even shared the prize money with her and two other female research assistants despite the fact that he was a notorious penny-pincher. Had the Nobel committee been aware of Robscheit-Robbins's work and awarded the prize to her along with Whipple, Robscheit-Robbins would have been only the second woman, after Marie Curie, and the first American woman to receive the prize.[21]

I have encountered no similarly documented stories about any archaeologist specializing in Greek archaeology, which means either these principal investigators were generous in their acknowledgment of their research assistants and associates or transgressions occurred but no one publicized them. Perusing the *Corinth* volumes suggests that research associates received a great deal of respect as their names appear repeatedly as authors, coauthors, coeditors, and contributors. Research associates wrote the very first volume of the *Corinth* series to appear in print. Ida Thallon Hill and Lida Shaw King authored the catalog and analysis of the decorative architectural terracotta pieces excavated at Corinth.[22] Hill and King had first been offered the opportunity to work as research assistants and publish the material nearly three decades earlier before either had completed her degree. Other opportunities arose and the two moved onto other projects which earned them their degrees. Hill came back to the material later and completed the final work on it after her marriage to Bert Hodge Hill, then director of the American School, allowed her to quit her university post and move to Athens to focus exclusively on research.[23] This pattern was typical for the excavations at Corinth; the principal investigator would put either a graduate student or a research associate in charge of a particular category of material with the understanding that that person would have the right to publish the completed work as a chapter or volume in the *Corinth* series with the proper acknowledgment.

In classical archaeology the situation for research assistants is a bit more difficult to discern, although assistants may have been at a disadvantage when compared to the research associates since they were definitely subordinate to the principal investigator, unlike the research associates who were their peers. The names of some research assistants appear on the Corinth volumes such as Freeman, who was a research assistant at Johns Hopkins and is listed as a co-editor and contributor to *Corinth I.2*, and Arthur Parsons, who was a graduate student without a dissertation project but who is listed nonetheless as a contributor to *Corinth III.2*.[24] The names of research assistants are not common in the *Corinth* volumes published in the 1930s and 1940s. Were there other research assistants who should also have been acknowledged but who never were? Naturally we cannot answer that question with the available evidence but the fact that some were acknowledged indicates research assistants could hold some expectation of recognition.

In the bottom tier when it came to acknowledging contributions to publications were women professionals married to other professionals in the same field with whom they collaborated. The etiquette appears to have been that the amount of credit was completely up to the discretion of the husband; he controlled the intellectual property produced for any project on which they worked together. For instance, during the 1920s the couple Frederic and Edith (Schwartz) Clements, both of whom had PhDs in botany, traveled to remote parts of the American West gathering samples for their work on plant ecology which Frederic Clements published under his own name. Upon his death, Edith Clements felt the need to clarify her contributions to his published work and so wrote her own autobiography laying out their shared intellectual adventures and physical misadventures.[25] In the field of American archaeology, Ann Axtell and her husband Earl Morris excavated together in the 1920s through 1940s in the American Southwest and she wrote large portions of their technical reports although only his name appeared as author.[26] On the other hand Harold and Winifred Gladwin, also a married couple who excavated in the Southwest, published their work jointly. In Greek archaeology wives also did not always receive acknowledgment for their work. Ida Thallon Hill ghost-wrote major portions of her husband's reports on his Corinth excavations.[27] Although it has been said of archaeologist couples working in the American Southeast that their joint work is more likely to be published under the man's name rather than both the man and the woman's,[28] that truism can be extended to archaeologists working in the Mediterranean basin before and after World War II.

The etiquette of publishing in Robinson's day, therefore, was that the authors of theses and dissertations should have their names on publications of their work, research assistants and associates should receive some type of acknowledgment, although the extent was to be determined by the principal investigator, and wives would contribute to their husbands' work without necessarily expecting to be named as a coauthor or contributor. Since Ellingson was neither Robinson's wife nor research assistant or associate, the etiquette of the day was that he should have allowed her, or better yet helped her, publish her thesis and dissertation under her own name as part of the *Excavations at Olynthus* series. He had rendered such aid for his other graduate students and it only served to enhance his reputation as a professor. While I have heard rumors of disputes between principal investigators and their research assistants about whether or not the assistants were properly recognized for their contributions to a publication, I have never heard any accusation against any scientist or archaeologist other than Robinson that they had successfully misappropriated a graduate student's thesis or dissertation. Changing etiquette did not explain Robinson's behavior.

I had been seeking a simple explanation as to why the text in Ellingson's thesis and dissertation was identical to the text in two of Robinson's *Excavations at Olynthus* volumes, any explanation other than the obvious one. According to the rules at Johns Hopkins of which Robinson was clearly aware, according to Robinson's own stated definition of the term, according to the etiquette accorded the publication of theses and dissertations in the sciences and archaeology, what Robinson had done in publishing Ellingson's material without proper acknowledgment or her permission was plagiarism. That was the simple explanation.

Why had Robinson treated Ellingson differently from Mylonas, Graham, Clement, and others with whom he shared the credit for authorship on the front pages of the Olynthus volumes? Ellingson returned to Johns Hopkins to complete her PhD in 1938, six years after Robinson had published her thesis under his own name; she had to have known what he had done with her thesis. Was she bitter or angry? Did she ever complain to anyone? Did she ever find out he had published her dissertation under his own name? We found answers to some of these questions among Robinson's papers at Ole Miss.

ELLINGSON'S REACTION

Christine and I continued to pour over the papers in the Robinson collection for hours. At one point she nudged me and slid a letter across the table. It was from Ellingson to Robinson dated October 6, 1952, thanking him for sending her a copy of *Excavations at Olynthus XIV*. She wrote:

Volume XIV of the Olynthus publications gave me a very pleasant surprise,—I was delighted to see my dissertation in print, and to realize that you thought it worth including in the Olynthus publications, a most logical place for it. I do thank you for publishing it and for your very gracious acknowledgement of my work, and for the volume itself.[29]

We shuffled through the box, looking for a response. We found one. "I was very glad to use your good material," Robinson replied, adding defensively "and probably should have given you more credit but I had to change many things and to do a lot more work on it, as you noticed."[30] Considering that approximately 95 percent of the first chapter Robinson printed in *Olynthus XIV* repeats Ellingson's dissertation verbatim, his claim to have rewritten it is not convincing. Robinson's admission that he should have given Ellingson more credit shows that he knew what he had done was wrong. We could find no follow-up letter from Ellingson.

Despite Robinson's poor treatment of her, Ellingson had no regrets about her days in graduate school or at Olynthus. Her words to Robinson were quite genuine and not a polite response to an uncomfortable situation. The two remained lifelong friends; Robinson visited Ellingson at least once while she lived in Evansville.[31] The fact that he sent her a copy of *Excavations at Olynthus XIV*, the copy that contained her dissertation, also speaks to their admittedly complex friendship. Indeed, Ellingson never spoke with bitterness or expressed a feeling of having been used to her colleagues or students at the University of Evansville.[32] Ellingson's eldest daughter said her mother had mentioned what Robinson had done but then dismissed his actions with the excuse that times were different when she was in graduate school.[33] Ellingson was even given a chance to set the record straight not long before her death when she was interviewed by Marcus Diamond who was writing an article about women scholars at Johns

Hopkins University. Diamond has stated explicitly that during his interview he "was looking for something outrageous, some benchmark, I suppose, against which to mark progress."[34] I suspect that Diamond was looking for exactly the type of story that Ellingson could tell about the behavior of her former advisor. By the time of his interview most of the people involved in the Olynthus excavations had passed away so one would think Ellingson would feel free to discuss these matters openly. Nonetheless, Ellingson maintained her silence about her part in writing *Excavations at Olynthus VII* and portions of *Excavations at Olynthus XIV*. Diamond reports she spoke at length about her great fondness for the project and for Robinson and even shared her photo album with him.[35]

Underlying Ellingson's reaction to Robinson's decision to leave her name off the publications of the Olynthus terracotta figurines was an attitude that female scholars should not seek public acknowledgment for their work nor complain about their treatment. Ellingson told her daughter these attitudes were common among classical archaeologists in the 1930s.[36] Although it may strike many of us who have grown up in a society that celebrates female empowerment as difficult to believe, many women internalized these beliefs and were content to work quietly in the background, leaving their male colleagues to reap the rewards of public acknowledgment. Classical archaeologist Shelby Brown has pointed out that even today female archaeologists rarely complain about any mistreatment because they love being in the field and believe the occasional sexist colleague is simply something that must be endured. Brown notes that to excavate one must be prepared to experience extreme heat, mud and dust, inadequate funding, and sometimes poor living arrangements, conditions with which archaeologists deal by means of a macho, stoic attitude. Sexism is just one more challenge to be silently endured by women archaeologists.[37] In 1989 when trying to organize a symposium on women's contributions to, and challenges in,

American archaeology, organizers had a difficult time getting women to participate as many stated they faced no challenges different from men.[38] Women archaeologists who worked in the American Southeast during the 1930s reported absolutely no discrimination occurring even though few reports and publications have female authors or contributors while many women appear in the photos taken of these projects.[39]

After Ellingson retired from the post of director of the Department of Archaeology at the Evansville Public Museum in 1949 museum director Charles Boggs sent her a letter thanking her for her service in which he states, "I have been especially impressed by the fact that you have performed quietly, efficiently and gracefully without demanding attentions or popular praise."[40] Boggs nicely summed up the ideal behavior expected of women archaeologists and scholars at the time, an ideal which Ellingson exemplified.

REVIEWS OF *EXCAVATIONS AT OLYNTHUS* VII AND XIV

Knowing that Robinson was not the only person to write about the terracotta figurines published in the *Excavations at Olynthus* series forces us to read volume VII and the first chapter and a half of volume XIV in a new light. It also helps us better interpret the observations, praise, and criticisms of reviewers since, unbeknownst to them, they were reviewing the very lightly edited writings of a novice graduate student and not those of the widely experienced archaeologist Robinson. The reviews of *Excavations at Olynthus VII* were positive. Valentin Müller, a German expert on ancient Greek sculpture,[41] wrote:

> The catalogue is very carefully done. We find not only a detailed description of every specimen accompanied by the necessary

statements about provenience, measurements, technique, and date but also ample references to parallels and discussions of problems concerning the particular type. . . . The catalogue is preceded by an Introduction in which Mr. Robinson draws several important conclusions from the finds. As in the other fields of archaeology, e.g., in regard to architecture, so also for our knowledge of Greek terra cottas the excavation of Olynthus is proving extremely fruitful.[42]

George W. Elderkin, one of the leaders of the Princeton excavations at the Syrian site of Antioch,[43] agreed:

The terracottas are classified and arranged within groups in chronological sequence so that there results a ceramic history of Olynthus from the sixth century to the year 348 B.C. when the city was destroyed. The story is very interesting. All types of terracottas are represented. . . . Dr. Robinson has rendered the double service of finding and publishing a highly suggestive ceramic anthology of the Olynthians.[44]

Reviewers praised both the thoroughness of the catalog and the analysis of the finds. Müller added of Ellingson's analysis, "Robinson's assertions are all very convincing generally so that little is left for criticism."[45]

Reviewers were harsher in their assessment of the first two chapters of *Excavations at Olynthus XIV*, wondering what the point was of publishing information about terracotta figurines excavated at sites other than Olynthus, most of which had already been published elsewhere, in a site report about Olynthus. Reynold Higgins, a British archaeologist and curator of Greek terracotta figurines at the British Museum,[46] wished the first chapter had been omitted.[47] Ellingson had included information about material from Olynthus in her dissertation and compared it to the material from those other sites in order to synthesize the study of figurines from across northern Greece and the Balkans. Robinson included her analysis of the Olynthus material in the second chapter of the volume, destroying the unity of her dissertation. By dividing the material in this way he created the awkwardness that Higgins noted of a first chapter which had nothing to do with the Olynthus figurines.

The second chapter of *Excavations at Olynthus XIV* received better reviews. Ellingson's synthesis and analysis of all the terracotta figurines found at Olynthus over the four seasons of excavation received the most interest and praise. Higgins claimed "Chapter II, 'Summary and Statistics,' perhaps the most important part of the book, supplies much material on which future students can work."[48] He was impressed with what he believed was Robinson's archaeological analysis of the figurines' find spots, leading to an understanding of what the ancient people at Olynthus were doing with the figurines, a subject he called too often "neglected" by scholars analyzing terracotta figurines as *objets d'art*.[49] "Robinson's" conclusions, based on tables and statistical evidence, particularly caught the attention of other reviewers as well. Sterling Dow, an epigrapher and excavator in the Athenian Agora,[50] was intrigued that "Robinson" could use these numeric data to prove that the "terracottas are not used chiefly as grave furniture, nor is their cult significance primary; instead, they were for decoration and amusement," challenging contemporary interpretations of their use.[51] Although the book was about lamps and coins, as well as terracotta figurines, Robert Scranton, excavator at Corinth and Athens, concluded "the section on terracottas has genuine independent significance,"[52] a statement with which most other reviewers agreed.[53] Even if the portions of the *Excavations at Olynthus* series that she wrote did not bear her name, Ellingson had a great deal about which to be proud. We will never know if she read any of these reviews or, if she did, how she felt about seeing the reviewers comment on her work, thinking it had been written by Robinson.

A PORTRAIT AND AN APOLOGY

While the relationship Robinson and Ellingson shared was complicated, their letters indicate quite clearly that they both valued their friendship. Robinson was a very proud man for whom apologies must not have come easily, nonetheless I believe he offered Ellingson one for plagiarizing her work in his own inimitable way. On December 20, 1952, the University of Mississippi unveiled a painting of Robinson by an artist famed for his portraits, Stanislav Rembski (see figure 6.1); the painting currently hangs in the University of Mississippi Museum of Art.[54] The portrait shows Robinson surrounded by symbols of his accomplishments, symbols he no doubt selected. He wears regalia to show his pride in being an academic; behind him is a part of an early pebble mosaic he discovered at Olynthus depicting Achilles and Thetis; beside him is the head of a satyr, part of his personal collection of antiquities, resting on a base inscribed in Greek with the cryptic phrase, "criticism tests mortals"; behind him is a fragmented line of Greek text with Aeolic spellings, indicating his publications on Greek poetry and literature, particularly Sappho.[55] In his hands is a book open to the cover page with the title "Olynthus" clearly visible on the right side; the central location within the frame of the book and the bright colors in which it is painted clearly make it one of the first things the viewer notices and mark it as one of the achievements of which Robinson was most proud. On the left-hand page of the open book Rembski painted the frontispiece of the volume with such great care and in such detail that it is easy to identify; it is the frontispiece of *Excavations at Olynthus VII*, a watercolor painted by von Peschke when he was at Olynthus in 1931 (see figure 6.2). *Olynthus VII* is, of course, the publication of Ellingson's thesis, an extremely bizarre choice to include in this portrait. Of all the *Olynthus* volumes with which Robinson could have chosen to be portrayed to represent his greatest accomplishment, he chose the one volume of the series which he knew he had not written.

Figure 6.1. Front of a card David Robinson sent to Mary Ross Ellingson for the 1952 holiday season featuring a recently completed portrait of himself. (Image courtesy of the University of Evansville Archives)

One way to explain his peculiar selection of imagery is to suggest Robinson was trying to apologize to Ellingson, an unprovable supposition but one supported by a great deal of circumstantial evidence. Robinson would have known Ellingson would recognize the figurine in Rembski's portrait immediately. The figurine in the frontispiece is catalog number 185, which Ellingson found in the East Cemetery.[56] It was definitely a memorable find as it still retained distinct traces of the original paint with which it had been decorated. Paint rarely survives on terracotta figurines, making the painted lines decorating the woman's cap and the laurel wreath painted in white on the tambourine welcome discoveries. After excavating the piece, Ellingson measured its find spot, photographed it (see figure 2.11 on the far left), took measurements of the figurine for the project inventory, and wrote a detailed description of it for the catalog that formed the basis of her thesis. She may even have been writing to her family about this piece in an undated letter when she described finding two of the most beautiful dancer figurines she had ever seen. There can be no doubt Ellingson saw von Peschke's watercolor of the painted dancer. It is likely he showed it to her at Olynthus since she had excavated the figurine and since she had modeled

Figure 6.2. Frontispiece from *Excavations at Olynthus VII*, a watercolor by Georg von Peschke. (Image courtesy of the Johns Hopkins University Press)

for him, indicating her interest in his art. Her dissertation also contains numerous references to *Excavations at Olynthus VII*, proving she had consulted the volume often and no doubt saw the frontispiece repeatedly. Even though twenty-one years passed since Ellingson found the dancer, she would certainly have recognized the dancer's sinuous pose, the tambourine, and the unusual double base on which the figurine stands, all of which are clearly visible in Rembski's portrait of Robinson.

The timing of Robinson's gesture in including Ellingson's thesis in his portrait is also significant. The university presented the painting to the public in December 1952. When Robinson sat for the portrait or when he told Rembski which volume of *Excavations at Olynthus* to include is not recorded but presumably it was within weeks or at most a few months of the unveiling. The letter exchange quoted earlier between Ellingson and Robinson in which he offers his meek apology for publishing her dissertation took place in mid-October 1952, about two months prior to the public presentation of the portrait. I believe this is more than a coincidence of timing. Robinson's tiff with Ellingson must have been on his mind as well as the worry that he had jeopardized their friendship at the time he was telling Rembski which symbols to include. It was the perfect opportunity for a symbolic apology. Both Robinson and Ellingson had studied art history and had taught survey courses in the entire history of art; he knew she was used to reading the symbolism in a painting. He could not be certain she would ever come to Oxford, Mississippi to see the portrait, however, so he came up with an ingenious solution. For the 1952 holiday season Robinson had a Christmas card printed that featured Rembski's portrait in color on the front. Although reduced in size from the original, the details of the figurine on the frontispiece, the curve of the dancer's body, the paint, the tambourine, and the double base, are still easy to discern. The intended message of this elaborate scheme was an apology for publishing her work without proper attribution and an acknowledgment that she contributed to his success. Robinson may have delighted in the knowledge that he had publically, yet secretly, given Ellingson credit and also snickered at future art historians studying Rembski's work who would never fully understand the symbolism of the portrait although they would think they did.

Ellingson may have received Robinson's message. They corresponded a great deal as the many letters now in the archives at the University of Mississippi prove. Robinson saved copies of those he had sent to Ellingson and her responses; she kept only a couple of his letters. In her later years she moved twice, each time to a smaller place, shedding unnecessary possessions.[57] Interestingly the copy of *Excavations at Olynthus XIV* Robinson sent her in 1952 was one item that did not survive these purges but the Christmas card did. This card must have meant something very special to her for her to keep it until her death.

"PUBLISH OR PERISH"

As we drove home from Oxford, Christine and I talked excitedly about all we had discovered. This was by far the most egregious case of plagiarism in classical archaeology, perhaps also in all of archaeology and even the sciences, anyone had yet been able to document. We had found reams of primary source documents to back up this assertion and to begin to explain why it had happened. I began to form an idea, perhaps all this work had not been just an obsessive hobby. "Publish or perish"; it was time to publish.

SEVEN

"UNWRITTEN HISTORY"

Writing and publishing an academic article is a long and arduous process, especially for a relatively unknown and unpublished scholar early in his career. The first step is to present the idea as a conference paper. This provides the author with the opportunity to get some feedback from colleagues before writing the article. I presented a paper exposing Mary Ross Ellingson's authorship of portions of the *Excavations at Olynthus* volumes at the most prestigious conference for classical archaeologists in North America, the annual conference of the Archaeological Institute of America, in January 2005 in San Diego. The paper's title was intended to be provocative, "How Women Archaeologists Were Erased from the Early 20th Century History of Archaeology: A Case Study." The paper was a great success. People crowded around when it was done to ask questions, make comments, and encourage me to publish.

The next step in getting a scholarly article published is to write a draft and send it to a journal. The editor reads the draft and decides whether to send the article to reviewers, who are other scholars in the author's field. The peer reviewers assess whether the article is worthy of publication as is, worthy after making some revisions, or does not meet professional standards in the field. The author of the article never learns the identities of the reviewers so that the reviewers may feel free to be as honest as possible in their assessment; hence the entire process is sometimes called a "blind review." If the article is approved for publication, the author works with the editor to address the issues raised by the reviewers and once the editor is satisfied the article is scheduled for publication. This process requires many months, sometimes even years.

My first rejection was swift. The anonymous reviewers said that I was not telling the whole story and they made the accusation that Robinson had plagiarized others. More surprises awaited as I followed their suggestions and dug deeper, trying to separate myth from reality. I would write and rewrite the article a number of times, always augmenting it with new information. I had published peer-reviewed articles before but this was to become the most controversial piece I had ever written.

OTHER PLAGIARISM ACCUSATIONS AGAINST ROBINSON

The anonymous reviewers claimed Robinson had plagiarized several of his other graduate students in addition to Ellingson. One of the individuals they named was Graham. This is a rather extraordinary charge since Robinson listed Graham as a coauthor of *Excavations at Olynthus VIII* and published Graham's catalog of lamps found during the 1931 season in *Excavations at Olynthus V* in a chapter with Graham's name on it.[1] Since Graham did not participate in the 1938 season and he is only recorded as working on the lamps and the domestic architecture, it is hard to imagine what he could have written that remained unpublished. Graham earned his PhD in 1933 and found a teaching position in 1935, allowing him to leave Baltimore and Robinson, which again leaves little time for Graham to have written anything else that Robinson could have pilfered. In addition, Robinson worked very actively to promote Graham's early career, so plagiarizing his work would have been counterproductive to his goal of seeing Graham succeed.[2] The only truth I can find behind this charge is Shaw's comment that Graham's name should have come first on the title page of *Excavations at Olynthus VIII* rather than Robinson's since Graham wrote most of the volume.[3] While perhaps true, that is certainly not a serious enough ethical breach to sustain the charge of plagiarism.

Another name the reviewers gave as a victim of Robinson's plagiarism was Gladys Weinberg who, according to one reviewer, wrote the majority of *Excavations at Olynthus V: Mosaics, Vases, and Lamps of Olynthus Found in 1928 and 1931*. On the cover page of the volume and in the table of contents Robinson credits Graham with having written the section on lamps, Mylonas the section on pre-Persian pottery, and A. Xyngopoulos the section on Byzantine pottery. Since Donald Wilber and Freeman were in charge of architecture and, presumably, the mosaics during the 1931 season[4] and Weinberg the vases,[5] the reviewer must be claiming that Weinberg wrote the four remaining chapters on Corinthian wares, wares of uncertain origin, and the red- and black-figured pottery, totaling 201 printed pages. In the preface to the volume Robinson writes of Weinberg, referring to her by her maiden name, "For help on the inventory of the vases (now in the Archaeological Museum of Saloniki) I am indebted to Miss Gladys R. Davidson, now fellow of the American School of Classical Studies in Athens, who also lent efficient aid in supervising a section of the excavations."[6] Robinson's statement contradicts that of the reviewer in that Robinson claims he wrote the remaining sections on the vases with only the *assistance* of Weinberg.

In the absence of documentation we will never know which claim represents objective truth. Whatever Weinberg wrote after she returned to Baltimore in 1931 simply does not survive as she did not submit it as a master's thesis and no drafts of the volume remain among Robinson's papers or Weinberg's own, now archived at the American School. As demonstrated with Ellingson's thesis, Robinson had pilfered the work of one of his graduate students prior to the writing of *Excavations at Olynthus V*, a fact that lends credence to what the reviewer reported. On the other hand Robinson considered himself an expert on, and lover of, Greek pottery, so it seems unlikely he would have left the writing of what he must have considered to be one of the best parts of the volume to a graduate student. Since the volume was assembled and published quickly, appearing in print in 1933, and these four chapters were so long, it is easy to imagine Robinson and Weinberg working on the chapters together. It may be that Robinson believed he had given Weinberg sufficient credit for her contribution in the preface, particularly as she had not written her pottery catalog entries as part of a thesis which would have accorded her more publishing rights.[7] Weinberg may have had an equally strong belief that her work on one or more of these four chapters earned her credit equal to that of her fellow graduate student and research assistant, Graham, whom Robinson credited as the author of the chapter on lamps even though Graham never submitted his work as a thesis or dissertation either. While it seems likely some of Weinberg's work appears in these four chapters, even if the amount is impossible to determine with the surviving evidence, the reviewer's claim she wrote the majority of the volume seems impossible when so much of the volume is devoted to material Weinberg clearly did not study and it seems unlikely she could have written the other four chapters completely on her own in the time available.

The anonymous reviewer who reported hearing Weinberg's stories about her time working with Robinson also stated Weinberg had said that Robinson had scoffed at the notion she could publish her dissertation under her own name. This extraordinary claim appears highly dubious, perhaps something went awry in the repeated transmission of the story. Weinberg wrote about material from Corinth, not Olynthus, thus Robinson had no control whatsoever over that material and whether or not he thought she could publish it under her own name or someone else's was irrelevant. In addition, the encouraging sentiments Robinson wrote to

Weinberg about the excellence of her dissertation is at complete odds with this secondhand story.[8]

The anonymous reviewers had more familiar names of Robinson's alleged plagiarism victims including Clement, a curious claim as Clement was one of Robinson's students who chose not to write a dissertation on an Olynthus-related topic. Instead he wrote on the ancient cults of Thessaly[9] and although he did not publish his dissertation, Robinson did not publish on this subject either. Clement joined the Olynthus team in 1934, several years after he had completed his dissertation, spending the season cataloging the coins.[10] Robinson and Clement published the coins jointly in 1938 in *Excavations at Olynthus IX*.[11] The next year Clement published his review of *Excavations at Olynthus VIII*, which led to the feud between him and Robinson[12] and certainly an end to any collaborative projects that would have given Robinson access to his work. In addition there is no record of Clement working on any material other than the coins published in *Excavations at Olynthus IX*. Again the veracity of this charge is suspect based on the surviving evidence.

The reviewers did not stop with these three names, they had two more. One of these was William McDonald. McDonald's name is well known among archaeologists for his innovative work on the Minnesota-Messina regional survey[13] and as a professor at the University of Minnesota where he created the experimental interdisciplinary Graduate Center for Ancient Studies. Long before that as a graduate student at Johns Hopkins he received his field training at Olynthus under Robinson.[14] During the final season at Olynthus in 1938 he was in charge of inventorying the bronzes and lamps.[15] McDonald chose not to write his dissertation on a subject related to Olynthus but instead completed *The Political Meeting Places of the Greeks* in 1940.[16] This was published three years later in the Johns Hopkins Studies in Archaeology series.[17] As editor of the series, Robinson not only helped to get McDonald's dissertation into print but even found money to finance the book's publication.[18] One anonymous reviewer of my article claimed Robinson had plagiarized McDonald, publishing an edited version of his dissertation as an entry in the *Realency-clopädia der Classischen Altertumswissenschaft*, commonly called the "*RE*" or the "Pauly-Wissowa" after its earliest editors. The *RE* is the most widely respected general encyclopedia on all issues in the classical world routinely consulted by experts in the field. Robinson made his last contribution to the encyclopedia in 1938, two years before McDonald finished his dissertation. In that entry Robinson wrote about houses, not about public space which was McDonald's chosen subject.[19] Robinson also did not publish any general article on Greek public space in 1940 or later. Plagiarism is a strange accusation in this case as not only was McDonald's dissertation published, making detection of such an action likely, but again Robinson helped McDonald publish it in the series Robinson had created. In addition, Robinson gave McDonald permission to publish a reconstruction of a building he was working on from Olynthus that Robinson himself had not yet published.[20] If there is some truth behind this charge, I have been unable to find it.

The final person the reviewers claimed Robinson had plagiarized is another well-known archaeologist, George Hanfmann. Hanfmann is best known for his excavations at the site of Sardis in Turkey while he was a professor at Harvard University and the curator of ancient art at Harvard's Fogg Art Museum. First joining the faculty at Harvard in 1935, he spent his entire professional career there. Prior to his arrival in the United States, Hanfmann completed a dissertation on Etruscan art at the Friedrich-Wil-helms-Universität in Berlin in 1934. That same year he fled Nazi anti-Semitic policies taking up an invitation from Robinson to come to Johns Hopkins and serve as the Charles A. W. Vogeler Fellow in Greek Archaeology for the academic year 1934 to 1935. During his brief tenure at Johns Hopkins he completed a second PhD.[21] Although he appears to have been unable to visit Saloniki where the artifacts from the Olynthus excavations were stored, Hanfmann used the excavation records and Robinson's own notes in order to write about the metal objects found at the site, the basis for his Johns Hopkins dissertation.[22]

An anonymous reviewer suggested that Robinson had compiled most of *Excavations at Olynthus X: Metal and Miscellaneous Finds* from Hanfmann's dissertation. I compared the text of *Excavations at Olynthus X* to a copy of Hanfmann's dissertation I obtained from the Johns Hopkins University archives to test the validity of this claim. While the subject matter is similar, the scope of each text is significantly different. Hanfmann's catalog of metal finds from Olynthus includes 565 entries describing artifacts found in the 1928, 1931, and 1934 seasons. Robinson's catalog includes 2,683 entries describing artifacts found in all four seasons of excavation. As Robinson's text contains almost five times the number of entries as Hanfmann's, Hanfmann clearly could not have written the majority of *Excavations at Olynthus X*. Nonetheless the catalog entries repeated in both documents are nearly identical, although more than half of the entries are quite short describing the numerous beads and arrowheads found at the site, sometimes listing only an inventory number and a length or diameter. Since Hanfmann had not actually seen the material or taken his own measurements, he had to have been copying this information straight out of the excavation notebooks, the same source Robinson used. This does not explain why the remaining two hundred or so longer catalog entries are nearly identical; however, Robinson must have copied them from Hanfmann's dissertation.[23] Robinson had little interest in Hanfmann's forty-nine-page synthesis and analysis of the metal objects, the only sections of the dissertation outside of the catalog that he used were the discussions Hanfmann wrote preceding and following groups of artifacts, explaining the categories into which he divided them.[24] After comparing every word in *Olynthus X* with Hanfmann's dissertation, I estimate that approximately 15 percent of Robinson's text was in fact written by Hanfmann with little or no modification. Robinson did not use Hanfmann's work without acknowledgment, however. The thank-you in the preface of the volume is worth quoting in full:

> In studying the metal objects I have been much helped by my former student, Dr. George Hanfmann, now instructor in Fine Arts at Harvard, and by Dr. Sarah Elizabeth Freeman, who has rendered invaluable service in preparing for the printer the manuscript and plates and who drew the new plan on Plate XLXXII, based on our excavation plan and that of Dr. Saul Weinberg.[25]

Note that Robinson failed to mention the existence of Hanfmann's dissertation, to which there is no reference in the entire work, and that Hanfmann must share his acknowledgment in the sentence with two others.

Does this example constitute plagiarism? Since this material comes from a dissertation, the simple answer is yes according to the standards of the time. Did Robinson see it as plagiarism? That question is, of course, unanswerable but it is easy to see how he could have justified what he was doing. Hanfmann and Robinson were working from the same notebooks to write their texts and Robinson did not use Hanfmann's analysis, which constituted his original thoughts but instead borrowed only his catalog entries and introductory paragraphs. Also so little of the finished text of the volume was Hanfmann's that Robinson may have felt his thank-you was sufficient.

As I looked again at the anonymous reviewers' comments, I was quite struck by how the rumors of plagiarism still dogged Robinson's reputation a half century after his death. I was certain no one had ever heard of Ellingson and of the people the reviewers had cited, only one had a documentable claim to the charge of plagiarism, which did not seem to me to be a strong enough reason for this vague accusation to have continued to haunt his memory. Might the rumors be right but pertain to other people the reviewers had not mentioned? To find out, I tracked down the names of all graduate students who worked with Robinson at Olynthus and wrote theses or dissertations under him. Between my own research and the suggestions of the reviewers I had already explored the cases of ten of his former students[26] and I found an additional eleven names of people who had worked with him at Olynthus. Of these, seven either wrote on subjects not related to Olynthus, about which Robinson did not publish either, or if they did, he helped them publish their work under their own names.[27] One had written a dissertation with a title similar to something Robinson had published but after comparing the two texts it seemed clear they were independent.[28] Of the remaining three, the titles of Frank Albright's thesis and dissertation indicate that they covered a topic about which Robinson also wrote; unfortunately a copy of neither the thesis nor the dissertation exists in the Johns Hopkins University archives, so it is impossible to compare the texts.[29] As for the two remaining graduate students, I discovered Robinson borrowed catalog entries from both just as he had from Hanfmann.

Eleanor B. Lay, who later married and became Eleanor Ross, wrote a dissertation from which Robinson plagiarized some catalog entries. Ross participated in the 1934 season at Olynthus when she was in charge of inventorying the terracotta figurines.[30] She used this inventory as the basis for writing her dissertation, which she completed in 1936. That same year Ross joined the faculty at Syracuse University as an Instructor in Latin, a post she held for several more decades.[31] Some sixteen years after Ross completed her dissertation Robinson published the terracotta figurines found in 1934 and 1938 in *Excavations at Olynthus XIV* incorporating edited versions of some of her catalog entries, about 75 percent of the text remains unchanged, into the second chapter.[32] That chapter is a combination of Ross's catalog entries and the synthesis and analysis from Ellingson's dissertation. Robinson did not use any of Ross's analysis. In the introduction to *Excavations at Olynthus XIV* Robinson offers Ross a general thank-you but never mentions using text from her dissertation.[33] This cutting and pasting explains an observation one reviewer made of *Excavations at Olynthus XIV* the year after it was published. Unbeknownst to the reviewer, or anyone else, Ellingson wrote the first chapter of the volume and half of the second covering the terracotta figurines, Ross wrote half of the second chapter on the figurines, and Robinson wrote the remaining chapters on the lamps and coins. The reviewer stated, "The three chief divisions of *Olynthus XIV* are totally different in character and treatment."[34] Naturally this seemed odd since only Robinson's name appeared on the cover; one would have expected more consistency from a single author.

The other woman whose catalog entries Robinson copied was named Christina B. Meredith who took the name Vestling after she married. Vestling entered the graduate program in mathematics at Johns Hopkins in the fall of 1934. After her first year she came to the Department of Art and Archaeology and in 1937 completed her master's thesis on the finger rings found at Olynthus during the 1931 and 1934 excavation seasons.[35] She did not complete a dissertation at Johns Hopkins. Because she arrived at Johns Hopkins after the 1934 excavation season and left before the 1938 season, she did not excavate at Olynthus and her thesis was based on the excavation diaries, photographs, and inventories rather than observation of the material in the museum in Saloniki or in the field at Olynthus.[36] She appears to have left academia after marrying.

Robinson published the finger rings in *Excavations at Olynthus X*. To the forty-six rings discussed by Meredith Vestling, Robinson added twelve more found in the 1928 and 1938 seasons. As in the cases of Hanfmann's and Ross's dissertations, Robinson seems only to have been interested in Vestling's catalog entries, very little of her analysis and synthesis found its way into

Robinson's introduction to the rings. Also like the other two dissertations, Robinson did some editing of the entries, leaving about 75 percent of the original text.[37] Curiously, Robinson failed to mention Vestling in the preface of *Excavations at Olynthus X* at all and no reference to her or her thesis appears anywhere in the volume. Her name never appears in anything written about Olynthus.

After I had put in many months of research the final tally for graduate students Robinson had plagiarized was four: Ellingson, Hanfmann, Ross, and Vestling. Still, Ellingson's case was different from the rest. Robinson had copied catalog entries from Hanfmann, Ross, and Vestling, as well as some transitional material from Hanfmann, and had integrated it into the text he was writing. While according to the rules at Johns Hopkins and the wider practice at the time, he should not have been using material from other people's dissertations without permission and proper acknowledgment, some subsequent reviewers of my article did not see this as plagiarism as they were only catalog entries and not analysis. In the case of Ellingson, however, Robinson edited her master's thesis very lightly and then published it as a single, unified volume. He also took large sections of her dissertation and published them as one complete chapter and the half of another. In no other case did he lift so much text from one source and in no other case did he use the original author's analysis. Even by the yardstick of Robinson's own behavior, his plagiarism of Ellingson was shocking.

Why Robinson failed to give these four people proper credit will remain a mystery. It might be that he wanted the prestige of being a prolific author and simply took a shortcut to get there. Ellingson, Ross, and Vestling all married, which at the time was understood to mean their academic careers were over.[38] Precious few women were able to manage an academic archaeological career and marriage; the majority of successful professional female scholars either never married or faced a high rate of divorce.[39]

Marrying and leaving the field left their academic work unpublished and forgotten and thus ripe, it appears in Robinson's mind at least, for appropriation. Why Robinson did not give Hanfmann more credit is a particularly curious question since Hanfmann was already well on his way into a promising career when Robinson published his work. It would have enhanced Robinson's status if he had put Hanfmann's name on the cover of an *Excavations at Olynthus* volume as a contributor as he had done with other of his former students; he could have appeared to be the generous patron helping his younger protégé.

The anonymous reviewers of the article had given me some useful ideas. Excited by these new discoveries, I wrote a completely new article. The next editor to whom I submitted it did not bother to send it to anonymous reviewers; she rejected it on sight, without offering a specific reason.

LACK OF CONTEXT

I worked up a lecture on Ellingson's adventures at Olynthus and Robinson's plagiarism for a popular audience and tried it out around Evansville at any venue I could find. People who knew Ellingson would approach me, astonished by what they learned. She had rarely spoken of her life before she arrived in Evansville. Their interest gave me the idea of writing an article for a popular magazine about Ellingson's time at Olynthus including quotes from her letters and photos from her album. Maybe it was too hard to publish a scholarly article about plagiarism, surely a popular article would do better. I wrote her story and sent it to the editor of a popular archaeology magazine. He never wrote back.

My frequently reworked scholarly article titled "Who Wrote the *Excavations at Olynthus* Volumes" fared little better. I felt that I was making progress when I received a rejection letter *after* the editor had sent it to the reviewers. That editor was kind enough to send me the reviewers' comments which complained about a lack of social context for the story. It was a highly useful critique. Much of the material in the earlier chapters of this book was missing from that scholarly article. I found it difficult to explain Ellingson's full story and Robinson's plagiarism with enough background material in the limited number of words available for an article. I reworked the article again from top to bottom, and sent it off hopefully to another journal. Another rejection followed; I was not getting the balance right. "Publish or perish." My tenure review was not far off so I had to focus on other work I knew I could publish. I returned to rework the Ellingson article in stolen moments I could find between teaching classes, grading assignments, writing up my Roman streets research for publication as articles, and, eventually, a book. Time began to slip by; the Ellingson story remained on my mind even if I was finding less and less time to work on the article.

NO STORY HERE

My work on Roman streets was starting to gain some attention. The Archaeological Institute of America (AIA) contacted me about participating in their lecture program. The AIA has more than one hundred chapters in cities across North America as well as a few abroad. Every year they choose archaeologists doing interesting work who are good public speakers to join the ranks of their lecturers. Being an AIA lecturer is by invitation only and being asked to participate is a great honor. Speakers write abstracts for a couple of lectures. The AIA informs chapter presidents whom they will be sending and when, and makes the abstracts available to them. I wrote three abstracts. One was for a lecture about work I had done at a Roman site in Spain. Another was about my work on Roman streets focusing on the site of Pompeii, which is always a crowd-pleaser. The last was based on

Ellingson's story. Presidents of the chapters I was being sent to all chose the Ellingson lecture. Audiences at all of the lectures, and at the AIA chapters where I gave this lecture the next year when I was invited back to the program, were supportive and enthusiastic. At one stop some in the audience members remained for an hour after the completion of the lecture to ask questions and discuss the implications of all they had heard. Clearly the lack of interest from journal editors was not shared by a broader audience.

So far reasons for rejecting the article had been that I had not found everyone Robinson plagiarized and that the article lacked context. I was able to address the first critique successfully but continued to struggle with the second. A third criticism that emerged from subsequent rejections was that there was no story here; it just did not matter. According to the reasoning of some editors and reviewers, what Robinson did represented the standard behavior at that time; he did nothing wrong. Other reviewers and editors argued the opposite; Robinson was an outlier whom everyone knows was a rogue. Regardless of the reason, the conclusion was the same that there was nothing in the article that was new. Of course there is an obvious counterargument to each of these reasons for rejecting the article. If archaeologists of previous generations commonly plagiarized their graduate students, and now that behavior is considered unacceptable, we are obligated to document the shift in our own intellectual culture so that future generations will have a better understanding of how the interpretations of archaeological data produced in the past, many of which are still considered valid today, developed. As for the opposite reason for rejecting the article, that only Robinson plagiarized his students, again that is worth documenting for the exact same reason.

There was another, deeper issue, however, leading to the conclusion that there was nothing worth printing in the article; the people we tend to remember and write about for the history of classical archaeology are those who directed an excavation, wrote articles and books, taught at research institutions, and trained graduate students, activities which men have dominated. To find the feminine footprint in our history we have to look harder since, like Ellingson, women often did not have the same career trajectories as men. Writing about women in North American archaeology, archaeologist and historian Dena Dincauze makes a statement equally true of the women in classical archaeology:

> The routes to powerful positions within the profession are the same as they have always been; those routes have not traditionally been the paths women trod. Whether on account of training, personal predilection, or the obstacles of discrimination, women conventionally took other ways, ways that led to some personal fulfillment but less often to professional recognition. Such choices are part of the diversity of women's experiences in archaeology, today as well as in the past.[40]

Margaret Root, another archaeologist who has written on the history of women in the field, points out the consequences of ignoring people like Ellingson who participated in the field but did not follow the career path of her male counterparts:

> It is an unintended, but no less unfortunate, disservice to denigrate this type of archaeological achievement because it has been tainted by association with the limitations imposed by society upon the female sex—in effect a form of double prejudice. Far better to acknowledge and deplore the factors that have led to the channeling of many women's efforts into certain areas of research and scholarly production and then to dignify their work with energetic critical assessment.[41]

The next editor did not find Root's argument persuasive. She sent me a very polite note rejecting the article because she did not believe her readers would find the story very interesting, a statement I have no doubt she truly believed.

UNWRITTEN HISTORY

There was one final common thread that ran through many of the letters and anonymous reviews I received that was much more disturbing than any of the previously mentioned reasons for the rejection of the article. American classical archaeology has an extremely strong strain of conservatism, especially in Greek archaeology. Part of this conservatism is the understanding that one does not criticize those who came before. Robinson stated this clearly to Graham nearly seventy years ago[42] and it still remains true today. Stephen Dyson blames the system whereby any American who wants credibility as, and the opportunity to become, a Greek archaeologist must attend the American School and participate in its excavations at Corinth or in the Athenian Agora, a system which creates and feeds this conservatism. Dyson compares Greek archaeology to the work of a famed American anthropological archaeologist, stating, "Time spent at the American excavations at Corinth is more likely to encourage the development of an archaeological Confucius devoted to the word of the ancestors rather than a classical Lewis Binford, willing to challenge received tradition."[43]

Resistance to sharing Ellingson's story did not come from editors and anonymous reviewers alone. While on the road doing lectures for the AIA I spoke at a university where one of Robinson's students had taught. Although that person had passed away long before I spoke there, several people who had trained under this person were now teaching and conducting research there and they remembered hearing stories about Robinson and Olynthus. Intense discussion followed my lecture. Many in the audience believed this was an important story that needed to be told since it offered a new view of how the Olynthus project was completed and shone a light on the role of women in classical archaeology in the 1930s. Those who had heard stories of Olynthus from their mentor disagreed and argued I should not be delivering this lecture. They saw me as embarrassing classical archaeology in general, and Robinson in particular, when none of it mattered any more as all the participants were gone and Ellingson had never gone on to make a name for herself in the field.

Journal editors and anonymous reviewers continued to reject the article while I met with intense interest in Ellingson's tale on the lecture circuit. By this time I had written several completely different versions of the article, incorporating suggestions from a number of anonymous reviewers, to no avail. Not a single editor even encouraged me to rework it and resubmit the article. In frustration I turned to a mentor of mine from graduate school, a senior scholar who understood these matters better than I. He warned me to stop trying to publish this story until I had tenure at my university. He explained that while the conservative bent of American classical archaeology was powerful there was another issue. Robinson had helped such a large number of students through graduate school and many were now senior scholars holding positions of editors and peer reviewers at journals and publishing houses in North America. If I was able to publish Ellingson's story and angered them by embarrassing their former teacher, they might try to block publication of anything else I wrote in the future. "Publish or perish." Being unable to publish could kill the career of an untenured faculty member and even cost him or her a job. I thought long and hard about what he had said. I had a great deal of respect for him but found it hard to believe there could be such a far-reaching conspiracy of silence organized by the people who wrote the forty-one theses and seventy-four dissertations Robinson had supervised.

I started again to write another version of the Ellingson-Robinson story with a blank computer screen. Again I reread the comments from all the anonymous reviewers and editors who had rejected my past efforts and tried to address their concerns. When it was done, I sent it to a journal published outside of North America. It was rejected. One of the anonymous reviewers was adamant the editor not publish the article. The reviewer's comments did not fault the article's research, arguments or writing. Instead he or she wrote:

> what you are dealing with here is part of the unwritten history of classical archaeology. Best to leave it unwritten.

It was the most devastating review I have ever read. Eleven editors and more than two dozen peer reviewers had spoken; no one was going to publish the article. All my work on this project over the last several years now appeared wasted. I put the photo album, letters, and newspaper clippings back into the large white envelope in which I had found them and put it all back on top of a shelf, burying it with office supplies and hoping I and everyone else would forget they were there.

EPILOGUE

The University of Evansville has a tradition of planting a tree on campus honoring faculty when they retire. Back when I had first discovered Ellingson's photo album and seen her personnel file, I had read the program for Ellingson's tree-planting ceremony, which was included in the file. I was quite startled when I read the location of her tree. In fact I was so surprised, I immediately put on my coat and went out to find the tree with its tiny plaque commemorating the retired professor. Her tree was not fifty feet from my Tin City excavation trench. Tin City is the name of a former student-family housing complex used on the University of Evansville campus between 1947 and 1961. The thirteen surplus military barracks that made up Tin City were reserved for World War II and the Korean War student-veterans who had families. As part of a class in which I teach aspiring archaeologists the techniques of the trade, I had begun an excavation at the Tin City site. Without knowing it, I had chosen a location for our trench which Ellingson's tree overlooked. The coincidence was immensely satisfying at the time. I could almost see Ellingson's spirit embodied in that tree, protecting and guiding a new generation of eager, young archaeologists. Sometimes when all of my students were contentedly scraping the dirt away layer by layer from their units, I would wander over to the tree and reread the plaque attached to it, seeking the strength to rework and resubmit the article about Ellingson one more time. The summer after I gave up the idea of publishing and put away the photo album the tree died, a fitting symbol of my dashed hopes.

The years passed and I moved onto projects other than Ellingson's until a little over a year ago when I received an email from Ellingson's oldest daughter. She had heard about one of the lectures I had given about her mother and wanted to express her pleasure at seeing her mother's work and memory being kept alive. Guilt is a powerful motivator. I picked up the phone and called the groundskeepers to see if it was possible to replace Ellingson's dead tree and now-missing plaque; I even offered to pay whatever it would cost (see figure E.1). After hanging up, I got the photo album back down from the shelf for the first time in years and flipped through its pages. An idea began to form in my mind; perhaps my mistake had been trying to contain such a large and complicated story within the confines of a brief article, maybe Ellingson's story would make a better book.

Despite what I have been told repeatedly, I still believe Ellingson's story is worth telling for the sake of her generation. They were the second generation of women to enter the field of classical archaeology and they had to carve their own niches circumscribed

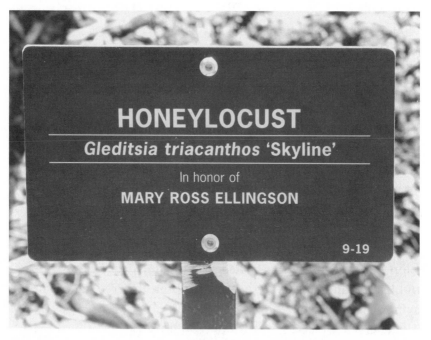

Figure E.1. New plaque beside Mary Ross Ellingson's replacement tree on the University of Evansville campus. (Photo by the author)

by gender expectations and by an economy that limited their job prospects more severely than it had for the previous, or would for the subsequent, generations. Ellingson, Weinberg, and Freeman each made her career on the margins of academia but nonetheless found a way to make contributions to the field. Ellingson's contributions may seem small, she excavated for one season, wrote one volume, and contributed a chapter and a half to a second volume but that does not mean she deserves to be forgotten. Because we can trace the stories of Ellingson, Weinberg, and Freeman they are worth telling as they represent the unknown tales of many other women in archaeology and the sciences who left less evidence behind but who nonetheless participated in their fields in similar and meaningful ways.

Ellingson's story is worth telling for the sake of the current generation of classical archaeologists as well. This story has clearly made some of my fellow archaeologists who serve as journal editors and anonymous reviewers extremely uncomfortable. Their way to deal with that discomfort was to dismiss the entire affair, an instinct which is understandable but not healthy. By keeping this tale out of print we abet Robinson in his victimization of Ellingson, a taint I think we would all prefer to avoid. To date, what Robinson did is the most egregious case of plagiarism yet recorded in the history of classical archaeology, perhaps in all of archaeology, but a number of anonymous reviewers claimed there were other cases, some much worse than the one documented in the previous pages. I am hopeful that by having finally broken the silence through the publication of this book, all those who know more of the hidden history of classical archaeology will now be emboldened to document what they know. Even if they merely record the unverified rumors they have heard, perhaps in published reviews of this book, we can start to have a frank discussion of classical archaeology's history rather than contribute to the creation of a mythological past. The number of articles and books Robinson wrote is staggering, it even appears heroic; to know that he had unacknowledged aid with his publications helps to bring him down to a human level. Keeping knowledge like this suppressed leaves him a myth, not a man.

Ellingson's story is also worth telling for the sake of future generations. When I was an undergraduate about half of my classmates were female, now women make up about 85 percent of the undergraduate archeology majors at the University of Evansville. By the next generation, men will no longer dominate the field. All archaeology students, male and female, deserve to read about the women who came before them, women who made a place for themselves on the margins but by doing so gave future generations a base from which to work their way further into the field and higher up into positions of leadership. The new generation of budding archaeologists, even scientists and other scholars, should understand how the intellectual culture and expected gender roles in the field of archaeology have changed dramatically over the last decades. Sharing the truth with this rising generation will allow them to appreciate the extraordinary pressures under which women in all fields worked in the past and which make any accomplishment all the more impressive. Ellingson can also serve as a role model for the new generation. Satisfactorily balancing a career, fieldwork, and family is difficult, indeed it is a common concern I hear about from my students as they envision their futures. Yet Ellingson was able to strike that balance in a way that satisfied her; her example should give us hope that it is possible for us as well.[1]

Among Ellingson's photos is one of herself, Weinberg, and Freeman taken in a park near Johns Hopkins in the winter of 1930–1931 as the three were preparing to depart for Olynthus. Each woman is in her typical pose, Freeman with chin down and a demure look on her face, Weinberg with her head thrown back in a hearty laugh, and Ellingson chin up and a broad smile on her face. Ellingson wrote in the margin of the photo "the 3 archaeologists." At that moment I suspect each woman had confidence

Figure E.2. From left to right Sarah Freeman, Gladys Weinberg, and Mary Ross Ellingson in a park near Johns Hopkins in late 1930 or early 1931. (Photo courtesy of Barbara Petersen)

that she would be able to make the future career she envisioned happen; none could foresee how the economy, changing attitudes about gender roles, war, and the actions of their advisor would shape their futures. This photo resonates with me because every spring I see our graduates gathering with a few of their friends at their favorite outdoor spots on campus to snap a similar photo. My students do not realize that as they upload these photos to social media, perhaps with the label "the 3 archaeologists," they have many more opportunities for making their dreams come true because of people like Gladys Weinberg, Sarah Freeman, and Mary Ross Ellingson.

APPENDIX
The Vlach Wedding Letter

Throughout this book are numerous edited versions of Mary Ross Ellingson's letters. While I quoted an edited part of her letter from April 21, 1931, in an earlier chapter, this letter is different from the others and deserves to be printed in its full, unedited version for two reasons (figure A.1). The letter captures Ellingson's personality better than most. Her sense of humor, *joie de vivre*, and total embrace of her experience abroad shine through in her vivid description of participating in a Vlach wedding. The letter also highlights her journalistic training, which is the other reason it is worth printing in full. Vlach culture is disappearing from modern Greece and it is not clear that weddings like this are even performed anymore. Future generations of Vlachs as well as anthropologists and historians studying their culture may find something useful for their research in the great detail with which Ellingson describes the ceremony. Note as well how her eye as an archaeologist has developed; she is particularly interested in the role of material culture in the ceremony, describing how all participants use artifacts.

To preserve the flavor of the original, I have transcribed the letter exactly. It is worth preserving her abbreviations and errors in spelling and punctuation as I think they serve to remind us she was writing this letter by hand while watching over dozens of men excavating on the hill at Olynthus. As for the ambiguous portions, of which there are several, I leave those to the reader to interpret. Ellingson refers to the Vlachs as "Clefts," a term she later corrects to "Vlachs" in the undated newspaper clipping written by Thelma Atkinson.

Figure A.1. First page of Mary Ross Ellingson's April 21, 1931, letter. (Image courtesy of the University of Evansville Archives)

April 21
Main Trench,
Hill R,
Olynthus.

Dear Family—

I have so much to tell you. I know it's foolish to start writing it when I could do it so much faster on the typewriter, but then I never have time to write anywhere but at the dig.

Well such excitement as there was on Sunday! Yours truly rode in a wedding procession, and right beside the bridegroom in the place of honor, at that! The Greeks still have the same custom as they had in ancient days—the bridegroom sets out from his home—(this one was in Mariana, not far from Myrio-phyto) in his cart & horse with 2 other carts, and the father riding horseback in front, kind of a herald glorified. He drives to the home of the bride, (at Cassandra, about 10 miles from Myriophyto), & she gets in one of the carts with her attendants, 3 women, 2 small girls, & her mother, & the party starts back again. Well here's where I came in. It was Sunday, & I had been typing a letter for Davey, & the others had gone swimming (I wanted to go, but Davey's letter had to be rushed), so when I got thru, Davey & I walked over to the next village, Hagias Mamas, to look at some inscriptions on stone [see figure A.2]. We had the most exciting time—I wouldn't have missed it for worlds,—but more of that later, I must get back to the wedding, the big event.

We were walking along the road, when we heard the tramp of horses' feet, and the rhythmic song of the Clefts (spelling doubtful)[1] approaching. Turning around, we saw horses, carts, people, banners approaching at a great rate of speed [see figures 3.8 and A.3]. Much shouting and firing of guns and pis-tols. The party stopped when they got to us. The bridegroom rode in the first cart, a gay orange one with blue paintings on it. The marriage banner was waved aloft by one of the attendants. It was a long pole, with a cross-bar near the top. On the end of the pole, was stuck a big red rosy apple. On the two ends of the cross-bar, small green apples. And below was attached the

Figure A.2. David Robinson making a squeeze of an ancient inscription reused as a block in the wall of a modern house. (Photo courtesy of the David M. Robinson Collection, Archives and Special Collections, University of Mississippi Libraries)

banner—of fine white linen, a heavy lace edge, Greek script embroidered in gay colors, ribbons and lace hanging from various places. Other ribbons were attached at the edge of the banner, about 4 inches apart and a jingle-bell on the end of each one. The groom was very resplendent in a new tailored suit of navy blue, patent leather oxfords with brown insets (new) a loud, very loud, blue silk handkerchief in his pocket, on one lapel, a spray of purple flowers (known as βιολέττα²—violetta here), and on the left lapel a glorious Easter lily. The crowning touch—a straw sailor hat, bedecked with tinsel. The bride's

Figure A.3. Mary Ross Ellingson (to the left of the man standing in the forefront of the cart, the groom Athanasios) and David Robinson (on the man's other side) ride in a wedding procession. (Photo courtesy of the University of Evansville Archives)

costume was almost too complicated to describe. She had rows and rows and rows of frills and embroidery (very very beautiful), & a jacket, and some kind of queer hat of white linen & lace that looked like a cross between a Mother Hubbard cap & a boudoir cap. Her attendants are all very gorgeously dressed, too, but they wear dark handkerchiefs on their heads.

Well as I was saying, when they caught up to us, they stopped, & some got out, they passed the cognac around, and invited Davey & me to come along. Which we did, I being very anxious to ride in a bridal procession. The groom got out, if you please, & got in a car & drove to Myriophyto, & there awaited the procession. So we rode in his cart, me on the front seat, between the driver & one of the male attendants. Now I must explain about these carts. There is a board across the front, to sit on, but no place to put your feet or brace yourself. There isn't anything in the back to sit on except the sides of the cart. Well off we went, me feeling very tickled the while at this bit of local colour. Bump no. 1.—Mary slips back a little on the seat. Pistol shot, no. 1., horses lurch forward, Mary falls back into the cart, upon Davey & other members of the bridal party. After resuming my original place—on we go. Bump no.2.—Mary slips back a little. Pistol shot, no. 2.—horses lurch forward, & Mary, by dint of hard pulling on case, & a few friendly pushes from the back, retains seat. Bump no 3.—I have to have more room, but don't like to push the driver off the seat, because then we mightn't get there. I don't like to push the attendant off the seat, because that might complicate matters. Finally he fell off anyway, & I rode along in peace & comfort for a while, till he jumped on again. Oh I forgot to say that he told Dr. Robinson he would like to marry me, & thought I was very beautiful (this being my 3rd proposal during the course of the afternoon). Finally we arrive at Myriophyto, where the whole village, exclusive of our bunch, was out to greet us. Much firing of pistols, etc. I forgot to say, they sang the song of the Clefts (an old rogue song effect—something to do with marriage) all the way along. Andoni, the cook, was out to see it, too, & when he saw Davey & me sitting up in the front cart, as large as life, & twice as natural,—well his eyes just about popped. After recovering his first surprise, he made one dive for the house, & shrieked at the bunch—M'sieur Robinson . . . Mam'selle. . . Marriage! They didn't know what it was all about, & wondered if Davey & I were eloping, Mrs. R. being away in Saloniki for the week-end. They came running out in great awe & admiration. By this time, the bridegroom had taken his place beside me, & the marriage banner was back in the cart, we started off once more. Halfway thru the village, a lot of people had rope stretched across the road & a line of people behind it. That was all very well, just a playful gesture, as customary at weddings, but what did our 2 horses do, but rear up & take to the fields. Finally order was restored. More pistol shots—& the horses were well away. Well, this time I was in a fix. I couldn't shove the driver off, because then we couldn't get there. And as for shoving the bridegroom off—well—. However I finally acquired the knack of staying on the seat, and outside of the fact that the man who was holding the marriage banner kept biffing me on the head, all went smoothly. Finally we arrived at Mariana. (The bunch had hired a truck & followed us.) (I forgot to say that some of the villagers thought I was the bride, & thru rice etc. at me.) We stopped at the threshold of the town, while the groom's father approached from the house! (Alex had taken a lot of pictures meanwhile). Then the groom descended, & followed by the marriage banner entered the house for a few last words (or more probably drinks). Then the bride, who had remained behind some distance, approached. In front of the house, she took a plate of things that look like skinny jelly beans, & thru them over her back. (I managed to get one in the scramble.) Then she entered the house (us tripping after.) We were shown to an upper room, where we sat & waited. Finally they passed around a tray, with about 10 tiny glasses on it, with cognac, & a plate of loucoumi (Turkish delight). Everybody took a sip, & then put the glass back for the next fellow, & took a piece of loucoumi. The groom follows the man who was passing it, & kept filling the glasses. Finally they decided to have the wedding downstairs instead. There-upon we went downstairs, in a small low-ceilinged stuffy room. There was kind of a wooden altar effect in the middle of the room, & on it a huge Bible, covered with wine velvet & brass. Leaning against the mantle piece were 2 white candles tied with orange blossoms & white ribbon. The priest started things going by lighting 2 candles which 2 small children held for him while he read out of the Bible in a sing song voice. The bride & groom, Eleutheria & Athanasios were their names, stood side by side. Her mother held her arms around her all the time clasping her hands. All during the ceremony she kept her eyes shut. I forgot to say that 2 rings lay on top of the Bible. The priest lifted his censor, & swung it around so that the room was filled with smoke & incense. He took the rings & waved 'em around, touching different parts of the bride's & groom's face & then finally, put them on. Then he put on an extra robe from under the altar all embroidered in gold. Then the chief singer sang some marriage hymns in mournful tones. Then the priest lit another pair of candles, the 2 on the mantelpiece, & put the others out. Then he took a long pink shawl effect with ribbons & lace hanging on it, & put it around the bride & groom. Then he took a glass of cognac, blessed it, gave the groom a swallow, then the bride—his hand shaking terribly the while—he is a very old man, & feeble then gave the rest of it to the best man, who stood behind the 2 during the ceremony. More sing-song, then the priest asks άξιος- axios? (I think it means—who is worthy? Or something like that.) Then somebody lifts the best man off the ground 3 times, why, I do not know. More sing-song. Then a box is produced from somewhere & from it are taken two wreaths of orange-blossoms. The priest makes all manner of mystic passes with them, putting them first, on one head & then on the other, finally leaving one on the head of the each, & tying them with a long string. Two small sprays of orange blossom are stuck somewhere, I just forget where. Then the priest kisses the pair, and then kind of pulls them around the altar 3 times the mother of the bride & 2 attendants having to support her as she is just about dead by this time. (her eyes still closed). Then the final blessing by the priest. Then the relations come up, kiss the bride & groom, & put some money on a brass plate for the priest—They are married! (I forgot to say the marriage banner hung outside the house all this while).

Before all this excitement started, Davey & I had been looking at some inscriptions. One was in the yard of a priest, & when we come along he asked us in, & of course I had to see the inside of the house so we went in. It was just a small affair, with very low roof & dirt floor—but I never saw such a clean house in my life. The priest's daughter I guess it was, was lying down on some rugs in one corner, suffering from the rheumatic. Then her husband got us something to drink. He passed us a tray with 3 tiny glasses on it, each with something different in. The one I chose was chipero[3]—something like uzo only more concentrated, & just about knocks you out, but leaves the nicest taste in your mouth. We all clinked our glasses together & said Χριστός Ἀνέστη—Christ is risen (This saying goes on for 40 days after Easter)

Oh yes, I forgot to say that the priest's daughter wanted me to marry her eldest son. And on the way over to the village, the village school master, just a young chap, walked quite a way with us. And he told Davey (all these people spoke Gk. & I couldn't understand a word of it) that he would make me an awfully good husband. He had a house of his own, & he could cook. There now, how's that for one afternoon?

No other news of note just now.

Had a letter from Helen, & she says she is arriving in Athens June 4. As things are now, I can't be there, so I don't know what to do. I'll just hope she comes later. Davey wants us all to stay later than June 1. If she is still in Edm[onton]. when you get this Mother will you please tell her about it; if she would like to come up to the excavation, the railway fare is $7, & I could meet her at the train in Saloniki. If she doesn't want to, I'll come down to Athens, regardless of Davey because I am working hard now. I wrote Helen a letter to the boat, one to her home, telling her I'd meet the Byron, Athens June 4. If she doesn't change her mind and come later, I'll cable her to the boat, and she can cable back what she wants to do. I can be in Athens then, I suppose, because I am keeping my inventory up to date. I told Davey the other day that Helen was coming to meet me June 4, and he said that some of us would have to plan to stay, so I don't think he'd mind a bit if I left before the others.

If anybody (I mean the girls) complains that I haven't written them, please tell them that I am awfully busy—I really don't have a minute except on Sundays, and then I like to rest in the morning and have church, and in the afternoon we usually go someplace and during the week it keeps me hopping to get my report and inventory done after we come back from the dig.

One thing, we have lots of clean clothes here and don't need to economize on washing. And another thing, Andoni has been making us the most wonderful lunches lately.

Heaps o' love,
Mary

NOTES

1. The proper term is Vlach.
2. The proper modern Greek spelling is βιολέτα.
3. The proper transliteration is *tsipouro*. Since Ellingson was writing these foreign words after having only heard them, it is not surprising she would make some mistakes.

NOTES

INTRODUCTION

1. Cf. David M. Robinson, *Excavations at Olynthus XIV: Terracottas, Lamps, and Coins Found in 1934 and 1938* (Baltimore: Johns Hopkins University Press, 1952), v–vi.

2. For a recent assessment of the advancements and shortfalls represented by the Olynthus excavations see Nicholas Cahill, *Household and City Organization at Olynthus* (New Haven, CT: Yale University Press, 2002), 61ff.

3. Cahill, *Household*, 24–25.

4. Cahill, *Household*, 46.

CHAPTER 1

1. This information is contained in a form in Ellingson's personnel file dated September 11, 1973, now in the archives at the University of Evansville.

2. Barbara Petersen, interview with the author on December 11, 2013.

3. "Pioneer Residents of Edmonton to Mark 67th Wedding Day," *Edmonton Bulletin*, December 31, 1940.

4. "Excavations in Old Greece Are Recounted," *Evansville Courier and Press*, March 3, 1940, 4.

5. "Wins Degree," *Edmonton Bulletin*, June 12, 1939.

6. Barbara Petersen, interview with the author on December 11, 2013.

7. Stephen L. Dyson, *Ancient Marbles to American Shores: Classical Archaeology in the United States* (Philadelphia: University of Pennsylvania Press, 1998), 158–59. For a contemporary view that passionately expresses the alarm felt by those who loved, and feared the loss of, Greek culture, see Eva Palmer-Sikelianos, *Upward Panic: The Autobiography of Eva Palmer-Sikelianos*, translated by John P. Anton (Philadelphia: Harwood Academic Publishers, 1993), 175–80.

8. Helen M. M. Ross, "The Terra Cotta Industry at Olynthus" (MA thesis, Johns Hopkins University, 1932), 69.

9. Mariam K. Chamberlain, *Women in Academe: Progress and Prospects* (New York: Russell Sage Foundation, 1988), 5.

10. Julia B. Morgan, *Women at the Johns Hopkins University: A History* (Baltimore: Johns Hopkins University Press, 1986), 20.

11. Margaret W. Rossiter, *Women Scientists in America: Struggles and Strategies to 1940* (Baltimore: Johns Hopkins University Press, 1982), 206.

12. Dyson, *Ancient Marbles*, 193.

13. Paul N. Perrot. "Gladys Davidson Weinberg (1909–2002)," *Journal of Glass Studies* 44 (2002): 211.

14. Aleisa Fishman, "Gladys Davidson Weinberg 1909–2002," in *Jewish Women in America: An Historical Encyclopedia*, eds. E. Paula Hyman and Debora D. Moore (New York: Routledge, 1997), 1462; Pierre de Miroschedji, Obituary for Gladys Davidson Weinberg, *Israel Exploration Journal* 52, no. 2 (2002): 97.

15. Harriet Pass Freidenreich, "Joining the Faculty Club: Jewish Women Academics in the United States," *Nashim: A Journal of Jewish Women's Studies and Gender Issues* 13 (2007): 72. See also Dyson, *Ancient Marbles*, 224.

16. David O. Levine, *The American College and the Culture of Aspiration, 1915–1940* (Ithaca, NY: Cornell University Press, 1986), 147–50.

17. Freidenrich, "Joining the Faculty Club," 93.

18. David M. Robinson, "Mosaics from Olynthus," *American Journal of Archaeology* 36, no. 1 (1932): 16, no. 2.

19. "In Memoriam: Sarah Elizabeth Freeman 1907–1986," *Ákoue*, Spring 1986, 12.

20. "Four College Girls Join Olynthus Quest," *New York Times*, February 15, 1931, 33.

21. "Students to Assist in Greek Excavation," *Baltimore Evening Sun*, February 14, 1931.

22. Lydia C. Carr, *Tessa Verney Wheeler: Women and Archaeology before World War II* (Oxford: Oxford University Press, 2012), 15 and 249.

23. "Four College Girls," 33. The fourth woman mentioned in the title, Dorothy Hill, chose at the last minute not to go to Olynthus. A year earlier the *Daily Mail* in London printed a similar article title about a British excavation: "Girl Excavators." For a discussion of this title and the fascination the press has had with women working in the field, see Carr, *Tessa Verney Wheeler*, 200–203.

24. Dyson, *Ancient Marbles*, 53.

25. Dyson, *Ancient Marbles*, 173.

26. Dyson, *Ancient Marbles*, 102 and 159.

27. Dyson, *Ancient Marbles*, 86.

28. Louis E. Lord, *A History of the American School of Classical Studies at Athens 1882–1942* (Cambridge, MA: Harvard University Press, 1947), 89 and 231.

29. Dyson, *Ancient Marbles*, 86.

30. Lord, *History of the American School*, 15.

31. Dyson, *Ancient Marbles*, 88.

32. See their biographies: Mary Allsebrook, *Born to Rebel: The Life of Harriet Boyd Hawes* (Oxford: Oxbow Books, 1992); Vasso Fotou and Ann Brown, "Harriet Boyd Hawes, 1871–1945," in *Breaking Ground: Pioneering Women Archaeologists*, eds. Getzel M. Cohen and Martha S. Joukowsky (Ann Arbor: University of Michigan Press, 2004), 198–273; Diane L. Bolger, "Ladies of the Expedition: Harriet Boyd Hawes and Edith Hall at Work in Mediterranean Archaeology," in *Women in Archaeology*, ed. Cheryl Claassen (Philadelphia: University of Pennsylvania Press, 1994), 41–50.

33. See her biography: Machteld J. Mellink and Kathleen M. Quinn, "Hetty Goldman 1881–1972," in *Breaking Ground: Pioneering Women Archaeologists*, eds. Getzel M. Cohen and Martha S. Joukowsky (Ann Arbor: University of Michigan Press, 2004), 298–350.

34. Margaret C. Root, "Introduction: Women of the Field, Defining the Gendered Experience," in *Breaking Ground: Pioneering Women Archaeologists*, eds. Getzel M. Cohen and Martha S. Joukowsky (Ann Arbor: University of Michigan Press, 2004), 19.

35. For example, Mortimer and Tessa Wheeler, see Carr, *Tessa Verney Wheeler*, 16. Aileen Fox was managing her own trench and directing two workmen during excavations at the site of Richborough in 1929, even before she met her husband, the archaeologist Cyril Fox; see her autobiography, Aileen Fox, *Aileen: A Pioneering Archaeologist* (Leominster, Herefordshire, UK: Gracewing, 2000), 48.

36. The concept of "containment" as a way to deal with women seeking to enter science and academia was first articulated by Margaret W. Rossiter, *Women Scientists in America*, 216.

37. Carr, *Tessa Verney Wheeler*, 8, 55, 167, and 201. My thanks to an anonymous reviewer from Rowman and Littlefield who pointed me to an early example of the strategy of putting women in charge of "small finds," thus keeping them out of the field. The example comes from the Roman site in Britain of Lydney Park, excavated in the early nineteenth century by William H. Bathurst. Bathurst put his daughter, Charlotte Bathurst, in charge of cataloging the coins. See William H. Bathurst, *Roman Antiquities at Lydney Park, Gloucestershire* (London: Longmans, Green, 1879). The text is available online at https://archive.org/details/romanantiquitie00bathgoog.

38. Quoted in Mary Ann Levine, "Creating Their Own Niches: Career Styles among Women in Americanist Archaeology Between the Wars," in *Women in Archaeology*, ed. Cheryl Claassen (Philadelphia: University of Pennsylvania Press, 1994), 17. This article is a reworked and improved version of paper the author presented at a conference and then published in the conference proceedings, Mary Ann Levine, "Presenting the Past: A Review of Research on Women in Archaeology," in

Equity Issues for Women in Archaeology, eds. Margaret C. Nelson, Sarah M. Nelson, and Alison Wylie. Archaeological Papers of the American Anthropological Association Number 5 (Arlington, VA: American Anthropological Association, 1994).

39. Root, "Introduction," 12.

40. Dyson, *Ancient Marbles*, 182–84.

41. Cynthia Irwin-Williams, "Women in the Field: The Role of Women in Archaeology before 1960," in *Women of Science: Righting the Record*, eds. G. Kass-Simon and Patricia Farnes (Bloomington: University of Indiana Press, 1990), 14.

42. Mellink and Quinn, "Hetty Goldman 1881–1972," 317.

43. Edith Hall, Boyd Hawes' collaborator, earned her PhD at Bryn Mawr; see Dyson, *Ancient Marbles*, 100.

44. Frederica de Laguna received her PhD from Columbia University, see Levine, "Creating Their Own Niches," 12.

45. Dyson, *Ancient Marbles*, 191.

46. Judith G. Touchton and Lynn Davis, *Fact Book on Women in Higher Education* (New York: Macmillan, 1991), 2. For a decade-by-decade breakdown of these figures along with related statistics on women in higher education, see chapter 4.

47. Rossiter, *Women Scientists in America*, 164.

48. The *Roma* was to have a very curious afterlife, being transformed into Italy's first aircraft carrier. With the outbreak of World War II the Italians rebuilt the ship for its new purpose, renaming it the *Aquila*. The transformation was nearly complete when Italy signed the armistice with the Allies; the crew damaged the ship to make certain the Germans could not use it. The *Aquila* was scrapped in the 1950s. David Brown, *Aircraft Carriers* (New York: Arco Publishing, 1977), 11–12.

49. Joseph W. Shaw, "James Walter Graham 1906–1991," *American Journal of Archaeology* 96, no. 2 (1992): 325; "Miss Annie C. Hare Is Married in London to Dr. J. Walter Graham, Archaeologist," *New York Times*, July 26, 1934, 16.

50. Shaw, "James Walter Graham," 325.

51. "Four College Girls," 33.

52. "Students to Assist."

53. George Mylonas, "Biographical Sketch," in *Studies Presented to David Moore Robinson on His Seventieth Birthday*. Vol. 1, ed. George Mylonas (St. Louis: Washington University, 1951), vii.

54. "Dr. Robinson Dies; Archaeologist, 77," *New York Times*, January 3, 1958, 21.

55. Mylonas, "Biographical Sketch," vii.

56. Dyson, *Ancient Marbles*, 28 and 102.

57. Mylonas, "Biographical Sketch," viii.

58. Dyson, *Ancient Marbles*, 193.

59. Mylonas, "Biographical Sketch," vii.

60. Mylonas, "Biographical Sketch," vii.

61. Dyson, *Ancient Marbles*, 96–98.

62. Jennifer K. West, "Observations on Selected Papers of David Moore Robinson from the University of Mississippi Archives" (MA thesis, University of Mississippi, 1995), 128.

63. Dyson, *Ancient Marbles*, 193.

64. For a complete list of Robinson's professional accomplishments, see George Mylonas, "Biographical Sketch."

65. David M. Robinson, "Greek and Latin Inscriptions from Asia Minor," *Transactions and Proceedings of the American Philological Association* 57 (1926): 195, n. 1.

66. David M. Robinson, foreword to *Excavations at Olynthus I. The Neolithic Settlement*, by George Mylonas (Baltimore: Johns Hopkins University Press, 1929), vii.

67. Virginia Polytechnic Institute and State University in Blacksburg.

68. Raymond Dessy, *Exile from Olynthus. Women in Archaeology.com. Mentoring and Networking in Greece, 1927–1928*, 2005, http://scholar.lib.vt.edu/faculty_archives/dessy/T_HOME-PAGE.htm, 36–38, 41.

69. For example, A. Philip McMahon, "Review of *Excavations at Olynthus, Part III. The Coins Found at Olynthus in 1928* by David M. Robinson," *Parnassus* 3, no. 8 (1931): 34; Franklin P. Johnson, "Review of *Excavations at Olynthus, Part III. The Coins Found at Olynthus in 1928* by David M. Robinson and *Excavations at Olynthus, Part IV. The Terra-cottas of Olynthus, Found in 1928* by David M. Robinson," *Classical Philology* 26, no. 3 (1931): 339–40.

70. Edith H. Dohan, "Review of *Excavations at Olynthus, Part IV. The Terra-cottas of Olynthus, Found in 1928* by David M. Robinson," *American Journal of Archaeology* 36, no. 2 (1932): 207–8. One peer reviewer from Rowman and Littlefield who read an earlier version of this book made the interesting suggestion that having women like Dohan critique his work may have made Robinson more open to trust the ability of women as fieldworkers. This could explain his differential treatment of van Ingen and Couch in 1928 and Ellingson, Weinberg, and Freeman in 1931; the former pair spent most of their season cataloging in the dig house while the latter trio spent their season in the trenches. Naturally such a suggestion cannot be proven.

71. Linda M. Medwid, *The Makers of Classical Archaeology* (New York: Humanity Books, 2000), 301–3.

72. Alan Wace, "Review of *Excavations at Olynthus. Part II. Architecture and Sculpture: Houses and Other Buildings* by David M. Robinson," *Classical Review* 45, no. 2 (1931): 87.

73. Winifred Lamb, "Review of *Excavations at Olynthus. Part II: Architecture and Sculpture* by David M. Robinson," *Journal of Hellenic Studies* 51 (1931): 114–15.

74. Quoted in Raymond Dessy, *Exile from Olynthus*, 34.

75. For example, Carl W. Blegen, "Review of *Excavations at Olynthus, Part II, Architecture and Sculpture: Houses and Other Buildings* by David M. Robinson," *American Journal of Archaeology* 36, no. 3 (1932): 368–69; Lord, *A History of the American School*, 251.

76. Dessy, *Exile from Olynthus*, *passim*.

77. While I have come across no evidence that Robinson ever participated in an extramarital affair with Ellingson or anyone else, his wife may have been fully aware of his flirtatious behavior. For a similar but much more extreme case, see the relationship between British archaeologist Mortimer Wheeler, who had serial affairs, and his wife, Tessa, who was known to console the young ladies Wheeler abandoned when he found a new love interest; Carr, *Tessa Verney Wheeler*, 182.

78. Quoted in Dessy, *Exile from Olynthus*, 33.

79. Quoted in Dessy, *Exile from Olynthus*, 36.

80. Dessy, *Exile from Olynthus*, 42 and 46.

81. Dessy, *Exile from Olynthus*, 45.

82. There are numerous references among Robinson's, Ellingson's, and van Ingen's correspondence to grants, fellowships, and scholarships for which Robinson pushed his students to apply and helped them to obtain.

83. Natalia Vogeikoff-Brogan, "The Modern Greek Exam, 'Professor Blank's' Method, and Other Stories from the 1930s," *From the Archivist's Notebook*, October 1, 2013, http://nataliavogeikoff.com/category/women-studies/.

84. Natalia Vogeikoff-Brogan, "The Modern Greek Exam," http://natalia vogeikoff.com/category/women-studies/.

85. Dyson, *Ancient Marbles*, 193.

86. Dessy, *Exile from Olynthus*, 28.

87. Lord, *A History of the American School*, 204.

88. Dessy, *Exile from Olynthus*, 3.

89. Robinson, "Greek and Latin Inscriptions," 195, n. 1.

90. Robinson, "Greek and Latin Inscriptions," 195, n. 1.

91. The dispute is documented in Jennifer K. West, "Observations on Selected Papers," 121.

92. David M. Robinson, "The *Res Gestae Divi Augusti* as Recorded on the Monumentum Antiochenum," *American Journal of Philology* 47, no. 1 (1926): 3.

93. Mylonas, "Biographical Sketch," ix.

94. "Mrs. Robinson's Rites Tomorrow," *Baltimore Evening Sun*, May 16, 1960.

95. Barbara Petersen, interview with the author on December 11, 2013.

96. Mylonas, "Biographical Sketch," ix–x.

97. Lord, *A History of the American School*, 176; Spyros Iakovidis, "George Emmanuel Mylonas, 1898–1988," *American Journal of Archaeology* 93 (1989): 235.

98. David M. Robinson, foreword to *Excavations at Olynthus I*, ix; Medwid, *The Makers of Classical Archaeology*, 211; Spyros Iakovidis, "George Emmanuel Mylonas," 235.

99. George E. Mylonas, *Excavations at Olynthus I. The Neolithic Settlement*. Johns Hopkins University Studies in Archaeology 6 (Baltimore: Johns Hopkins University Press, 1929).

CHAPTER 2

1. "Students to Assist in Greek Excavation," *Baltimore Evening Sun*, February 14, 1931.

2. According to a news clipping among Ellingson's papers at the University of Evansville Thelma Atkinson was the maid of honor at Ellingson's wedding, so presumably they were old friends and she had read Ellingson's letters and spoken with her about her time at Olynthus. The clipping about the wedding is titled "Mary Ross Is Married Quietly at Family Residence, Saturday" and, unfortunately, lacks a masthead or any indication of in which paper it was originally published.

3. J. Walter Graham, "Excavations at Olynthus Second Campaign 1931," Box 37, David M. Robinson Collection, Archives and Special Collections, University of Mississippi Libraries.

4. David M. Robinson, "Mosaics from Olynthus," *American Journal of Archaeology* 36, no. 1 (1932): 16.

5. For details on a few other women who directed crews of local workmen at foreign and domestic sites see Lydia C. Carr, *Tessa Verney Wheeler: Women and Archaeology before World War II* (Oxford: Oxford University Press), 11.

6. German and French archaeologists had done more work on Greek houses than American archaeologists prior to the commencement of Robinson's excavations at Olynthus, see Theodor Wiegand and Hans Schrader, *Priene: Ergebnisse der Ausgrabungen und Untersuchungen in den Jahren 1895–1898* (Berlin: G. Reimer, 1904); Joseph Chamonard, *Exploration archéologique de Délos. Fascicule viii. Le Quartier du Théâtre* (Paris: E. de Boccard, 1924); Hetty Goldman, "Excavations of the Fogg Museum at Colophon," Paper presented at the fourteenth annual meeting of the Archaeological Institute of America, Washington, DC, December 29, 1922. *American Journal of Archaeology* 27 (1923): 67–68. In 1933, after Robinson had completed two seasons at Olynthus, Chamonard would publish another important addition to the corpus of household studies: *Exploration archéologique de Délos. Fascicule xiv. Les mosaïques de la Maison des Masques* (Paris: E. de Boccard, 1933).

7. Stephen L. Dyson, *Ancient Marbles to American Shores: Classical Archaeology in the United States* (Philadelphia: University of Pennsylvania Press, 1998), 86–87.

8. For example, Franklin P. Johnson, "Review of *Excavations at Olynthus, Part II: Architecture and Sculpture: Houses and Other Buildings* by David M. Robinson," *Art Bulletin* 12, no. 4 (1930): 421–22; and Alfred Merlin, "Review of *Excavations at Olynthus, Part II: Architecture and Sculpture: Houses and Other Buildings* by David M. Robinson," *Revue Historique* 165, no. 2 (1930): 348–50.

9. Jennifer K. West, "Observations on Selected Papers of David Moore Robinson from the University of Mississippi Archives" (MA thesis, University of Mississippi, 1995), 126.

10. Nicholas Cahill, *Household and City Organization at Olynthus* (New Haven, CT: Yale University Press, 2002), 63; Dyson, *Ancient Marbles* 194–95.

11. Cahill, *Household*, 63.

12. Alan Wace, "Review of *Excavations at Olynthus. Part II. Architecture and Sculpture: Houses and Other Buildings* by David M. Robinson," *Classical Review* 45, no. 2 (1931): 87.

13. Cahill, *Household*, 61–63.

14. Both logs are preserved in Box 37, David M. Robinson Collection, Archives and Special Collections, University of Mississippi Libraries.

15. Cahill, *Household*, 62–63.

16. For a full description of this house and its architecture, see David M. Robinson and J. Walter Graham, *Excavations at Olynthus VIII: The Hellenic House; a Study of the Houses Found at Olynthus with a Detailed Account of Those Excavated in 1931 and 1934*, Johns Hopkins University Studies in Archaeology 25 (Baltimore: Johns Hopkins University Press, 1938), 117–18.

17. For more on Hippodamus of Miletus and the origins of urban planning, see Richard E. Wycherly, *How the Greeks Built Cities* (London: Macmillan, 1949), chapter 2. Although it is a bit dated now, Wycherly provides a highly readable account of the development of Greek city planning.

18. David M. Robinson, foreword to *Excavations at Olynthus I. The Neolithic Settlement*, by George Mylonas (Baltimore: Johns Hopkins University Press, 1929), viii.

19. These photos are in Box 42, David M. Robinson Collection, Archives and Special Collections, University of Mississippi Libraries.

20. David M. Robinson, "Mosaics from Olynthus," *American Journal of Archaeology* 36, no. 1 (1932): 16, no. 2.

21. David M. Robinson, *Excavations at Olynthus XI: Necrolynthia, a Study of Greek Burial Customs and Anthropology*, Johns Hopkins University Studies in Archaeology 32 (Baltimore: Johns Hopkins University Press, 1942), vii.

22. David M. Robinson, *Excavations at Olynthus V: Mosaics, Vases, and Lamps of Olynthus Found in 1928 and 1931* (Baltimore: Johns Hopkins University Press, 1933), xi.

23. David M. Robinson, *Excavations at Olynthus VII: The Terra-Cottas of Olynthus Found in 1931* (Baltimore: Johns Hopkins University Press, 1933), viii.

CHAPTER 3

1. Compare Ellingson's experiences discovering Greek culture with her near contemporary and another American woman, Eva Palmer-Sikelianos, *Upward Panic. The Autobiography of Eva Palmer-Sikelianos*. Translated by John P. Anton (Philadelphia: Harwood Academic Publishers, 1993), 53–56.

2. "Edmonton Girl Finds Interest in Archaeology," *The Albertan*, September 18, 1931.

3. "Excavations in Old Greece Are Recounted," *The Evansville Courier and Press*, March 3, 1940, 4.

4. For a brief summary of this tragic period in Greek history, see Richard Clogg, *A Short History of Modern Greece* (New York: Cambridge University Press, 1979), 117–22.

5. The old women sitting together and spinning in figure 3.6 brings to mind the words of Eva Palmer-Sikelianos: "Spinning with a distaff is a most sociable occupation, especially when old women gather round their neighbor's fire-place to sit spinning and gossiping at the same time, which aways seemed a pleasanter way of paying a visit than our stand-up-and-do-nothing tea parties." Palmer-Sikelianos, *Upward Panic*, 76.

6. For more on the impact of the refugee settlement in Aegean Macedonia, see John Shea, *Macedonia and Greece: The Struggle to Define a New Balkan Nation* (Jefferson, NC: McFarland and Company, 1997), 105–7.

7. Stephen L. Dyson, *Ancient Marbles to American Shores: Classical Archaeology in the United States* (Philadelphia: University of Pennsylvania Press, 1998), 194.

8. This estimate comes from Tom J. Winnifrith, *The Vlachs: The History of a Balkan People* (New York: St. Martin's Press, 1987), 3. Winnifrith gives an excellent account of the development of the Vlach language and the history of the Vlach people.

9. This excerpt gives a taste for the letter, the full text with Ellingson's account of more of her misadventures as well as a meticulously detailed account of the ceremony is presented in the appendix.

10. Ellingson has made a mistake in her Latin here. The ending should be ablative; *Bello.*

11. Kostis Kourelis, "Byzantium and the Avant-Garde: Excavations at Corinth 1920s–1930s," *Hesperia* 76 (2007): 423–24.

12. The museum was moved out of the building in 1965 and today the former mosque is a civic building used for public displays. To see modern photos of the building, including one that was taken from nearly the same angle as Ellingson's, see http://wikimapia.org/1479811/Geni-Mosque.

CHAPTER 4

1. Mary Ann Levine, "Creating Their Own Niches: Career Styles among Women in Americanist Archaeology between the Wars," in *Women in Archaeology*, ed. Cheryl Claassen (Philadelphia: University of Pennsylvania Press, 1994), 22–23.

2. Margaret W. Rossiter, *Women Scientists in America: Struggles and Strategies to 1940* (Baltimore: Johns Hopkins University Press, 1982), 215–16; Carol S. Hollenshead, Stacey A. Wenzel, Barbara B. Lazarus, and Indira Nair, "The Graduate Experience in the Sciences and Engineering: Rethinking a Gendered Institution," in *The Equity Equation. Fostering the Advancement of Women in the Sciences, Mathematics, and Engineering*, eds. Cinda-Sue Davis, Angela B. Ginorio, Carol S. Hollenshead, Barbara B. Lazarus, and Paula M. Rayman (San Francisco: Jossey-Bass, 1996), 126.

3. Quoted in Natalia Vogeikoff-Brogan, "The Modern Greek Exam, 'Professor Blank's' Method, and Other Stories from the 1930s," *From the Archivist's Notebook*, October 1, 2013, http://nataliavogeikoff.com/category/women-studies/.

4. These data are based on the fall enrollment numbers for the given academic year; Thomas D. Snyder, ed. *120 Years of American Education: A Statistical Portrait* (National Center for Educational Statistics, U.S. Department of Education, Office of Educational Research and Improvement, 1993), 75. http://nces.ed.gov/pubs93/93442.pdf.

5. Snyder, *120 Years of American Education*, 75.

6. Judith G. Touchton and Lynn Davis, *Fact Book on Women in Higher Education* (New York: Macmillan, 1991), 222.

7. Lilli S. Hornig, "Affirmative Action through Affirmative Attitudes," in *Women in Academia: Evolving Policies toward Equal Opportunities*, eds. Elga Wasserman, Arie Y. Lewin, and Linda H. Bleiweis (New York: Praeger Publishers, 1975), 9.

8. C. Robert Pace, *They Went to College: A Study of 951 Former University Students* (Minneapolis: University of Minnesota Press, 1941), 56.

9. Levine, "Creating Their Own Niches," 16; Cynthia Irwin-Williams, "Women in the Field: The Role of Women in Archaeology before 1960," in

Women of Science: Righting the Record, ed. G. Kass-Simon and Patricia Farnes (Bloomington: University of Indiana Press, 1990), 25.

10. Irwin-Williams, "Women in the Field," 14; Lucia Nixon, "Gender Bias in Archaeology," in *Women in Ancient Societies: An Illusion of Night*, eds. Léonie J. Archer, Susan Fischler, and Maria Wyke (New York: Routledge, 1994), 16.

11. Rossiter, *Women Scientists in America*, 168.

12. Julie Des Jardins, *The Madame Curie Complex: The Hidden History of Women in Science* (New York: Feminist Press of the City University of New York, 2010), 5–8.

13. Rossiter, *Women Scientists in America*, 165–66.

14. American Association of University Professors, "Academic Freedom and Tenure," *Bulletin of the American Association of University of Professors* 26, no. 1 (1940): 49–54.

15. Rossiter, *Women Scientists in America*, 194–95.

16. Rossiter, *Women Scientists in America*, 168 and 176; Hollenshead et al., "The Graduate Experience," 126.

17. Chase Going Woodhouse, "Women," *American Journal of Sociology* 37, no. 6 (1932): 958–59.

18. Mary E. Cookingham. "Combining Marriage, Motherhood, and Jobs before World War II: Women College Graduates, Classes of 1905–1935," *Journal of Family History* 9, no. 2 (1984): 189.

19. Rossiter, *Women Scientists in America*, 195–96.

20. Lynne P. Sullivan, "Madeline D. Kneberg Lewis: Leading Lady of Tennessee Archaeology," in *Grit-Tempered: Early Women Archaeologists in the Southeastern United States*, eds. Nancy M. White, Lynne P. Sullivan, and Rochelle A. Marrinan (Gainesville: University Press of Florida, 1999), 86–87.

21. Hollenshead et al., "The Graduate Experience," 126.

22. Jane H. Kelley, "Being and Becoming," in *Rediscovering Our Past: Essays on the History of American Archaeology*, ed. Jonathan E. Reyman (Aldershot: Avebury, 1992), 86.

23. Pace, *They Went to College*, 56.

24. Rossiter, *Women Scientists in America*, 139.

25. Sharon B. McGrayne, *Nobel Prize Women in Science. Their Lives, Struggles, and Momentous Discoveries* (New York: Brick Lane Press, 1993), 144.

26. Cookingham. "Combining Marriage, Motherhood, and Jobs," 179.

27. Cookingham. "Combining Marriage, Motherhood, and Jobs," 178–79 and 186; Barbara Sicherman, "College and Careers: Historical Perspectives on the Lives and Work Patterns of Women College Graduates," in *Women and Higher Education in American History*, eds. John M. Faragher and Florence Howe (New York: W. W. Norton, 1988), 142–43.

28. Pace, *They Went to College*, 41 and 56.

29. Nixon, "Gender Bias in Archaeology," 17; Levine, "Creating Their Own Niches," 16–17.

30. Getzel M. Cohen and Martha S. Joukowsky, eds., *Breaking Ground: Pioneering Women Archaeologists* (Ann Arbor: University of Michigan Press, 2004), 557.

31. Cookingham. "Combining Marriage, Motherhood, and Jobs," 179.

32. Alva Myrdal and Viola Klein, *Women's Two Roles. Home and Work*, 2nd ed. (London: Routledge and Kegan Paul, 1968), 44–45; Sicherman, "College and Careers," 143.

33. Levine, "Creating Their Own Niches," 36.

34. Quoted in Vasso Fotou and Ann Brown, "Harriet Boyd Hawes, 1871–1945," in *Breaking Ground: Pioneering Women Archaeologists*, eds. Getzel M. Cohen and Martha S. Joukowsky (Ann Arbor: University of Michigan Press, 2004), 235.

35. For a lament of the interest in the history of women in classical archaeology and for an assessment of the employment landscape for women in the field, see Tracey Cullen, "Contributions to Feminism in Archaeology," *American Journal of Archaeology* 100, no. 2 (1996): 412.

36. Published in David M. Robinson, *Excavations at Olynthus VII: The Terra-Cottas of Olynthus found in 1931* (Baltimore: Johns Hopkins University Press, 1933), #182, 51–52.

37. For an independent assessment of her thesis, see Walter R. Agard, "Review of *Excavations at Olynthus, Part VII. The Terra-Cottas Found in 1931* by David M. Robinson," *Classical Journal* 30, no. 3 (1934): 173–74; Valentin Müller, "Review of *Excavations at Olynthus* by David M. Robinson," *Classical Philology* 31, no. 1 (1936): 92–93; George W. Elderkin, "Review of *Excavations at Olynthus, Part VII. The Terra-Cottas Found in 1931* by David M. Robinson," *American Journal of Archaeology* 38, no. 3 (1934): 497.

38. "Excavations in Old Greece Are Recounted," *Evansville Courier and Press*, March 3, 1940, 4.

39. David Robinson to W. H. Alexander, June 21, 1932. The original letter is in the possession of Barbara A. Petersen and a copy is on file in the archives at the University of Evansville.

40. For an independent assessment of her dissertation, see Reynold A Higgins, "Review of *Excavations at Olynthus. Part XIV, Terracottas, Lamps and Coins Found in 1934 and 1938* by D. M. Robinson," *Journal of Hellenic Studies* 75 (1955): 180; Reynold A. Higgins, "Review of *Excavations at Olynthus. Part XIV, Terracottas, Lamps and Coins Found in 1934 and 1938* by D. M. Robinson," *Antiquaries Journal* 35 (1955): 97; Sterling Dow, "Review of *Excavations at Olynthus. Part XIV* by David M. Robinson," *American Historical Review* 58, no. 3 (1953): 586–87; William A. McDonald, "Review of *Excavations at Olynthus Part XIV. Terracottas, Lamps and Coins Found in 1934 and 1938* by David

M. Robinson," *Classical Journal* 50, no. 2 (1954): 94–95; Robert Scranton, "Review of *Excavations at Olynthus, Part XIV: Terracottas, Lamps, and Coins Found in 1934 and 1938* by David M. Robinson," *Classical Philology* 49, no. 2 (1954): 143–44; R. M. Cook, "Review of *Excavations at Olynthus. Part XIV, Terracottas, Lamps and Coins Found in 1934 and 1938* by D. M. Robinson," *Classical Review* 5, no. 3/4 (1955): 326–27; R. C. Wood, "Review of *Excavations at Olynthus. Part XIV, Terracottas, Lamps and Coins Found in 1934 and 1938* by D. M. Robinson," *American Journal of Archaeology* 57, no. 3 (1953): 227–28.

41. Helen M. M. Ross, 1939. "The Terra-cotta Figurines of Macedonia and Thrace" (PhD diss., Johns Hopkins University, 1939), 132–45.

42. This information comes from a newspaper article among Ellingson's papers at the University of Evansville archives titled "Mary Ross Is Married Quietly at Family Residence Saturday." The name of the paper is missing but someone has written "August 1939" on it.

43. Barbara Petersen, interview with the author on December 11, 2013.

44. The letter is dated May 27, 1939, and is addressed to W. H. Alexander. It is currently in the possession of Barbara Petersen; a copy is on file in the archives at the University of Evansville.

45. Cookingham, "Combining Marriage, Motherhood, and Jobs," 182; Sicherman, "College and Careers, 139.

46. October 5, 1941 letter from Mary Ellingson, to David Robinson; October 15, 1941, Robinson to Ellingson; November 4, 1941, Ellingson to Robinson; all three letters are in Box 5, David M. Robinson Collection, Archives and Special Collections, University of Mississippi Libraries. Copies are filed in the archive at the University of Evansville.

47. David Robinson to Mary Ellingson, October 15, 1941, Box 5, David M. Robinson Collection, Archives and Special Collections, University of Mississippi Libraries, a copy is in the archive at the University of Evansville.

48. Mary Ellingson to David Robinson, March 18, 1941, Box 5, David M. Robinson Collection, Archives and Special Collections, University of Mississippi Libraries, a copy is in the archive at the University of Evansville.

49. Barbara Petersen, interview with the author on December 11, 2013.

50. George Klinger, *We Face the Future Unafraid: A Narrative History of the University of Evansville* (Evansville, IN: University of Evansville Press, 2003), 105.

51. Klinger, *We Face the Future Unafraid*, 135.

52. Archaeological Institute of America, "Archaeological Institute of America Award for Distinguished Service Gladys Davidson Weinberg," *American Journal of Archaeology* 90, no. 2 (1986): 173.

53. Gladys R. Davidson, "Miscellaneous Finds from Corinth, 1896-1933" (PhD diss., Johns Hopkins University, 1935).

54. David Robinson to Gladys Weinberg, October 21, 1942, Box 5, David M. Robinson Collection, Archives and Special Collections, University of Mississippi Libraries, a copy is in the archive at the University of Evansville.

55. Gladys D. Weinberg, *Corinth, Results of Excavations Conducted by the American School of Classical Studies at Athens XII. The Minor Objects* (Princeton, NJ: American School of Classical Studies at Athens, 1952).

56. Sharon C. Herbert, "Saul S. Weinberg, 1911–1992," *American Journal of Archaeology* 97, no. 3 (1993): 567.

57. Aleisa Fishman, "Gladys Davidson Weinberg 1909–2002," in *Jewish Women in America: An Historical Encyclopedia*, eds. E. Paula Hyman and Debora D. Moore (New York: Routledge, 1997), 1462; and Susan H. Allen, *Classical Spies: American Archaeologists with the OS in World War II Greece* (Ann Arbor: University of Michigan Press, 2011), 256 and 304.

58. Pierre de Miroschedji, Obituary for Gladys Davidson Weinberg, *Israel Exploration Journal* 52, no. 2 (2002): 97.

59. Herbert, "Saul S. Weinberg," 567.

60. Harriet Pass Freidenreich, "Joining the Faculty Club: Jewish Women Academics in the United States," *Nashim: A Journal of Jewish Women's Studies and Gender Issues* 13 (2007): 68 and 76.

61. I have heard the rumor repeated by several people that had Saul Weinberg not been Jewish, he would have been considered to head the American School. Such a rumor is impossible to confirm and no one who has told me this rumor was willing to state it on the record.

62. Herbert, "Saul S. Weinberg, 1911–1992," 567; Archaeological Institute of America, "Saul S. Weinberg," *American Journal of Archaeology* 90, no. 2 (1986): 174.

63. Obituary for Saul Weinberg, *Israel Exploration Journal* 43, no. 2/3 (1993): 199; Paul N. Perrot, "Gladys Davidson Weinberg (1909–2002)," *Journal of Glass Studies* 44 (2002): 211–15.

64. Herbert, "Saul S. Weinberg," 567.

65. Nixon, "Gender Bias in Archaeology," 16–17.

66. Perrot, "Gladys Davidson Weinberg (1909–2002)," 211.

67. Levine, "Creating Their Own Niches," 17.

68. Fishman, "Gladys Davidson Weinberg 1909–2002," 1462.

69. Perrot, "Gladys Davidson Weinberg—A Tribute," *Journal of Glass Studies* 24 (1982): 9.

70. Archaeological Institute of America, "Archaeological Institute of America Award," 173–74.

71. Obituary for Saul Weinberg, *Israel Exploration Journal* 43, no. 2/3 (1993): 199; Perrot, "Gladys Davidson Weinberg (1909–2002)," 211.

72. Sarah E. Freeman, "The Excavation of a Roman Temple at Corinth" (PhD diss., Johns Hopkins University, 1934) and "Temple E at Corinth," in *Corinth, Results of Excavations Conducted by the American School of Classical Studies at Athens* I.2: *Architecture*, eds. Richard Stillwell, Robert L. Scranton and Sarah E. Freeman (Princeton, NJ: American School of Classical Studies at Athens 1941), 166–236.

73. Special Collections, Milton S. Eisenhower Library, Johns Hopkins University, "Freeman (Sarah Elizabeth) 1906–1986, Papers 1944–1969, MS. Gar30," n.d. http://old.library.jhu.edu/collections/specialcollections/manuscripts/msregisters/msgar30freeman.pdf.

74. David M. Robinson and J. Walter Graham, *Excavations at Olynthus VIII: The Hellenic House; A Study of the Houses Found at Olynthus with a Detailed Account of Those Excavated in 1931 and 1934,* Johns Hopkins University Studies in Archaeology 25 (Baltimore: Johns Hopkins University Press, 1938), ix; David M. Robinson, *Excavations at Olynthus X: Metal and Minor Miscellaneous Finds, an Original Contribution to Greek Life,* Johns Hopkins University Studies in Archaeology 31 (Baltimore: Johns Hopkins University Press, 1941), xi.

75. Rossiter, *Women Scientists in America*, 207.

76. George Mylonas, "Biographical Sketch," in *Studies Presented to David Moore Robinson on His Seventieth Birthday.* Vol. 1, ed. Geroge Mylonas (St. Louis, MO: Washington University, 1951), xvii.

77. Max B. Spiegel, "The Garrett Collection: Coins, Medals, and Archives at the American Numismatic Society," *American Numismatic Society Magazine* 5, no. 3 (2006). http://ansmagazine.com/Winter06/Garrett; "In Memoriam: Sarah Elizabeth Freeman 1907–1986," *Ákoue*, Spring 1986.

78. "Man Convicted of Murdering Retired Professor," *AP News Archive*, July 7, 1987, http://www.apnewsarchive.com/1987/Man-Convicted-of-Murdering-Retired-Professor/id-7498088409c4759742230947017034d8.

79. Rossiter, *Women Scientists in America*, 184–86.

80. Rossiter, *Women Scientists in America*, 205–6.

81. Levine, "Creating Their Own Niches," 23.

CHAPTER 5

1. J. Walter Graham, "Domestic Architecture in Classical Greece," PhD diss., Johns Hopkins University, 1933.

2. "Miss Annie C. Hare Is Married in London to Dr. J. Walter Graham, Archaeologist," *New York Times*, July 26, 1934, 16.

3. David M. Robinson, "Mosaics from Olynthus," *American Journal of Archaeology* 36, no. 1 (1932): 16, no. 2.

4. Robinson describes this episode in a letter dated January 10 or 17 (the last digit is smudged), 1953 now in the Graham folder, Box 6, David M. Robinson Collection, Archives and Special Collections, University of Mississippi Libraries. A copy is now on file at the University of Evansville Archives.

5. David M. Robinson, "The Third Campaign at Olynthus," *American Journal of Archaeology* 39, no. 2 (1935): 210, no. 1.

6. David M. Robinson, *Excavations at Olynthus XIII: Vases Found in 1934 and 1938*, Johns Hopkins University Studies in Archaeology 38 (Baltimore: Johns Hopkins University Press, 1950), vi.

7. Paul A. Clement, "Review of *Excavations at Olynthus, Part VIII: The Hellenic House, a Study of the Houses Found at Olynthus with a Detailed Account of Those Excavated in 1931 and 1934* by David M. Robinson and J. Walter Graham," *L'Antiquité Classique* 8 (1939): 474.

8. "Miss Annie C. Hare Is Married," 16; Joseph W. Shaw, "James Walter Graham 1906–1991," *American Journal of Archaeology* 96, no. 2 (1992): 325.

9. Homer Thompson, "In Memoriam: J. Walter Graham 1906–1991," *Åkoue* (Fall 1991): 15.

10. Shaw, "James Walter Graham," 325.

11. David M. Robinson and J. Walter Graham, *Excavations at Olynthus VIII: The Hellenic House; a Study of the Houses Found at Olynthus with a Detailed Account of those Excavated in 1931 and 1934*, Johns Hopkins University Studies in Archaeology 25 (Baltimore: Johns Hopkins University Press, 1938), v.

12. Shaw, "James Walter Graham," 325.

13. Later to marry and become Lucy Shoe Meritt.

14. Lucy T. Shoe, "Review of *Excavations at Olynthus, Part VIII: The Hellenic House, a Study of the Houses Found at Olynthus with a Detailed Account of Those Excavated in 1931 and 1934* by David M. Robinson and J. Walter Graham," *American Journal of Archaeology* 43, no. 4 (1939): 707–8.

15. Nicholas Cahill, *Household and City Organization at Olynthus* (New Haven, CT: Yale University Press, 2002), ix and 61–64.

16. George E. Mylonas, "Biographical Sketch," in *Studies Presented to David Moore Robinson on His Seventieth Birthday*. Vol. 1, ed. George E. Mylonas (St. Louis, MO: Washington University, 1951), xvii; Shaw, "James Walter Graham," 325; Thompson "In Memoriam," 15.

17. Mylonas, "Biographical Sketch," ix.

18. David M. Robinson, *Excavations at Olynthus XIV: Terracottas, Lamps, and Coins Found in 1934 and 1938* (Baltimore: Johns Hopkins University Press, 1952), vii.

19. Letter from Robinson to Graham, October 30, 1947, Graham folder, Box 6, David M. Robinson Collection, Archives and Special Collections, University of Mississippi Libraries.

20. Linda M. Medwid, *The Makers of Classical Archaeology* (New York: Humanity Books, 2000), 258.

21. Robinson, *Olynthus XIV*, v.

22. Sterling Dow, "Review of *Excavations at Olynthus. Part XIV* by David M. Robinson," *American Historical Review* 58, no. 3 (1953): 58.

23. Richard E. Wycherley, "Review of *Excavations at Olynthus. Part X. Metal and Minor Miscellaneous Finds: An Original Contribution to Greek Life* by David M. Robinson" "*Excavations at Olynthus. Part XI. Necrolynthia: A Study in Greek Burial Customs and Anthropology* by David M. Robinson," *Journal of Hellenic Studies* 62 (1942): 104.

24. Richard E. Wycherley. "Review of *Excavations at Olynthus XII: Domestic and Pubic Architecture* by D. M. Robinson," *Journal of Hellenic Studies* 66 (1946): 135.

25. Robert Scranton. "Review of *Excavations at Olynthus, Part XIV: Terracottas, Lamps, and Coins Found in 1934 and 1938* by David M. Robinson," *Classical Philology* 49, no. 2 (1954): 144.

26. Cahill, *Household*, 61.

27. Louis E. Lord, *A History of the American School of Classical Studies at Athens 1882–1942* (Cambridge, MA: Harvard University Press, 1947), 261.

28. William A. McDonald, "Review of *Excavations at Olynthus Part XIV. Terracottas, Lamps and Coins Found in 1934 and 1938* by David M. Robinson," *Classical Journal* 50, no. 2 (1954), 94.

29. Stephen L. Dyson, *Ancient Marbles to American Shores: Classical Archaeology in the United States* (Philadelphia: University of Pennsylvania Press, 1998), 194.

30. Letter from Robinson to Graham, October 30, 1947, Graham folder, Box 6, David M. Robinson Collection, Archives and Special Collections, University of Mississippi Libraries.

31. George M. A. Hanfmann, *The David Moore Robinson Bequest of Classical Art and Antiquities* (Boston: Harvard University Press, 1961), 3.

32. Mylonas, "Biographical Sketch," xi–xxi.

33. Jennifer K. West, "Observations on Selected Papers of David Moore Robinson from the University of Mississippi Archives" (MA thesis, University of Mississippi, 1995), 125.

34. Clement, "Review of *Excavations at Olynthus, Part VIII*," 474–77; and J. Walter Graham, "Review of *Excavations at Olynthus XII: Domestic and Pubic Architecture* by D. M. Robinson," *American Historical Review* 53, no. 1 (1947): 145–46.

35. Robinson, "The Third Campaign at Olynthus," 210, no. 1.

36. Robinson, *Excavations at Olynthus XIII*, 36.

37. "big book."

38. Graham, "Review of *Excavations at Olynthus XII*," 145–46.

39. Letter from Robinson to Graham, October 30, 1947, Graham folder, Box 6, David M. Robinson Collection, Archives and Special Collections, University of Mississippi Libraries.

40. Clement, "Review of *Excavations at Olynthus, Part VIII*," 474.

41. Robinson is exaggerating here, although in truth he was very generous in underwriting the excavation; see Lord, *A History of the American School*, 261.

42. Letter from Robinson to Graham, January 10 or 17, 1953, Graham folder, Box 6, David M. Robinson Collection, Archives and Special Collections, University of Mississippi Libraries. Presumably Robinson is referring to a public lecture Graham had delivered in Cleveland.

43. West, "Observations on Selected Papers," 121.

44. "Dr. Robinson Dies; Archaeologist, 77," *New York Times*, January 3, 1958, 21.

45. Letter from Robinson to Graham, October 30, 1947, Graham folder, Box 6, David M. Robinson Collection, Archives and Special Collections, University of Mississippi Libraries.

46. West, "Observations on Selected Papers," 121, 126.

47. "Dr. Robinson Dies," 21.

48. West, "Observations on Selected Papers," 118–28 has a summary of Robinson's later career as well as an assessment of his complex personality.

49. "G. E. Mylonas, 89, Archeologist Who Led Greek Excavations, Dies," *New York Times*, May 2, 1988, D14.

50. This letter is now in the Mylonas folder, Box 12, David M. Robinson Collection, Archives and Special Collections, University of Mississippi Libraries.

51. Letter from Robinson to Graham, January 10 or 17, 1953, Graham folder, Box 6, David M. Robinson Collection, Archives and Special Collections, University of Mississippi Libraries.

52. Raymond Dessy, *Exile from Olynthus. Women in Archaeology.com. Mentoring and Networking in Greece, 1927–1928*, 2005, 16. http://scholar.lib.vt.edu/faculty_archives/dessy/T_HOME-PAGE.htm.

53. Robinson, *Excavations at Olynthus XIII*, vi.

54. Linda M. Medwid, *The Makers of Classical Archaeology*, 211–12; Spyros Iakovidis, "George Emmanuel Mylonas, 1898–1988," *American Journal of Archaeology* 93 (1989): 237; "G. E. Mylonas, 89," D14.

55. Archaeological Institute of America, "Seventy-Second General Meeting of the Archaeological Institute of America," *American Journal of Archaeology* 75, no. 2 (1971): 194.

56. George E. Mylonas, ed., *Studies Presented to David Moore Robinson on His Seventieth Birthday*. Vol. 1; and George E. Mylonas and Doris Raymond,

eds. *Studies Presented to David Moore Robinson on His Seventieth Birthday* Vol. 2 (St. Louis, MO: Washington University, 1953).

57. Robinson, "The Third Campaign at Olynthus," 210, no. 1.

58. See Arthur W. Parsons, "The Long Walls to the Gulf," in *Corinth, Results of Excavations Conducted by the American School of Classical Studies at Athens* III.2: *The Defenses of Acrocorinth and the Lower Town*, eds. Rhys Carpenter and Antoine Bon (Princeton, NJ: American School of Classical Studies at Athens 1936), 84–127.

59. Lucy Shoe Meritt, *History of the American School of Classical Studies in Athens 1939–1980* (Princeton, NJ: American School of Classical Studies in Athens, 1984), 33; Mylonas, "Biographical Sketch," xix.

60. Susan H. Allen, *Classical Spies: American Archaeologists with the OS in World War II Greece* (Ann Arbor: University of Michigan Press, 2011), 31.

61. Allen, *Classical Spies*, 47.

62. Allen, *Classical Spies*, 66–67.

63. Arthur W. Parsons, "Klepsydra and the Paved Court of the Pythion" PhD diss., Johns Hopkins University, 1942.

64. Arthur W. Parsons, "Klepsydra and the Paved Court of the Pythion," *Hesperia* 12, no. 3 (1943): 191–267.

65. Meritt, *History of the American School*, 33; Mylonas, "Biographical Sketch," xix.

66. "Dr. Arthur Parsons," *New York Times*, October 1, 1948, 26.

67. Wayne T. Pitard, "Alexander the Great: How Grad Student Alexander Schulz Became a Key Figure in the Museum's History," *Spurlock Museum Magazine* (Fall 2012): 6.

68. Alexander H. G. Schulz, "The Burials and Burial Customs of Prehistoric Greece" (MA thesis, Johns Hopkins University, 1935).

69. "Student Rebuilds Ancient Bathtub," *Baltimore Sun*, November 24, 1935.

70. Wayne T. Pitard. "Alexander the Great," 6.

71. Wayne T. Pitard, personal communication.

72. Kostis Kourelis, "Byzantium and the Avant-Garde: Excavations at Corinth 1920s–1930s," *Hesperia* 76 (2007): 423–24; and Kostis Kourelis, *Peschke: Colors of Greece* (Lancaster, PA: Franklin and Marshall College, 2012).

73. October 20, 1931, letter from Euripides Melanides to Mary Ellingson, the original is in the possession of Barbara Petersen, a copy is in the archives at the University of Evansville.

74. Robinson, "The Third Campaign at Olynthus," 210, n. 1; David M. Robinson and George E. Mylonas, "The Fourth Campaign at Olynthus," *American Journal of Archaeology* 43, no. 1 (1939): 48, n. 1.

75. "Italians Raid Salonika," *New York Times*, January 27, 1941, 2; "Allies Bomb Salonika Bases," *New York Times*, October 28, 1943, 3.

76. March 13, 1941, letter from Mary Ellingson to David Robinson, Box 5, David M. Robinson Collection, Archives and Special Collections, University of Mississippi Libraries; a copy is filed in the archive at the University of Evansville.

77. Robinson, *Excavations at Olynthus XIV*, vii.

CHAPTER 6

1. David M. Robinson, *Excavations at Olynthus VII: The Terra-Cottas of Olynthus Found in 1931* (Baltimore: Johns Hopkins University Press, 1933), viii.

2. David M. Robinson, *Excavations at Olynthus XIV: Terracottas, Lamps, and Coins Found in 1934 and 1938* (Baltimore: Johns Hopkins University Press, 1952), vii.

3. E. C. Hills, "The Degree of Doctor of Philosophy," *Bulletin of the American Association of University Professors* 12, no. 3 (1927), 172–73.

4. Ellingson to Robinson October 5, 1941; Robinson to Ellingson October 15, 1941; Ellingson to Robinson November 4, 1941; Robinson to Ellingson November 7, 1941, now in the Ellingson folder, Box 5, David M. Robinson Collection, Archives and Special Collections, University of Mississippi Libraries. Copies of all these letters are on file in the archives at the University of Evansville.

5. Saul Weinberg to Robinson, October 2, 1940; Robinson to Weinberg October 5, 1940, Weinberg folder, Box 18, David M. Robinson Collection, Archives and Special Collections, University of Mississippi Libraries; Robinson to Gladys Davidson Weinberg October 21, 1942; Robinson to Davidson Weinberg November 4, 1942, Davidson folder, Box 4, David M. Robinson Collection, Archives and Special Collections, University of Mississippi Libraries. Copies of all these letters are on file in the archives at the University of Evansville.

6. David M. Robinson, *Excavations at Olynthus X: Metal and Minor Miscellaneous Finds, an Original Contribution to Greek Life*, Johns Hopkins University Studies in Archaeology 31 (Baltimore: Johns Hopkins University Press, 1941), v.

7. David M. Robinson, *Excavations at Olynthus XIII: Vases Found in 1934 and 1938*, Johns Hopkins University Studies in Archaeology 38 (Baltimore: Johns Hopkins University Press, 1950), 36.

8. George E. Mylonas, *Excavations at Olynthus I. The Neolithic Settlement.* Johns Hopkins University Studies in Archaeology 6 (Baltimore: Johns Hopkins University Press, 1929), xi–xii.

9. George M. A. Hanfmann, *The David Moore Robinson Bequest of Classical Art and Antiquities* (Boston: Harvard University Press, 1961), 3.

10. Quoted in Jennifer K. West, "Observations on Selected Papers of David Moore Robinson from the University of Mississippi Archives" (MA thesis, University of Mississippi, 1995), 62.

11. Quoted in Jennifer K. West, "Observations on Selected Papers," 60–61.

12. See chapter 1.

13. See chapter 5.

14. David M. Robinson, *Excavations at Olynthus VII*, viii.

15. Gladys D. Weinberg, *Corinth, Results of Excavations Conducted by the American School of Classical Studies at Athens XII: The Minor Objects* (Princeton, NJ: American School of Classical Studies at Athens, 1952).

16. Sarah E. Freeman, "Temple E at Corinth," in *Corinth, Results of Excavations Conducted by the American School of Classical Studies at Athens I.2: Architecture*, eds. Richard Stillwell, Robert L. Scranton and Sarah E. Freeman (Princeton, NJ: American School of Classical Studies at Athens, 1941), 166–236.

17. Cynthia Irwin-Williams, "Women in the Field: The Role of Women in Archaeology before 1960," in *Women of Science: Righting the Record*, eds. G. Kass-Simon and Patricia Farnes (Bloomington: University of Indiana Press, 1990), 20 and 25.

18. Mary Ann Levine, "Creating Their Own Niches: Career Styles among Women in Americanist Archaeology between the Wars," in *Women in Archaeology*, ed. Cheryl Claassen (Philadelphia: University of Pennsylvania Press, 1994), 13; Irwin-Williams, "Women in the Field," 25.

19. Margaret W. Rossiter, *Women Scientists in America: Struggles and Strategies to 1940* (Baltimore: Johns Hopkins University Press, 1982), 204.

20. Rossiter, *Women Scientists in America*," 213.

21. Rossiter, *Women Scientists in America*," 213–14.

22. Ida Thallon Hill and Lida Shaw King, *Corinth, Results of Excavations Conducted by the American School of Classical Studies at Athens IV, Part I: Decorated Architectural Terracottas* (Princeton, NJ: American School of Classical Studies at Athens, 1929).

23. Natalia Vogeikoff-Brogan, "Ida Thallon Hill (1875–1954)," *Breaking Ground: Women in Old World Archaeology* (n.d.), http://www.brown.edu/Research/Breaking_Ground/bios/Hill_Ida%20Thallon.pdf.

24. Richard Stillwell, Robert L. Scranton, and Sarah E. Freeman, eds., *Corinth, Results of Excavations Conducted by the American School of Classical Studies at Athens I.2: Architecture* (Princeton, NJ: American School of Classical Studies at Athens, 1941); Arthur W. Parsons, "The Long Walls to the Gulf," in *Corinth, Results of Excavations Conducted by the American School of Classical Studies at Athens III.2: The Defenses of Acrocorinth and the Lower Town*, eds. Rhys Carpenter and Antoine Bon (Princeton, NJ: American School of Classical Studies at Athens, 1936), 84–127.

25. Rossiter, *Women Scientists in America*," 208–9.

26. Levine, "Creating Their Own Niches," 28–29.

27. Vogeikoff-Brogan, "Ida Thallon Hill (1875–1954)."

28. Nancy M. White, "Women in Southeastern U.S. Archaeology," in *Grit-Tempered: Early Women Archaeologists in the Southeastern United States*, eds. Nancy M. White, Lynne P. Sullivan, and Rochelle A. Marrinan (Gainesville: University Press of Florida, 1999), 21.

29. Mary Ellingson to David M. Robinson, October 6, 1952, Box 5, David M. Robinson Collection, Archives and Special Collections, University of Mississippi Libraries. A copy of this letter is now on file with Ellingson's papers in the University of Evansville Library Archives.

30. David M. Robinson to Mary Ellingson October 14, 1952, Box 5, David M. Robinson Collection, Archives and Special Collections, University of Mississippi Libraries. A copy of this letter is now on file with Ellingson's papers in the University of Evansville Library Archives.

31. Mary Ellingson to David M. Robinson, October 6, 1952, Box 5, David M. Robinson Collection, Archives and Special Collections, University of Mississippi Libraries. A copy of this letter is now on file with Ellingson's papers in the University of Evansville Library Archives.

32. George Klinger, chair of the Department of English during Ellingson's tenure, personal communication; Mike Carson, a student and later colleague of Ellingson's at the University of Evansville Department of English, personal communication.

33. Barbara A. Petersen, interview with author on April 5, 2004.

34. Marcus Diamond to Barbara A. Petersen, February 15, 1994. This letter is now on file with Ellingson's papers in the University of Evansville Library Archives.

35. Marcus Diamond, interview with the author on March 6, 2004.

36. Barbara A. Petersen, interview with author on April 5, 2004.

37. Shelby Brown, "Feminist Research in Archaeology: What Does It Mean? Why Is It Taking so Long?" in *Feminist Theory and the Classics*, eds. Nancy Sorkin Rabinowitz and Amy Richlin (New York: Routledge 1993), 241–43.

38. White, "Women in Southeastern U.S. Archaeology," 21.

39. Jonathan E. Reyman, "Women in American Archaeology: Some Historical Notes and Comments," in *Rediscovering Our Past: Essays on the History of American Archaeology*, ed. Jonathan E. Reyman (Aldershot: Avebury, 1992), 71–72.

40. Boggs to Ellingson, June 22, 1949, University of Evansville Library Archives.

41. See Valentin Müller, *Frühe plastik in Griechenland und Vorderasien; ihre typenbildung von der neolithischen bis in die griechisch-archaische zeit (rund 3000 bis 600 v. Chr.)* (Augsburg: B. Filser, 1929).

42. Valentin Müller, "Review of *Excavations at Olynthus* by David M. Robinson," *Classical Philology* 31, no. 1 (1936): 92.

43. George Wicker Elderkin, *Antioch-on-the-Orontes* I (Princeton, NJ: Princeton University Press, 1934).

44. George Wicker Elderkin, "Review of *Excavations at Olynthus, Part VII. The Terra-Cottas Found in 1931* by David M. Robinson," *American Journal of Archaeology* 38, no. 3 (1934): 497.

45. Müller, "Review of *Excavations at Olynthus*," 92.

46. Linda M. Medwid, *The Makers of Classical Archaeology* (New York: Humanity Books, 2000), 152–53.

47. Reynold A. Higgins, "Review of *Excavations at Olynthus. Part XIV, Terracottas, Lamps and Coins Found in 1934 and 1938* by D. M. Robinson," *Journal of Hellenic Studies* 75 (1955): 180.

48. Reynold A. Higgins, "Review of *Excavations at Olynthus. Part XIV, Terracottas, Lamps and Coins Found in 1934 and 1938* by D. M. Robinson," *Antiquaries Journal* 35 (1955): 97.

49. Higgins, "Review of *Excavations at Olynthus. Part XIV*," 180.

50. Medwid, *The Makers of Classical Archaeology*, 96–8.

51. Sterling Dow, "Review of *Excavations at Olynthus. Part XIV*, by David M. Robinson," *American Historical Review* 58, no. 3 (1953): 587.

52. Robert Scranton, "Review of *Excavations at Olynthus, Part XIV: Terracottas, Lamps, and Coins Found in 1934 and 1938* by David M. Robinson," *Classical Philology* 49, no. 2 (1954): 143.

53. For example, William A. McDonald. "Review of *Excavations at Olynthus Part XIV. Terracottas, Lamps and Coins Found in 1934 and 1938* by David M. Robinson," *Classical Journal* 50, no. 2 (1954): 94–95; R. M. Cook, "Review of *Excavations at Olynthus. Part XIV, Terracottas, Lamps and Coins Found in 1934 and 1938* by D. M. Robinson," *Classical Review* 5, no. 3/4 (1955): 326–27; R. C. Wood, "Review of *Excavations at Olynthus. Part XIV, Terracottas, Lamps and Coins Found in 1934 and 1938* by D. M. Robinson," *American Journal of Archaeology* 57, no. 3 (1953): 227–28.

54. David M. Robinson to Mary Ellingson, undated card celebrating Christmas 1952, now on file with Ellingson's papers in the University of Evansville Library Archives. To see a photo of the painting, see http://thaumazein-albert.blogspot.com/2011/12/works-from-david-m-robinson-collection.html.

55. I am indebted to Jim Ware of the University of Evansville for his analysis of the ancient Greek in this painting.

56. David M. Robinson, *Excavations at Olynthus VII: The Terra-Cottas of Olynthus Found in 1931* (Baltimore: Johns Hopkins University Press, 1933), #185, 53.

57. Barbara Petersen, personal communication.

CHAPTER 7

1. J. Walter Graham, "Lamps from Olynthus, 1931," in *Excavations at Olynthus V: Mosaics, Vases, and Lamps of Olynthus Found in 1928 and 1931*, ed. David M. Robinson (Baltimore: Johns Hopkins University Press, 1933), 265–84.

2. For a summary of Graham's career and of the relationship between Robinson and Graham, see chapter 5.

3. Joseph W. Shaw, "James Walter Graham 1906–1991," *American Journal of Archaeology* 96, no. 2 (1992): 325.

4. David M. Robinson, "Mosaics from Olynthus," *American Journal of Archaeology* 36, no. 1 (1932): 16 no. 2.

5. David M. Robinson, *Excavations at Olynthus V: Mosaics, Vases, and Lamps of Olynthus Found in 1928 and 1931* (Baltimore: Johns Hopkins University Press, 1933), xi.

6. Robinson, *Excavations at Olynthus V*, xi.

7. See chapter 6.

8. See chapter 4 for quotes from their letters on the matter of her dissertation.

9. Paul A. Clement Jr., *Thessalian Cults* (PhD diss., Johns Hopkins University, 1930).

10. David M. Robinson, "The Third Campaign at Olynthus," *American Journal of Archaeology* 39, no. 2 (1935): 210, no. 1.

11. David M. Robinson and Paul A. Clement, *Excavations at Olynthus IX: The Chalcidic Mint and the Excavation Coins Found in 1928–1934*. Johns Hopkins University Studies in Archaeology 26 (Baltimore: Johns Hopkins University Press, 1938).

12. See chapter 5.

13. William A. McDonald and George R. Rapp Jr., eds., *The Minnesota Messenia Expedition: Reconstructing a Bronze Age Regional Environment* (Minneapolis: University of Minnesota Press, 1972).

14. Stephen L. Dyson, *Ancient Marbles to American Shores: Classical Archaeology in the United States* (Philadelphia: University of Pennsylvania Press, 1998), 248.

15. David M. Robinson and George E. Mylonas, "The Fourth Campaign at Olynthus," *American Journal of Archaeology* 43, no. 1 (1939): 48 no. 1.

16. William A. McDonald, *The Political Meeting Places of the Greeks* (PhD diss., Johns Hopkins University, 1940).

17. William A. McDonald, *The Political Meeting Places of the Greeks*. Johns Hopkins Studies in Archaeology 34 (Baltimore: Johns Hopkins University Press, 1943).

18. McDonald, *The Political Meeting Places of the Greeks*, viii.

19. David M. Robinson, "Prähistorische und Griechische Häuser," in *Realencyclopädia der Classischen Altertumswissenschaft*, Supplementband 7, edited by August Pauly and Georg Wissowa, 224–78 (Stuttgart: E. B. Metzler, 1940).
20. McDonald, *The Political Meeting Places of the Greeks*, vi.
21. George M. A. Hanfmann, *Metal Objects from Olynthus* (PhD diss., Johns Hopkins University, 1935), 218; David G. Mitten, "George Maxim Anossov Hanfmann, 1911–1986," *American Journal of Archaeology* 91, no. 2 (1987): 259; Stephen L. Dyson, *Ancient Marbles*, 225–26 and 234.
22. Hanfmann, *Metal Objects from Olynthus*, 219; Mitten, "George Maxim Anossov Hanfmann, 1911–1986," 260; George Mylonas, ed., *Studies Presented to David Moore Robinson on His Seventieth Birthday.* Vol. 1 (St. Louis, MO: Washington University, 1951), xviii.
23. As a fairly typical example, the entries below are for the same bronze piece and share about 85 percent of the text. The first is a direct quote from Hanfmann, *Metal Objects from Olynthus*, 100–101:

Incised Bronze Work Piece:
A. 375, pl. 109.
H. 0.055 m., W. 0.035 m.
   This is an extremely intricate and brilliant piece of incising. It has to be examined from all sides in order to bring out everything that the artist has represented. There were certainly four palmettes, one at each side of the object. Fragments of two of them are preserved. Two vertically standing spirals support one palmette on each side. If viewed on the longer axis we see two calices reversed, resting on spirals, with palmettes which point in opposite directions. Later sixth century B.C.
   Such intricate designs are generally archaic although they could survive for a considerable period.1 Similar are especially compositions prevalent in Ionic schools, and the single parts of this ornament also argue for an Ionic origin,2 although it must be admitted that Attic artists of the sixth century were equally fond of such designs.3 It may be of interest to observe similar designs also on Chalcidic vases, since there are few possible other connections between Chalcis and Olynthus in art. 4
   1 Cf. Jacobsthal, Ornamente griechischer Vasen, 1929, pls. 10, c; 24, c; 137, a. Survival: pl. 132.
   2 Cf. Jacobsthal, op. cit., pls. 22, b; 24; 35; 39.; Ducati Pontische Vasen, pl. 3.
   3 Jacobsthal, op. cit., pls. 28, 30, 39.
   4 Pfuhl, fig. 161; Rumpf, op. cit. pl. XII, XLV XLVIII, LVII f, LXVI f

Compare the text of Hanfmann's entry to the following quote from David M. Robinson, *Excavations at Olynthus* X: *Metal and Minor Miscellaneous Finds*,

an Original Contribution to Greek Life. Johns Hopkins University Studies in
Archaeology 31 (Baltimore: Johns Hopkins University Press, 1941), 41:

Pl. V. 22. Inv. 28.375. Bronze piece with incised decoration. H. 0.055 m., W.
0.035 m. Broken.

This is an extremely intricate and brilliant piece of incising. It has to be
examined from all sides in order to bring out everything that the artist has represented. There were certainly four palmettes, one at each side of the object.
Fragments of two of them are preserved. Two vertically standing spirals support one palmette on each side. If viewed on the longer axis we see two calices,
reversed, resting on spirals with palmettes which point in opposite directions.
From the South Hill, Apotheke G 7.192

Such intricate designs are generally archaic, although they could survive
for a considerable period. 193 Especially similar are compositions prevalent
in Ionic schools, and the single parts of this ornament also argue for an Ionic
origin,194 although it must be admitted that Attic artists of the sixth century
were equally fond of such designs.195 It may be of interest to observe similar
designs which also occur on Chalcidic vases, since there are only a few other
possible connections between Chalcis and Olynthus in art. 196 This piece is
to be dated in the late sixth century B.C.

192 Cf. *Olynthus*, II, p. 27.

193 Cf. Jacobsthal, *Ornamente griechischer Vasen*, 1927, Pls. 10 c; 24 c;
137 a. Survival: Pl. 132.

194 Cf. Jacobsthal, *op. cit.*, Pls. 22 b; 24; 35; 39. Also Ducati *Pontische
Vasen*, Pl. 3.

195 Cf. Jacobsthal, *op. cit.*, Pls. 28, 29, 30.

196 Pfuhl, *Malerie und Zeichnung der Griechen*, Fig. 161; Rumpf, *Chalki-
dische Vasen* Pls. XII, XLV, XLVIII, LVII f., LXVI ff.

24. Compare the following two quotes. The first quote is from George M. A.
Hanfmann, *Metal Objects from Olynthus*, 140:

The Olynthian earrings show a variety which is especially surprising in view of
the comparative monotony existing among the other ornaments. Eighteen va-
rieties are represented, which may however be divided into seven main groups
according to their shape. The material is usually bronze but silver earrings
occurred in three graves.

The second quote is from Robinson, *Excavations at Olynthus X*, 79:

The Olynthian earrings show a variety which is especially surprising in view of
the comparative monotony existing among the other ornaments. Eighteen vari-
eties are represented, which may, however, be divided into seven main groups

according to their shape. The material is usually bronze but silver earrings occurred in three graves.

25. Robinson, *Excavations at Olynthus X*, x–xi.

26. Mary Ross Ellingson, Gladys Davidson Weinberg, Sarah Freeman, George Mylonas, Alexander Schulz, Arthur Parsons, J. Walter Graham, Paul Clement, William McDonald, and George Hanfmann.

27. John A. Alexander, "Potidaea" (PhD diss., Johns Hopkins University, 1939), later published as *Potidaea* (Athens: University of Georgia Press, 1963). Herbert N. Couch, "Sources for the Study of Sardis" (MA thesis, Johns Hopkins University, 1926) and "Treasuries of the Greeks and Romans" (PhD diss., Johns Hopkins University, 1927) later published as *Treasuries of the Greeks and Romans* (Menasha, Wisc.: George Banta Co., 1929). John R. Craft, "The City Drainage at Olynthus" (MA thesis, Johns Hopkins University, 1939) and "The Civic Water Supply of Ancient Greece" (PhD diss., Johns Hopkins University, 1940). Mabel Gude, "A History of Olynthus" (PhD diss., Johns Hopkins University, 1930), later published as *A History of Olynthus, with a Prosopographia and Testimonia*. Johns Hopkins University Studies in Archaeology 17 (Baltimore: Johns Hopkins University Press, 1933). Mary W. McGehee, "Replicas of Scenes on Attic Red-figured Vases" (MA thesis, Johns Hopkins University, 1926) and "Replica Scenes of Attic Red-figured Vases" (PhD diss., Johns Hopkins University, 1932). Eunice B. Stebbins, "The Letters of Augustus Preserved in Greek Inscriptions and in the Greek Writers" (MA thesis, Johns Hopkins University, 1926); "The Dolphin in the Literature and Art of Greece and Rome, Including Pre-Hellenic Civilizations" (PhD diss., Johns Hopkins University, 1927), published as *The Dolphin in the Literature and Art of Greece and Rome, Including Pre-Hellenic Civilizations* (Menasha, WI: George Banta, 1929). Lillian M. Wilson, "A Study of the Roman Toga" (PhD diss., Johns Hopkins University, 1924); *The Roman Toga*. Johns Hopkins University Studies in Archaeology 1 (Baltimore: Johns Hopkins University Press, 1924); "The Loom Weights," in *Excavations at Olynthus II Architecture and Sculpture: House and Other Buildings* edited by D. M. Robinson, 118–28. Johns Hopkins University Studies in Archaeology 9 (Baltimore: Johns Hopkins University Press, 1930).

28. Saul S. Weinberg, *The Prehistoric House of the Mainland of Greece* (PhD diss., Johns Hopkins University, 1936) and David M. Robinson, "Prähistorische und Griechische Häuser" published in 1938.

29. The thesis is Frank P. Albright, *Red Figured Vases of Olynthus Found in 1934* (MA thesis, Johns Hopkins University, 1936); Robinson published on this subject in *Excavations at Olynthus XIII: Vases Found in 1934 and 1938*. Johns Hopkins University Studies in Archaeology 38 (Baltimore: Johns Hopkins University Press, 1950). Robinson acknowledges Albright in the preface but fails to mention his thesis. Albright's dissertation was "Funeral Customs of the Greeks" (PhD diss., Johns Hopkins University, 1940), parts of which seem to have wound up in Robinson's

Excavations at Olynthus XI: Necrolynthia, a Study of Greek Burial Customs and Anthropology. Johns Hopkins University Studies in Archaeology 32 (Baltimore: Johns Hopkins University Press, 1942) on which Albright is listed as a contributor.

30. Robinson, "The Third Campaign at Olynthus," 210 no. 1.

31. George Mylonas, "Biographical Sketch," in *Studies Presented to David Moore Robinson on His Seventieth Birthday.* Vol. 1, ed. Geroge Mylonas (St. Louis, MO: Washington University, 1951), xviii.

32. For example, compare the description each wrote of the same figurine. The following quote is from Eleanor B. Lay, "Terra-cottas Found at Olynthus in 1934" (PhD diss., Johns Hopkins University, 1936), 34–35:

No. 28. Inv. 121. Female mask. House A V 9, b̲, at a depth of 1.25 m. Ht. 0.187. W. 0.139. Th. 0.055. Complete except for large fragment at right base of mask and small fragment at right base of neck of figure. Coarse bluish grey clay shading to yellowish buff with numerous fine particles of mica. White slip. Blue paint on stephane and veil. Red paint on hair and eyes. Blue paint on under garment. Buff incrustation. Two holes in top for suspension.

The hair, parted in the center, is drawn to either side in fine small but distinct waves and falls to the shoulders in heavy rope-like curls. On the head is worn a stephane adorned with a palmette design and a veil descends to the shoulders and along the outer edge, widening out in a graceful curve at the shoulders and again becoming narrower as it follows the line of the upper arm to the base of the mask. The features are typically archaic, the eyes wide set, the nose long, the mouth small and placed close beneath the nose, the lips thick and protruding, the chin firm. The garment, probably a chiton, is especially indicated by the V at the neck. The upper arms are held close to the body. At the elbow the arms are bent sharply and the hand are held over the breast, the left somewhat higher than the right. Type of the fifth century.1

1 Cf. OL. IV, no. 278; OL. VII, nos. 35, 383. For palmette design compare OL. IV, nos. 297–8, 410; Pottier, Diphilos et Les Modeleurs de T. C. Grecques, no. 203, pl. X.

Compare with this quote from David M. Robinson, *Excavations at Olynthus XIV: Terracottas, Lamps, and Coins Found in 1934 and 1938* (Baltimore: Johns Hopkins University Press, 1952), 89:

30. Female mask. Inv. 34.121. From House A v 9, room *b* (*Olynthus*, VIII, pp. 96–97). H. 0.187 m. W. 0.139 m. Th. 0.055 m. Coarse bluish gray clay, shading to yellowish buff, with numerous fine particles of mica. White slip; blue paint on stephane, veil and under-garment; red paint on hair and eyes. Buff incrustation. Complete except for a large fragment at the right of the base

of the mask and a small fragment at the right base of the neck of the figure. Two holes in top for suspension.

The hair, parted in the middle, is drawn to either side in fine, distinct, but small waves and falls to the shoulders in heavy rope-like curls. On the head the stephane is adorned with a palmette and rosette design as in the Cybele mould (cf. *Olynthus*, IV, 410). A veil descends to the shoulders and along the outer edge, widening in a graceful curve at the shoulders and again becoming narrower as it follows the line of the upper arm to the base of the mask. The features are typically archaic; the eyes wide set, the nose long, the mouth small and placed close beneath the nose, the lips thick and protruding, the chin firm. The garment, probably a chiton, is indicated by the V at the neck. The upper arms are held close to the body; at the elbow the arms are bent sharply and and [sic] the hand are held over the breasts, which are far apart as in early Greek art (e.g. the "Ludovisi Throne"), the left somewhat higher than the right. From the same mould as nos. 28 and 46. Cf. Olynthus, IV, 278, 284, and VII, 383; Pottier, Diphilos et les Modeleurs de terres cuites grecques, pl. X, 197, 203. Now in the D. M. Robinson Collection at the University of Mississippi.

Fifth Century B.C.

33. From David M. Robinson, *Excavations at Olynthus XIV*, vii: "I thank especially my former students and members of my staff, Mary Ross (now Mrs. R. C. Ellingson of Evansville, Ind.), Eleanor Lay (now Mrs. Arthur Ross of Syracuse, New York), and I owe much to my deceased daughter (Mrs. Wilson)."

34. R. C. Wood, "Review of *Excavations at Olynthus. Part XIV, Terracottas, Lamps and Coins Found in 1934 and 1938* by D. M. Robinson," *American Journal of Archaeology* 57, no. 3 (1953): 227.

35. Christina B. Meredith, "The Finger Rings Found at Olynthus in 1931 and 1934" (MA thesis, Johns Hopkins University, 1937), 50.

36. Meredith, "The Finger Rings Found at Olynthus," 3–4.

37. The following quote from Meredith, "The Finger Rings Found at Olynthus," 29:

No. 12. Inv. 686. Location unknown. Diary reference unknown. For photograph see Plate 64.1931. Bronze ring with pointed oval bezel. Complete. L. of bezel 0.01 m. W. of bezel 0.008 m. D. of band 0.02 m.

Design at right angles to the band. Bezel very worn. Cock to the left. The feathers are done in long fine lines. The legs do not show. Compare the treatment of the dog on no. 29. The cock on no. 32 is quite different. Our cock, unlike the usual representations, has feathers all over his body and not merely on the wings and tail. This cock belongs to the less elongated Corinthian breed.1) For a similar treatment of birds see the Mycenaean sardonyx from Vaphio2) and the silver coin of the early fifth century from Himera.3)

First half of fourth century B.C.

1) Cf. Morin-Jean, pp. 112–114, Figs. 124–127 for various breeds of cocks.

2) Furtwängler I–II, Plate III, No. 54; Εφ. Αρχ. 1889, Taf. 10, No. 19.

3) MacDonald, Greek Coins in the Hunterian Collection I, Plate XIII, No. 17.

The following quote is from David M. Robinson, *Excavations at Olynthus X*, 151:

Pl. XXVII. 477. Inv. 31.686. Bronze finger-ring. Same type as preceding. Pointed oval bezel. L. of bezel 0.01 m., W. of bezel 0.008 m., Dm. of band 0.02 m. The design would have been right side up when worn. It represents a cock to the left. The feathers are done in long fine lines. The legs do not show. Compare the treatment of the dog on no. 464. The cock on no. 467 is quite different. This cock, unlike the usual representations, has feathers all over his body and not merely on the wings and tail. He belongs to the less elongated Corinthian breed.305

Exact provenience unknown. First half of fourth century B.C.

305 Cf. Morin-Jean, *Le Dessin des Animaux en Grèce d'après les Vases Peints*, pp. 112–114, Figs. 124–127 for various breeds of cocks.

38. See chapter 4.

39. Susan H. Allen, "The Archaeology of the AIA: An Introduction," in *Excavating Our Past: Perspectives on the History of the Archaeological Institute of America*, Colloquia and Conference Papers 5, ed. Susan H. Allen (Boston: Archaeological Institute of America, 2002), 18.

40. Dena F. Dincauze, "Exploring Career Styles in Archaeology," in *Rediscovering Our Past: Essays on the History of American Archaeology*, ed. Jonathan E. Reyman (Aldershot: Avebury, 1992): 136.

41. Margaret C. Root, "Introduction: Women of the Field, Defining the Gendered Experience," in *Breaking Ground: Pioneering Women Archaeologists*, eds. Getzel M. Cohen and Martha S. Joukowsky (Ann Arbor: University of Michigan Press, 2004), 13.

42. "It is generally considered bad etiquette for a student to review or criticize the work of his own chief." Letter from Robinson to Graham, October 30, 1947, Graham folder, Box 6, David M. Robinson Collection, Archives and Special Collections, University of Mississippi Libraries. A copy is on file at the University of Evansville archives.

43. Dyson, *Ancient Marbles to American Shores*, 86.

EPILOGUE

1. On the need to write about women of the past generation who can serve as role models for those of the present, see Lydia C. Carr, *Tessa Verney Wheeler: Women and Archaeology before World War II* (Oxford: Oxford University Press), 7.

REFERENCES

Agard, Walter R. "Review of *Excavations at Olynthus, Part VII. The Terra-Cottas Found in 1931* by David M. Robinson." *Classical Journal* 30, no 3 (1934): 173–74.

Albright, Frank P. "Red Figured Vases of Olynthus Found in 1934." MA thesis, Johns Hopkins University, 1936.

———. "Funeral Customs of the Greeks." PhD diss., Johns Hopkins University, 1940.

Alexander, John A. "Potidaea." PhD diss., Johns Hopkins University, 1939.

———. *Potidaea*. Athens: University of Georgia Press, 1963.

Allen, Susan H. "The Archaeology of the AIA: An Introduction." In *Excavating Our Past: Perspectives on the History of the Archaeological Institute of America*, edited by Susan H. Allen, Colloquia and Conference Papers 5, 1–28. Boston: Archaeological Institute of America, 2002.

———. *Classical Spies: American Archaeologists with the OS in World War II Greece*. Ann Arbor: University of Michigan Press, 2011.

"Allies Bomb Salonika Bases." *New York Times*, October 28, 1943, 3.

Allsebrook, Mary. *Born to Rebel: The Life of Harriet Boyd Hawes*. Oxford: Oxbow Books, 1992.

American Association of University Professors. "Academic Freedom and Tenure." *Bulletin of the American Association of University of Professors* 26, no. 1 (1940): 49–54.

Archaeological Institute of America. "Seventy-Second General Meeting of the Archaeological Institute of America." *American Journal of Archaeology* 75, no. 2 (1971): 194–217.

———. "Archaeological Institute of America Award for Distinguished Service Gladys Davidson Weinberg." *American Journal of Archaeology* 90, no. 2 (1986): 173.

———. "Saul S. Weinberg." *American Journal of Archaeology* 90, no. 2 (1986): 174.

Bathurst, William H. *Roman Antiquities at Lydney Park, Gloucestershire*. London: Longmans, Green, 1879. https://archive.org/detailsromanantiquitie 00bathgoog.

Blegen, Carl W. "Review of *Excavations at Olynthus, Part II, Architecture and Sculpture: Houses and Other Buildings* by David M. Robinson." *American Journal of Archaeology* 36, no. 3 (1932): 368–69.

Bolger, Diane L. "Ladies of the Expedition: Harriet Boyd Hawes and Edith Hall at Work in Mediterranean Archaeology." In *Women in Archaeology*, edited by Cheryl. Claassen, 41–50. Philadelphia: University of Pennsylvania Press, 1994.

Brown, David. *Aircraft Carriers*. New York: Arco Publishing, 1977.

Brown, Shelby. "Feminist Research in Archaeology: What Does It Mean? Why Is It Taking So Long?" In *Feminist Theory and the Classics*, edited by Nancy Sorkin Rabinowitz and Amy Richlin, 238–70. New York: Routledge, 1993.

Cahill, Nicholas. *Household and City Organization at Olynthus*. New Haven, CT: Yale University Press, 2002.

Carr, Lydia C. *Tessa Verney Wheeler: Women and Archaeology before World War II*. Oxford: Oxford University Press, 2012.

Chamberlain, Mariam K. *Women in Academe: Progress and Prospects*. New York: Russell Sage Foundation, 1988.

Chamonard, Joseph. *Exploration archéologique de Délos. Fascicule viii. Le Quartier du Théâtre*. Paris: E. de Boccard, 1924.

———. *Exploration archéologique de Délos. Fascicule xiv. Les mosaïques de la Maison des Masques*. Paris: E. de Boccard, 1933.

Clement, Jr., Paul Augustus. *Thessalian Cults*. PhD diss., Johns Hopkins University, 1930.

———. "Review of *Excavations at Olynthus, Part VIII: The Hellenic House, a Study of the Houses Found at Olynthus with a Detailed Account of Those Excavated in 1931 and 1934* by David M. Robinson and J. Walter Graham." *L'Antiquité Classique* 8 (1939): 474–77.

Clogg, Richard. *A Short History of Modern Greece*. New York: Cambridge University Press, 1979.

Cohen, Getzel M., and Martha S. Joukowsky, eds. *Breaking Ground: Pioneering Women Archaeologists*. Ann Arbor: University of Michigan Press, 2004.

Cook, R. M. "Review of *Excavations at Olynthus. Part XIV, Terracottas, Lamps and Coins Found in 1934 and 1938* by D. M. Robinson." *Classical Review* 5, no. 3/4 (1955): 326–27.

Cookingham, Mary E. "Combining Marriage, Motherhood, and Jobs before World War II: Women College Graduates, Classes of 1905–1935." *Journal of Family History* 9, no. 2 (1984): 178–95.

Couch, Hebert N. "Sources for the Study of Sardis." MA thesis, Johns Hopkins University, 1926.

———. "Treasuries of the Greeks and Romans." PhD diss., Johns Hopkins University, 1927.

———. *Treasuries of the Greeks and Romans*. Menasha, WI: George Banta, 1929.

Craft, John R. "The City Drainage at Olynthus." MA thesis, Johns Hopkins University, 1939.

———. "The Civic Water Supply of Ancient Greece." PhD diss., Johns Hopkins University, 1940.

Cullen, Tracey. "Contributions to Feminism in Archaeology." Review of *Women in Prehistory* by Margaret Ehrenberg; *Engendering Archaeology: Women and Prehistory* by Joan M. Gero and Margaret Conkey; *The Archaeology of Gender: Proceedings of the 22nd Annual Chacmool Conference* by Dale Waide and Noreen D. Willows; *Exploring Gender through Archaeology: Selected Papers from the 1991 Boone Conference* by Cheryl Claassen; *Women in Archaeology* by Cheryl Claassen; *Equity Issues for Women in Archaeology* by Margaret C. Nelson, Sara M. Nelson, and Alison Wylie; *Women in Ancient Societies: "An Illusion of the Night"* by Léonie J. Archer, Susan Fischler, and Maria Wyke. *American Journal of Archaeology* 100, no. 2 (1996): 409–14.

Davidson, Gladys R. "Miscellaneous Finds from Corinth, 1896–1933." PhD diss., Johns Hopkins University, 1935.

de Miroschedji, Pierre. "Obituary for Gladys Davidson Weinberg." *Israel Exploration Journal* 52, no. 2 (2002): 97–98.

Des Jardins, Julie. *The Madame Curie Complex: The Hidden History of Women in Science.* New York: Feminist Press of the City University of New York, 2010.

Dessy, Raymond. *Exile from Olynthus. Women in Archaeology.com. Mentoring and Networking in Greece, 1927–1928,* 2005. Accessed August 13, 2010. http://scholar.lib.vt.edu/faculty_archives/dessy/T_HOME-PAGE.htm.

Dincauze, Dena F. "Exploring Career Styles in Archaeology." In *Rediscovering Our Past: Essays on the History of American Archaeology,* edited by Jonathan E. Reyman, 131–36. Aldershot: Avebury, 1992.

"Dr. Arthur Parsons." *New York Times,* October 1, 1948, 26.

"Dr. Robinson Dies; Archaeologist, 77." *New York Times,* January 3, 1958, 21.

Dohan, Edith H. "Review of *Excavations at Olynthus, Part IV. The Terra-cottas of Olynthus, Found in 1928* by David M. Robinson." *American Journal of Archaeology* 36, no. 2 (1932): 207–8.

Dow, Sterling. "Review of *Excavations at Olynthus. Part XIV* by David M. Robinson." *The American Historical Review* 58, no. 3 (1953): 586–87.

Dyson, Stephen L. *Ancient Marbles to American Shores: Classical Archaeology in the United States.* Philadelphia: University of Pennsylvania Press, 1998.

"Edmonton Girl Finds Interest in Archaeology." *The Albertan,* September 18, 1931.

Elderkin, George Wicker. *Antioch-on-the-Orontes I.* Princeton, NJ: Princeton University Press, 1934.

———. "Review of *Excavations at Olynthus, Part VII. The Terra-Cottas Found in 1931* by David M. Robinson." *American Journal of Archaeology* 38, no. 3 (1934): 497.

"Excavations in Old Greece Are Recounted." *Evansville Courier and Press*, March 3, 1940.

Fishman, Aleisa. "Gladys Davidson Weinberg 1909–2002." In *Jewish Women in America: An Historical Encyclopedia*, edited by E. Paula Hyman and Debora D. Moore, 1462. New York: Routledge, 1997.

Fotou, Vasso, and Ann Brown. "Harriet Boyd Hawes, 1871–1945." In *Breaking Ground: Pioneering Women Archaeologists*, edited by Getzel M. Cohen and Martha S. Joukowsky, 198–273. Ann Arbor: University of Michigan Press, 2004.

"Four College Girls Join Olynthus Quest." *New York Times*, February 15, 1931, 33.

Fox, Aileen. *Aileen: A Pioneering Archaeologist*. Leominster, Herefordshire, UK: Gracewing, 2000.

Freeman, Sarah E. "The Excavation of a Roman Temple at Corinth." PhD diss., Johns Hopkins University, 1934.

———. "Temple E at Corinth." In *Corinth, Results of Excavations Conducted by the American School of Classical Studies at Athens* I.2: *Architecture*, edited by Richard Stillwell, Robert L. Scranton, and Sarah E. Freeman, 166–236. Princeton, NJ: American School of Classical Studies at Athens, 1941.

Freidenreich, Harriet Pass. "Joining the Faculty Club: Jewish Women Academics in the United States." *Nashim: A Journal of Jewish Women's Studies and Gender Issues* 13 (2007): 68–101.

"G. E. Mylonas, 89, Archeologist Who Led Greek Excavations, Dies." *New York Times*, May 2, 1988, D14.

Goldman, Hetty. "Excavations of the Fogg Museum at Colophon." Paper presented at the fourteenth annual meeting of the Archaeological Institute of America, Washington, DC, December 29, 1922. *American Journal of Archaeology* 27 (1923): 67–68.

Graham, J. Walter. "Domestic Architecture in Classical Greece." PhD diss., Johns Hopkins University, 1933.

———. "Lamps from Olynthus, 1931." In *Excavations at Olynthus V: Mosaics, Vases, and Lamps of Olynthus Found in 1928 and 1931*, edited by David M. Robinson, 265–84. Baltimore: Johns Hopkins University Press, 1933.

———. "Review of *Excavations at Olynthus XII: Domestic and Public Architecture* by D. M. Robinson." *American Historical Review* 53, no. 1 (1947): 145–46.

Gude, Mabel. "A History of Olynthus." PhD diss., Johns Hopkins University, 1930.

———. *A History of Olynthus, with a Prosopographia and Testimonia*. Johns Hopkins University Studies in Archaeology 17. Baltimore: Johns Hopkins University Press, 1933.

Hanfmann, George M. A. *Metal Objects from Olynthus*. PhD diss., Johns Hopkins University, 1935.

———. *The David Moore Robinson Bequest of Classical Art and Antiquities*. Boston: Harvard University Press, 1961.

Herbert, Sharon C. "Saul S. Weinberg, 1911–1992." *American Journal of Archaeology* 97, no. 3 (1993): 567–59.

Higgins, Reynold A. "Review of *Excavations at Olynthus. Part XIV, Terracottas, Lamps and Coins Found in 1934 and 1938* by D. M. Robinson." *Antiquaries Journal* 35 (1955): 97.

———. "Review of *Excavations at Olynthus. Part XIV, Terracottas, Lamps and Coins Found in 1934 and 1938* by D. M. Robinson." *Journal of Hellenic Studies* 75 (1955): 180–81.

Hill, Ida Thallon, and Lida Shaw King. *Corinth, Results of Excavations Conducted by the American School of Classical Studies at Athens IV, Part I: Decorated Architectural Terracottas*. Princeton, NJ: American School of Classical Studies at Athens, 1929.

Hills, E. C. "The Degree of Doctor of Philosophy." *Bulletin of the American Association of University Professors* 12, no. 3 (1929): 163–85.

Hollenshead, Carol S., Stacey A. Wenzel, Barbara B. Lazarus, and Indira Nair. "The Graduate Experience in the Sciences and Engineering: Rethinking a Gendered Institution." In *The Equity Equation: Fostering the Advancement of Women in the Sciences, Mathematics, and Engineering*, edited by Cinda-Sue Davis, Angela B. Ginorio, Carol S. Hollenshead, Barbara B. Lazarus, and Paula M. Rayman, 122–62. San Francisco: Jossey-Bass, 1996.

Hornig, Lilli S. "Affirmative Action through Affirmative Attitudes." In *Women in Academia: Evolving Policies toward Equal Opportunities*, edited by Elga Wasserman, Arie Y. Lewin, and Linda H. Bleiweis, 8–19. New York: Praeger Publishers, 1975.

Iakovidis, Spyros. "George Emmanuel Mylonas, 1898–1988." *American Journal of Archaeology* 93 (1989): 235–37.

"In Memoriam: Sarah Elizabeth Freeman 1907–1986." *Ákoue*, Spring 1986, 12.

Irwin-Williams, Cynthia. "Women in the Field: The Role of Women in Archaeology before 1960." In *Women of Science: Righting the Record*, edited by G. Kass-Simon and Patricia Farnes, 1–41. Bloomington: University of Indiana Press, 1990.

"Italians Raid Salonika." *New York Times*, January 27, 1941, 2.

Johnson, Franklin P. "Review of *Excavations at Olynthus, Part II: Architecture and Sculpture: Houses and Other Buildings* by David M. Robinson." *Art Bulletin* 12, no. 4 (1930): 421–22.

———. "Review of *Excavations at Olynthus, Part III. The Coins Found at Olynthus in 1928* by David M. Robinson and *Excavations at Olynthus, Part IV. The Terra-cottas of Olynthus, Found in 1928* by David M. Robinson." *Classical Philology* 26, no. 3 (1931): 339–40.

Kelley, Jane H. "Being and Becoming." In *Rediscovering Our Past: Essays on the History of American Archaeology*, edited by Jonathan E. Reyman, 81–90. Aldershot: Avebury, 1992.

Klinger, George. *We Face the Future Unafraid: A Narrative History of the University of Evansville*. Evansville, IN: University of Evansville Press, 2003.

Kourelis, Kostis. "Byzantium and the Avant-Garde: Excavations at Corinth 1920s–1930s." *Hesperia* 76 (2007): 391–442.

———. *Peschke: Colors of Greece*. Lancaster, PA: Franklin and Marshall College, 2012.

Lamb, Winifred. "Review of *Excavations at Olynthus. Part II: Architecture and Sculpture* by David M. Robinson." *Journal of Hellenic Studies* 51 (1931): 114–15.

Lay, Eleanor B. "Terra-cottas Found at Olynthus in 1934." PhD diss., Johns Hopkins University, 1936.

Levine, David O. *The American College and the Culture of Aspiration, 1915–1940*. Ithaca, NY: Cornell University Press, 1986.

Levine, Mary Ann. "Creating Their Own Niches: Career Styles among Women in Americanist Archaeology between the Wars." In *Women in Archaeology*, edited by Cheryl Claassen, 9–40. Philadelphia: University of Pennsylvania Press, 1994.

———. "Presenting the Past: A Review of Research on Women in Archaeology." In *Equity Issues for Women in Archaeology*, edited by Margaret C. Nelson, Sarah M. Nelson, and Alison Wylie, 23–36. Archaeological Papers of the American Anthropological Association Number 5. Arlington, VA: American Anthropological Association, 1994.

Lord, Louis E. *A History of the American School of Classical Studies at Athens 1882–1942*. Cambridge, MA: Harvard University Press, 1947.

"Man Convicted of Murdering Retired Professor." *AP News Archive*, July 7, 1987. Accessed November 21, 2013. http://www.apnewsarchive.com/1987/Man-Convicted-of-Murdering-Retired-Professor/id-7498088409c47597422 30947017034d8.

McDonald, William A. *The Political Meeting Places of the Greeks*. PhD diss., Johns Hopkins University, 1940.

———. *The Political Meeting Places of the Greeks*. Johns Hopkins Studies in Archaeology 34. Baltimore: Johns Hopkins University Press, 1943.

———. "Review of *Excavations at Olynthus Part XIV. Terracottas, Lamps and Coins Found in 1934 and 1938* by David M. Robinson." *Classical Journal* 50, no. 2 (1954): 94–95.

McDonald, William A., and George R. Rapp Jr., eds. *The Minnesota Messenia Expedition: Reconstructing a Bronze Age Regional Environment*. Minneapolis: University of Minnesota Press, 1972.

McGehee, Mary W. "Replicas of Scenes on Attic Red-figured Vases." MA thesis, Johns Hopkins University, 1926.

———. "Replica Scenes of Attic Red-figured Vases." PhD diss., Johns Hopkins University, 1932.

McGrayne, Sharon Bertsch. *Nobel Prize Women in Science. Their Lives, Struggles, and Momentous Discoveries*. New York: Brick Lane Press, 1993.

McMahon, Philip. "Review of *Excavations at Olynthus, Part III. The Coins Found at Olynthus in 1928* by David M. Robinson." *Parnassus* 3, no. 8 (1931): 34.

Medwid, Linda M. *The Makers of Classical Archaeology*. New York: Humanity Books, 2000.

Mellink, Machteld J., and Kathleen M. Quinn. "Hetty Goldman 1881–1972." In *Breaking Ground: Pioneering Women Archaeologists*, edited by Getzel M. Cohen and Martha S. Joukowsky, 298–350. Ann Arbor: University of Michigan Press, 2004.

Meredith, Christina B. "The Finger Rings Found at Olynthus in 1931 and 1934." MA thesis, Johns Hopkins University, 1937.

Merlin, Alfred. "Review of *Excavations at Olynthus, Part II: Architecture and Sculpture: Houses and Other Buildings* by David M. Robinson." *Revue Historique* 165, no. 2 (1930): 348–50.

Meritt, Lucy Shoe. *History of the American School of Classical Studies in Athens 1939–1980*. Princeton, NJ: American School of Classical Studies in Athens, 1984.

"Miss Annie C. Hare Is Married in London to Dr. J. Walter Graham, Archaeologist." *New York Times*, July 26, 1934, 16.

"Mrs. Robinson's Rites Tomorrow." *Baltimore Evening Sun*, May 16, 1960.

Mitten, David G. "George Maxim Anossov Hanfmann, 1911–1986." *American Journal of Archaeology* 91, no. 2 (1987): 259–66.

Morgan, Julia B. *Women at the Johns Hopkins University: A History*. Baltimore: Johns Hopkins University Press, 1986.

Müller, Valentin. *Frühe plastik in Griechenland und Vorderasien; ihre typenbildung von der neolithischen bis in die griechisch-archaische zeit (rund 3000 bis 600 v. Chr.)*. Augsburg: B. Filser, 1929.

———. "Review of *Excavations at Olynthus* by David M. Robinson." *Classical Philology* 31, no. 1 (1936): 92–93.

Mylonas, George E. *Excavations at Olynthus I. The Neolithic Settlement*. Johns Hopkins University Studies in Archaeology 6. Baltimore: Johns Hopkins University Press, 1929.

———. "Biographical Sketch." In *Studies Presented to David Moore Robinson on His Seventieth Birthday*, Vol. 1, edited by Geroge Mylonas, vii–x. St. Louis, MO: Washington University, 1951.

Mylonas, George E., and Doris Raymond, eds. *Studies Presented to David Moore Robinson on His Seventieth Birthday*, Vol. 2. St. Louis, MO: Washington University, 1953.

Myrdal, Alva, and Viola Klein. *Women's Two Roles. Home and Work*, 2nd ed. London: Routledge and Kegan Paul, 1968.

Nixon, Lucia. "Gender Bias in Archaeology." In *Women in Ancient Societies: An Illusion of Night*, edited by Léonie J. Archer, Susan Fischler, and Maria Wyke, 1–23. New York: Routledge, 1994.

Obituary for Saul Weinberg. *Israel Exploration Journal* 43, no. 2/3 (1993): 198–99.

Pace, C. Robert. *They Went to College: A Study of 951 Former University Students*. Minneapolis: University of Minnesota Press, 1941.

Palmer-Sikelianos, Eva. *Upward Panic. The Autobiography of Eva Palmer-Sikelianos*. Translated by John P. Anton. Philadelphia: Harwood Academic Publishers, 1993.

Parsons, Arthur W. "The Long Walls to the Gulf." In *Corinth, Results of Excavations Conducted by the American School of Classical Studies at Athens III.2: The Defenses of Acrocorinth and the Lower Town*, edited by Rhys Carpenter and Antoine Bon, 84–127. Princeton, NJ: American School of Classical Studies at Athens, 1936.

———. "Klepsydra and the Paved Court of the Pythion." PhD diss., Johns Hopkins University, 1942.

———. "Klepsydra and the Paved Court of the Pythion." *Hesperia* 12, no. 3 (1943): 191–267.

Perrot, Paul N. "Gladys Davidson Weinberg—A Tribute." *Journal of Glass Studies* 24 (1982): 8–9.

———. "Gladys Davidson Weinberg (1909–2002)." *Journal of Glass Studies* 44 (2002): 211–15.

"Pioneer Residents of Edmonton to Mark 67th Wedding Day." *Edmonton Bulletin*, December 31, 1940.

Pitard, Wayne T. "Alexander the Great: How Grad Student Alexander Schulz Became a Key Figure in the Museum's History." *Spurlock Museum Magazine* Fall (2012): 6–8.

Reyman, Jonathan E. "Women in American Archaeology: Some Historical Notes and Comments." In *Rediscovering Our Past: Essays on the History of American Archaeology*, edited by Jonathan E. Reyman, 69–80. Aldershot: Avebury, 1992.

Robinson, David M. "Greek and Latin Inscriptions from Asia Minor." *Transactions and Proceedings of the American Philological Association* 57 (1926): 195–237.

———. "The *Res Gestae Divi Augusti* as Recorded on the Monumentum Antiochenum." *American Journal of Philology* 47, no. 1 (1926): 1–54.

———. "Foreword to *Excavations at Olynthus I. The Neolithic Settlement* by George Mylonas." Johns Hopkins University Studies in Archaeology 6, vii–x. Baltimore: Johns Hopkins University Press, 1929.

———. "Mosaics from Olynthus." *American Journal of Archaeology* 36, no. 1 (1932): 16–24.

———. *Excavations at Olynthus V: Mosaics, Vases, and Lamps of Olynthus Found in 1928 and 1931.* Baltimore: Johns Hopkins University Press, 1933.

———. *Excavations at Olynthus VII: The Terra-Cottas of Olynthus Found in 1931.* Baltimore: Johns Hopkins University Press, 1933.

———. "The Third Campaign at Olynthus." *American Journal of Archaeology* 39, no. 2 (1935): 210–47.

———. "Prähistorische und Griechische Häuser." In *Realencyclopädia der Classischen Altertumswissenschaft*, Supplementband 7, edited by August Pauly and Georg Wissowa, 224–78. Stuttgart: E. B. Metzler, 1938.

———. *Excavations at Olynthus X: Metal and Minor Miscellaneous Finds, an Original Contribution to Greek Life.* Johns Hopkins University Studies in Archaeology 31. Baltimore: Johns Hopkins University Press, 1941.

———. *Excavations at Olynthus XI: Necrolynthia, a Study of Greek Burial Customs and Anthropology.* Johns Hopkins University Studies in Archaeology 32. Baltimore: Johns Hopkins University Press, 1942.

———. *Excavations at Olynthus XIII: Vases Found in 1934 and 1938.* Johns Hopkins University Studies in Archaeology 38. Baltimore: Johns Hopkins University Press, 1950.

———. *Excavations at Olynthus XIV: Terracottas, Lamps, and Coins found in 1934 and 1938.* Baltimore: Johns Hopkins University Press, 1952.

Robinson, David M., and Paul A. Clement. *Excavations at Olynthus IX: The Chalcidic Mint and the Excavation Coins Found in 1928–1934.* Johns Hopkins University Studies in Archaeology 26. Baltimore: Johns Hopkins University Press, 1938.

Robinson, David M., and J. Walter Graham. *Excavations at Olynthus VIII: The Hellenic House; a Study of the Houses Found at Olynthus with a Detailed Account of those Excavated in 1931 and 1934.* Johns Hopkins University Studies in Archaeology 25. Baltimore: Johns Hopkins University Press, 1938.

Robinson, David M., and George E. Mylonas. "The Fourth Campaign at Olynthus." *American Journal of Archaeology* 43, no. 1 (1939): 48–77.

Root, Margaret C. "Introduction: Women of the Field, Defining the Gendered Experience." In *Breaking Ground: Pioneering Women Archaeologists*, edited by Getzel M. Cohen and Martha S. Joukowsky, 1–33. Ann Arbor: University of Michigan Press, 2004.

Ross, Helen M. M. "The Terra Cotta Industry at Olynthus." MA thesis, Johns Hopkins University, 1932.

————. "The Terra-cotta Figurines of Macedonia and Thrace." PhD diss., Johns Hopkins University, 1939.

Rossiter, Margaret W. *Women Scientists in America. Struggles and Strategies to 1940.* Baltimore: Johns Hopkins University Press, 1982.

Schulz, Alexander H. G. "The Burials and Burial Customs of Prehistoric Greece." MA thesis, Johns Hopkins University, 1935.

Scranton, Robert. "Review of *Excavations at Olynthus, Part XIV: Terracottas, Lamps, and Coins Found in 1934 and 1938* by David M. Robinson." *Classical Philology* 49, no. 2 (1954): 143–44.

Shaw, Joseph W. "James Walter Graham 1906–1991." *American Journal of Archaeology* 96, no. 2 (1992): 325–26.

Shea, John. *Macedonia and Greece: The Struggle to Define a New Balkan Nation.* Jefferson, NC: McFarland, 1997.

Shoe, Lucy T. "Review of *Excavations at Olynthus, Part VIII: The Hellenic House, a Study of the Houses Found at Olynthus with a Detailed Account of Those Excavated in 1931 and 1934* by David M. Robinson and J. Walter Graham." *American Journal of Archaeology* 43, no. 4 (1939): 707–8.

Sicherman, Barbara. "College and Careers: Historical Perspectives on the Lives and Work Patterns of Women College Graduates." In *Women and Higher Education in American History*, edited by John M. Faragher and Florence Howe, 130–64. New York: W. W. Norton, 1988.

Snyder, Thomas D., ed. 1993. *120 Years of American Education: A Statistical Portrait.* National Center for Educational Statistics, U.S. Department of Education, Office of Educational Research and Improvement. Accessed January 22, 2014. http://nces.ed.gov/pubs93/93442.pdf.

Special Collections, Milton S. Eisenhower Library, Johns Hopkins University. N.D. "Freeman (Sarah Elizabeth) 1906–1986, Papers 1944–1969, MS. Gar30." Accessed August 1, 2013. http://old.library.jhu.edu/collections/specialcollections/manuscripts/msregisters/msgar30freeman.pdf.

Spiegel, Max B. "The Garrett Collection: Coins, Medals, and Archives at the American Numismatic Society." *American Numismatic Society Magazine* 5, no. 3 (2006). Accessed November 21, 2013. http://ansmagazine.com/Winter06/Garrett.

Stebbins, Eunice B. "The Letters of Augustus Preserved in Greek Inscriptions and in the Greek Writers." MA thesis, Johns Hopkins University, 1926.

————. "The Dolphin in the Literature and Art of Greece and Rome, Including Pre-Hellenic Civilizations." PhD diss., Johns Hopkins University, 1927.

————. *The Dolphin in the Literature and Art of Greece and Rome, Including Pre-Hellenic Civilizations.* Menasha, WI: George Banta, 1929.

Stillwell, Richard, Robert L. Scranton, and Sarah E. Freeman, eds. *Corinth, Results of Excavations Conducted by the American School of Classical Studies at*

Athens I.2: *Architecture*. Princeton, NJ: American School of Classical Studies at Athens, 1941.

"Student Rebuilds Ancient Bathtub." *Baltimore Sun*, November 24, 1935.

"Students to Assist in Greek Excavation." *Baltimore Evening Sun*, February 14, 1931.

Sullivan, Lynne P. "Madeline D. Kneberg Lewis: Leading Lady of Tennessee Archaeology." In *Grit-Tempered: Early Women Archaeologists in the Southeastern United States*, edited by Nancy M. White, Lynne P. Sullivan, and Rochelle A. Marrinan, 57–91. Gainesville: University Press of Florida, 1999.

Thompson, Homer. "In Memoriam: J. Walter Graham 1906–1991." *Ákoue* Fall (1991), 15.

Touchton, Judith G., and Lynn Davis. *Fact Book on Women in Higher Education*. New York: Macmillan, 1991.

Vogeikoff-Brogan, Natalia. "Ida Thallon Hill (1875–1954)." *Breaking Ground: Women in Old World Archaeology* (n.d.). Accessed February 2, 2014. http://www.brown.edu/Research/Breaking_Ground/bios/Hill_Ida%20Thallon.pdf.

———. "The Modern Greek Exam, 'Professor Blank's' Method, and Other Stories from the 1930s." *From the Archivist's Notebook*, October 1, 2013. Accessed December 3, 2013. http://nataliavogeikoff.com/category/women-studies/.

Wace, Alan. "Review of *Excavations at Olynthus. Part II. Architecture and Sculpture: Houses and Other Buildings* by David M. Robinson." *Classical Review* 45, no. 2 (1931): 87.

Weinberg, Gladys D. *Corinth, Results of Excavations Conducted by the American School of Classical Studies at Athens XII. The Minor Objects*. Princeton, NJ: American School of Classical Studies at Athens, 1952.

Weinberg, Saul S. "The Prehistoric House of the Mainland of Greece." PhD diss., Johns Hopkins University, 1936.

West, Jennifer K. "Observations on Selected Papers of David Moore Robinson from the University of Mississippi Archives." MA thesis, University of Mississippi, 1995.

White, Nancy M. "Women in Southeastern U.S. Archaeology." In *Grit-Tempered: Early Women Archaeologists in the Southeastern United States*, edited by Nancy M. White, Lynne P. Sullivan, and Rochelle A. Marrinan, 1–24. Gainesville: University Press of Florida, 1999.

Wiegand, Theodor, and Hans Schrader. *Priene: Ergebnisse der Ausgrabungen und Untersuchungen in den Jahren 1895–1898*. Berlin: G. Reimer, 1904.

Wilson, Lillian M. *The Roman Toga*. Johns Hopkins University Studies in Archaeology 1. Baltimore: Johns Hopkins University Press, 1924.

———. "A Study of the Roman Toga." PhD diss., Johns Hopkins University, 1924.

———. "The Loom Weights." In *Excavations at Olynthus* II *Architecture and Sculpture: House and Other Buildings* edited by D. M. Robinson, 118–28. Johns Hopkins University Studies in Archaeology 9. Baltimore: Johns Hopkins University Press, 1930.

Winnifrith, Tom J. *The Vlachs: The History of a Balkan People*. New York: St. Martin's Press, 1987.

"Wins Degree." *Edmonton Bulletin*, June 12, 1939.

Wood, R. C. "Review of *Excavations at Olynthus. Part XIV, Terracottas, Lamps and Coins Found in 1934 and 1938* by D. M. Robinson." *American Journal of Archaeology* 57, no. 3 (1953): 227–28.

Woodhouse, Chase Going. "Women." *American Journal of Sociology* 37, no. 6 (1932): 956–62.

Wycherley, Richard E. "Review of *Excavations at Olynthus. Part X. Metal and Minor Miscellaneous Finds: An Original Contribution to Greek Life* by David M. Robinson"; "*Excavations at Olynthus. Part XI. Necrolynthia: A Study in Greek Burial Customs and Anthropology* by David M. Robinson." *Journal of Hellenic Studies* 62 (1942): 103–4.

———. "Review of *Excavations at Olynthus XII: Domestic and Public Architecture* by D. M. Robinson." *Journal of Hellenic Studies* 66 (1946): 134–35.

———. *How the Greeks Built Cities*. London: Macmillan, 1949.

AUTHOR'S NOTE ON THE LOCATIONS OF THE MARY ROSS ELLINGSON AND DAVID MOORE ROBINSON PAPERS

Mary Ross Ellingson's papers and photographs are in two locations: with her daughter, Barbara Petersen and in the archives of the University of Evansville. As this book went to press the university was still processing the material and so had not yet assigned any of it to specific boxes. All references in this book to the material held by the university are necessarily vague as a result. Archivists and interns are at work digitizing much of this material some of which has been posted online; see *Olynthus 1931: The Mary Ross Ellingson Photo Archive* at http://faculty.evansville.edu/ak58/ellingson.

Materials at the David M. Robinson Collection in the Archives and Special Collections at the University of Mississippi Libraries are listed with their archival box number throughout this book. Since my visit there the archivists have done further processing of the Robinson material, as a result some of the material has been moved to new boxes rendering some of the references in the endnotes obsolete. Anyone interested in viewing or referencing the material from either library should feel free to contact the archivists at either institution; they know the material well and are always happy to help.

INDEX

ABOUT THE AUTHOR

Alan Kaiser is a professor of archaeology at the University of Evansville. He earned his PhD in archaeology from Boston University and has worked on archaeological projects in Greece, Italy, Spain, Britain, Israel, Rhode Island, Indiana, and on the Caribbean island of Nevis. Kaiser's published works include scholarly and popular articles as well as two books aimed at a scholarly audience, *The Urban Dialogue: An Analysis of the Use of Space in the Roman City of Empúries, Spain* (2000) and *Roman Urban Street Networks* (2011).